Education for Peoplehood

Essays on the Teaching Ministry of the Church

Walter

In appreciation for your friendship and colleagueship!

Ross

Ross T. Bender

Education for Peoplehood

Essays on the Teaching Ministry of the Church

Foreword by Daniel S. Schipani

Text Reader Series 8
1997
Institute of Mennonite Studies
Elkhart, Indiana

Text Reader Series

Series Titles:

1. *Essays on Biblical Interpretation: Anabaptist-Mennonite Perspectives.* Edited by Willard M. Swartley, 1984.
2. *One Lord, One Church, One Hope, and One God: Mennonite Confessions of Faith in North America.* Howard John Loewen, 1985.
3. *Monotheism, Power and Justice: Collected Old Testament Essays.* Millard C. Lind, 1990.
4. *So Wide a Sea: Essays on Biblical and Systematic Theology.* Edited by Ben C. Ollenburger, 1991.
5. *Essays in Anabaptist Theology.* Edited by H. Wayne Pipkin, 1995.
6. *Understanding Ministerial Leadership: Essays contributing to a developing theology of ministry.* Edited by John A. Esau, 1995.
7. *Theology for the Church: Writings by Marlin E. Miller.* Edited by Richard A. Kauffman and Gayle Gerber Koontz, 1997.

The Text Reader series is published by the Institute of Mennonite Studies with the encouragement of the Council of Mennonite Seminaries. The series seeks to make available significant resource materials for seminary classroom use. By using photographic reproduction and/or desktop publishing technology, and marketing primarily through individual channels, the series seeks to make available helpful materials at relatively low cost.

Priority in accepting manuscripts will be given to material that has promise for ongoing use in the seminary classroom, with orientation toward or interest in the Anabaptist-Mennonite theological tradition.

The Institute of Mennonite Studies is the research agency of the Associated Mennonite Biblical Seminary, 3003 Benham Ave., Elkhart, Indiana, 46517-1999.

ISBN 0-936273-25-0

Printed in the United States of America

Contents

Foreword

Ross T. Bender's Vision of the Teaching Ministry:
The Contours of Education for Peoplehood

The title chosen for this book—*Education for Peoplehood*—is especially fitting because it points to two fundamental convictions that permeate Bender's fruitful work and thought as educator and theologian spanning several decades. First is the conviction that God is deeply interested and involved in fashioning a people for Godself; second, that the church's teaching ministry has a privileged place and role for us to collaborate in such a process of learning, growth, formation and transformation. In the following paragraphs I will succinctly highlight a number of *normative hypotheses* that inform his vision of the teaching ministry as I understand it. Those hypotheses must be seen as interrelated and fleshed out in detail in the seventeen chapters that comprise the body of this book. My aim is to help us to better appreciate Bender's comprehensive philosophy of education which is both relevant for the times ahead as well as faithful to the gospel of the reign of God.

First of all, **we must appropriate anew the biblical mandate to teach with authority and with a sense of urgency**. A number of principles follow:

* Teaching for faith essentially involves guiding the learning of a special language and the grammar of the Christian faith; it also includes encouragement of critical reflection—the reflective wisdom of the believer—in tune with the reflective, probing, truth-seeking biblical foundation of our faith.

* Education for peoplehood can be viewed fundamentally as a conversation between generations in the uniquely suited contexts of family and congregation called to function in partnership with each other. Indeed, the educational function of the family as a place where God may be daily experienced "at home" must be appreciated afresh and supported as a top priority. The unique responsibility of parents and adults in general thus cannot be exaggerated.

* Sunday school (together with other church settings and programs for learning) must be viewed as a community of conversation around the Scriptures, oriented to decision, action, and obedience, that is, discipleship. Its task is to build a common Christian meaningful vocabulary and to become a place where people test the purpose of their lives and the implications of their choices. Participation in such a conversation provides a way of seeing and interpreting the world from a biblical perspective.

* The ministry of Jesus provides the needed paradigm for the teaching ministry of the church in all its forms and settings. The mandate we have received consists in carrying on what Jesus began as example, revealer, and change agent--making disciples, baptizing, and teaching people the way of life in light of God's reign.

Second, **the Bible must be reclaimed as the text for the people of God in the search for knowledge and values in tune with the way of Jesus.** This assertion suggests several guidelines for practice:

* The key to the integrity of our approach to Scriptures lies in the context in which we study the Bible and the mindset we bring to the task. Like the faithful early Anabaptists, we must be open to hear God's word and must be ready to respond as disciples, that is, in obedience and faith.

* Learning in the biblical sense is best accomplished in the context of engagement, involvement, and participation. A variety of teaching strategies need to be creatively utilized in the face of both the richness and diversity of people's ways of learning through their life cycles and the changing cultural environment and social conditions.

* Teachers must operate on the assumption that the Scriptures are a living, contemporary document and that, by studying them under the Spirit's guidance, we will be able to hear the living God of the text speaking to God's people again. Hence, we must engage in a hermeneutical process aimed at facilitating such a multiway communication.

* The task of teaching includes the goal of the revival of those conversations between God and the people. The ultimate purpose, however, is not merely to learn the content of the biblical story and

teaching but much more--to learn to live (think, love, and act) biblically!

Third, **the theory and practice of education for peoplehood necessitate a sound anthropological base subordinated to our biblical and theological norms and perspectives**. Some of the corresponding principles that guide the practice of our teaching ministry can be then highlighted:

* The educational task depends profoundly upon our understanding of human existence and of personhood. Personhood must be considered especially in relation to nature and the nonhuman environment, to community, society, and culture, and to relationship with God.

* Philosophical and scientific views and perspectives on being human and on education can serve as foundation material for theory and practice. Such material, however, must be critically appropriated in terms of the normative convictions stemming from our biblical and theological base and frame of reference.

* Educating for peoplehood and personhood must keep in focus both formation and transformation; they are distinct yet interrelated processes and experiences in the discipleship journey of persons and faith communities. On the one hand, the teaching ministry must deliberately seek to sponsor growth in the life of the Christian faith; on the other hand, we must realize that spiritual growth through conversion and maturation "to the measure of the full stature of Christ" (Ephesians 4:13) is a gift from God and the work of God's Spirit.

Fourth, **theological education must be viewed and practiced as a special dimension of the church's teaching ministry for the sake of peoplehood in the light of God**. Several practical ramifications follow:

* The context of theological education is the community of faith. And one of the common tasks shared by congregation and seminary is that of discerning the will of God for our day, including our total response of faith, obedience and love. Both function along the continuum as communities of discernment; their common goal is participating in God's mission in the world, especially the formation of a covenant community, a people for Godself.

* The organizing principle of the curriculum of theological education is the endeavor to perceive and to realize what it is to be the faithful people of God today, that is, the shapes of authentic peoplehood in the church as well as in its institutions, including the seminary.

* Christian education must be seen as a theological discipline which brings a number of contributions to the theological enterprise, including the interdisciplinary cooperation between theology and the human sciences (a case in point: the critical and creative appropriation of Jean Piaget's thought to educational theory and practice in areas such as cognitive development, learning readiness, active learning, and moral reasoning).

* A common, fundamental theory of Christian education must be visualized as an ongoing learning continuum with three stages or movements: *exploration* of the comprehensive range of subject matter (Bible, church teachings and theology, history, learners' experience, current events, etc.), which leads to *decision making* in light of our call to commitment, which in turn leads to pertinent, responsible *action*, that is, faith concretely and existentially lived out.

The first affirmation Ross Bender makes in this book concerning his vision of the teaching ministry is that he has long considered the text of Deuteronomy 6 the bedrock of his philosophy of education. It is a very appropriate reference because in that text we find all the essentials: a) Education for peoplehood is primarily a worshipful expression of praise to the only true God and a response to divine grace and sustaining care. b) Education for peoplehood is a matter of life over death for the people of God; their identity, their survival and prosperity and their vocation in the world is at stake. c) Everybody is involved in the teaching and learning, beginning with God's own guiding Spirit; yet adults, and especially parents, have a special responsibility to model, to lead, to reveal, and to actively sponsor growth in the life of faith. d) The overall goal of education for peoplehood is, primarily, to honor and glorify the creator, liberator, empowering God; and such a goal is simultaneously the formation and transformation of a people according to God's righteousness and justice. e) The process and the content of education for peoplehood are also nicely indicated in the Deuteronomy text: it consists in a conversation between generations; the centerpiece of the dialogue is the story of liberation and the vision of God's everlasting covenant and reign. f) Concerning timing, teaching and learning belong in a daily and ongoing process at home, in church, on the way, and everywhere. Yet, there are special, opportune "teachable moments" (e.g., when your children ask you..., v. 20) that adults must elicit by virtue of their faithful living and which they must be attentive to grasp and deal with in due time for the sake of faith.

Yes, Deuteronomy 6 does point to all the right, fundamental answers to the key questions that any sound philosophy of education must address—who are the persons involved in education for peoplehood?; why should they be so involved and what are the purpose and the goals of such an endeavor?; where and when will teaching and learning happen?; what should be the content and how will it be shared? In this collection of essays on the teaching ministry of the church Ross Bender gives us a kind of extended commentary on such a biblical foundation; it is a commentary that will help us to understand better education for peoplehood and to practice it more consistently and relevantly in a wide variety of settings and levels. And for such a gift we are deeply grateful.

Daniel S. Schipani
Professor of Christian Education and Personality
Associated Mennonite Biblical Seminary

Preface

Have you ever gone on a journey only to discover when you reached your destination that it was not the destination you had planned? That was my experience in preparing these papers for publication. What I set out to do was to assemble a number of papers I had written over the years on a wide variety of subjects and place this collection in the seminary library upon my retirement from the Associated Mennonite Biblical Seminary as professor of Christian education. The final collection of 20 articles (already narrowed down from a longer list) was still too long. With the counsel and encouragement of my colleague, Professor Daniel Schipani, I retained only those essays having to do with education (family life education, congregational education and theological education).

The exercise of reading through all of these papers written over a period of three and a half decades was personally very satisfying. It brought back many warm memories of friends, occasions and ideas. It evoked a sense of indebtedness to my teachers, mentors, colleagues and students who have enriched my thinking about the teaching ministry of the church as well as its wider ministries. Many of the essays were initially presented in seminars, workshops, consultations and classes over the years. In some cases I have revised the original papers to bring them up to date, especially with reference to the use of inclusive language. In those essays which have not been so revised, I beg the indulgence of the reader.

Several of the essays were originally published in various journals and periodicals and are reprinted here by permission. They are as follows:

> "Teaching the Bible in the Congregation" was published in the Text Reader series of the Institute of Mennonite Studies, *Essays on Biblical Interpretation: Anabaptist-Mennonite Perspectives*, edited by Willard M. Swartley (IMS 1984).
>
> "Nurture: Passing on the Faith" was published in *Gospel Herald* (March 6, 1990).

“Seminary and Congregation: Communities of Discernment” was published in *Mennonite Quarterly Review* (July 1965).

“Theological Education in the Free Church Tradition” was published in the journal of the Association of Theological Schools, *Theological Education* (Winter 1973).

“Anabaptist Education” was published in *Harper's Encyclopedia of Religious Education*, Iris V. Cully and Kendig Brubaker Cully, editors (Harper and Row, 1990), 27-29.

“Indoctrination” was published in *Harper's Encyclopedia of Religious Education*, Iris V. Cully and Kendig Brubaker Cully, editors (Harper and Row, 1990), 321-22.

“Christian Education in Theological Education” was published in the journal of the Religious Education Association, *Religious Education* (January-February 1967), 18-24.

My hope is that these essays will contribute to the ongoing conversation about the nature of the teaching ministry of the church to the end that it will be continually renewed and thus fulfil the stimulating and critical function it is intended to fulfil. The essays include reflections about the aims and processes of education, what it means to be and become a person, the meaning of conversion, the family and the Sunday school as contexts for education, the contribution of Jean Piaget to educational theory and practice, theological education as it is carried out in the seminaries, and some thoughts about Jesus as the Master Teacher, his content and methodology.

I wish to express my thanks to my colleagues Professor Daniel S. Schipani and Dean Willard M. Swartley for their counsel and encouragement. I also express my appreciation to Ruth Liechty, the Administrative Secretary in the Institute of Mennonite Studies for her invaluable assistance in preparing this manuscript for publication and to Mary Klassen of the AMBS staff for her work in designing the cover. It was a source of continuing amazement to me to see how Ruth Liechty whipped the manuscript into shape by pressing the magical buttons on her computer which while they did not remove mountains did move paragraphs and other objects around into their proper places.

Finally, and most of all, I express my appreciation to my wife, Ruth Steinmann Bender, who has been my co-teacher in our family, who gave me valued feedback, and who unselfishly encouraged me to carry out this project even though it meant yielding her priorities to mine in terms of the time and energy involved in putting together a manuscript for publication.

Ross T. Bender
Institute of Mennonite Studies
Associated Mennonite Biblical Seminary

I

Nurture and Instruction

The ministry of teaching finds its model in the ministry of Jesus who was himself a teacher and its mandate in the commission he gave his followers to make disciples, baptize and teach them.

1

Could Any Work Be More Important?

Not long ago *Newsweek* (October 8, 1990) magazine came out with a special issue called *How to Teach Our Kids*. The introductory article asks the question rhetorically, "Could any work be more important? The Bible commands us to teach our children when we sit in the house and when we walk by the way. Teach our children when we lie down and when we rise up. Teach our children so that our days may be multiplied."

It was striking to me that a secular magazine would draw on this ancient biblical wisdom, quoting from a text in Deuteronomy which I have long considered the bedrock of my philosophy of education. But even more striking is this sentence, also taken from the Introduction, "We teach them [*our children*] our stories, our facts, our theorems, our culture [*and I would add, our faith*], or we abandon the future to chance and nonsense."

The task is momentous. It is crucial. It is a holy calling. I agree with the writer's implied answer to his own question, "Could any work be more important?" The answer is a resounding NO!

Education in the public schools is being harshly criticized these days. Over and over again we hear it being discussed in the media as its alleged failures are scrutinized and analysed. National test scores are reported and compared and invariably we are told that we are losing ground. Critics complain that Johnny can't read, write, spell or add; that Jane can't draw, sing or dance; that both of them have a bad case of national amnesia when it comes to our country's history; and that they know only one language (English) and that they don't know that one very well.

All this bad press is very discouraging to teachers, many of whom decide to leave the profession or retire early. It is difficult to do your best and to try harder when your efforts are so unappreciated and undervalued.

Much of the criticism is based on lack of information, for example, of the nature of the tests and the test scores. One Indiana teacher in our area pointed out, correctly, in a letter to the editor that it is inappropriate to compare the scores of a state where most or all of the high school seniors write the test with a state where only that smaller percentage of the students planning to go on to college or university take the test.

My point in mentioning this is not to criticize our teachers and schools, nor to exonerate them for that matter. It seems to me that the reason for all this attention and concern is that education matters so much to the well-being and the future of our society. We can do better and we must do better and no matter how much improvement we make in years to come, there will still be a great deal of concern about the quality of our education.

Ernest Boyer, president of the Carnegie Foundation for the Advancement of Education, is frequently quoted in the media as an advocate for the improvement of public education and is quoted in the *Newsweek* issue as saying that "we are absolutely running out of time."

I believe that we must have the same sense of urgency when it comes to Christian education. What work could be more important? The early Jewish community saw the task of religious education as a comprehensive task, as we noted earlier, "when you lie down, when you rise up, when you go out, when you walk by the way, and when you return." It involved telling the faith stories, answering questions, feasts and fasts, rituals such as the lighting of the Sabbath candle, special articles of clothing, preparation for celebrating the Passover, etc. Fathers who neglected to teach their sons Torah were called "amharaatz", that is, a boor or ignoramus and were considered to be very irresponsible. It is only during the exile, when ordinary Jewish parents could no longer speak the holy language (Hebrew), that there developed the office of rabbi and the institution of the synagogue which had as one of its major functions that of being a school. From that point on, the family gave way to the school as the primary educational influence in the life of the child.

I note that halfway through the special issue of *Newsweek* there is a belated comment concerning the family's educational responsibility. The article is called, "Where are the parents?" A beleaguered educator bewails, "Some days it looks like nobody else is helping." It is abundantly clear that where you have a cooperative arrangement between the family and the school you get the best educational results. It is precisely at this point that most of the problems of our educational system have their roots. Where such cooperation flourishes there are good results. Where it is lacking, there are serious problems. Might there be a lesson there as well for our program of Christian education?

I have a strong conviction that Christian education is the primary responsibility of Christian parents and families and that the Sunday school is designed to help and support parents in carrying out their task, not the other way round

The last section of the special issue is entitled, "The Real World" and it speaks about the politics and the economics of education and how they affect the possibilities of educational reform. I want to talk a bit about the real world too but my thoughts are going in a little different direction, that is, the intersection of Christianity and society in which we focus on some of the challenges to the Christian education endeavor. Certainly we face some of the same challenges that our teaching colleagues in the public school are facing.

We too face criticism that our educational efforts are inadequate, that we're not getting the job done. And I guess there is some truth in the criticism. We're not getting the job done. We might say in our own defense that we are given only one hour a week in which to do it. And we might protest that the public schools have professional teachers while we have only lay teachers who work without pay on marginal time in our Sunday schools. And that these are very busy people with many other responsibilities in their families, communities and at their full time jobs.

Besides that, our Sunday school teachers are usually the same ones who do so many of the other jobs in the congregation. It hardly seems appropriate to criticize them when they are the backbone of the whole church. In our tradition it is the lay people, not the professionals first of all, to whom we have entrusted this most high calling of passing on the heritage of faith to the next generation. I return to the Introduction of the special issue where the editor states "Everyone can learn...and everyone can teach." And I believe that to be true for the most part. Christian education is not the preserve only of the experts.

One of the things that our Sunday school program must do is to teach our children and youth our "stories, our facts, our theorems, our culture" and as I said earlier, our faith. 1 like to think of this as the teaching of a language, the language of our faith. We are teaching a special vocabulary, the meaning of such words as love, faith, trust, obedience, service, patience, kindness, forgiveness and the like. The best way to teach such words is to live them and then to reflect on their meaning. Children learn to speak in the context of their families, of course; then when they go to school their teachers help them to learn the deeper meanings of their words as well as to expand their vocabularies, to put their words into sentences and their sentences into paragraphs, and their paragraphs into chapters and longer stories in the process of making ordered sense of the world and their place in it. The same is true when it comes to their specifically Christian vocabularies as they enlarge them and learn the grammar of the Christian faith and are able to relate these words to the realities of the expanding world in which they are living.

As they grow older and become teenagers their world continues to expand and their vocabularies also expand in ways that help them to understand that world, to make ordered sense of it and to cope with it. The Christian education program has its role to play in helping them to think Christianly about that world and where they fit into it.

What is going on in that world? The deficit in our national budget seems virtually unfixable as politicians wrestle and struggle to get it under control with minimal damage to their political careers.

There is growing concern for the environment. I mention only oil spills, pollution, the ozone layer, the spotted owl.

The political changes in eastern Europe are nothing short of mind-boggling. The Berlin Wall has come tumbling down and Germany is in the process of reuniting, a process that may take some years. Russia is in process of abandoning communism and becoming a capitalist country with private ownership and individual initiative.

All over the world and in our country as well, there is a growing hunger for spirituality and a search for ways to satisfy that hunger. In Russia there is growing openness to Christianity. In the Arab world, there is a growing Islamic fundamentalism. In our country, there is a growing movement known as the New Age.

All around the world, there is a growing movement in search of freedom, of human rights, of peace and justice. In 1992 America celebrated the 500th anniversary of Columbus' discovery of America. For America's native population the observance of this event was not good news. The coming of Europeans to their shores brought with it war, disease, loss of land and much human misery.

Ruth and I have several grandchildren. We love them very much and desire a good future for them. I'm worried about the kind of world they are inheriting from us. It is a world in which there is much poverty, sickness, hunger, injustice, illiteracy, spiritual hunger and confusion, international turmoil, environmental pollution and the like. Our grandchildren are among the lucky ones. They are well fed and clothed, they have the best of medical care, they are getting a good education and have the prospect of quality higher education. They go to Sunday school where they are learning the language of faith; they are well loved by parents and grandparents. While they are protected from the ills and misfortunes of so many of the children of this world, it is important that they understand that not all people are so blessed and fortunate as they are. Their view of the world must include the way it really is as well as a vision of how it ought to be and of how their lives can make a difference.

As I prepared for this presentation, the news reports told of a recent meeting at the United Nations which brought more than 70 heads of state together for the World Summit for Children. While America is preoccupied with improving the quality of education for our children, the Summit drew attention to the fact that "more than 100 million school-age children around the world, 60 per cent of them girls, never see the inside of a classroom. Another 100 million children will drop out before completing their education."

A second statistic: "Every day 40,000 children under the age of five die in developing countries. Even more shocking, most of these deaths are preventable at very little cost."

“The United States lags far behind most industrial nations in preventing childhood disease and injury. A quarter of preschoolers and a third of poor children under five are not immunized.”

“Reports of child abuse in the United States have been increasing steadily in the past decade.”

“Every day, about 150 million children under five in developing countries go to bed hungry.”

The *Newsweek* article makes another important point which applies also to our endeavor; it states that “the single most important skill that we must strive to master and then to impart is the ability to think and to think critically.... Teach them, too, not to be afraid but to welcome the new.”

While it is true that we want to teach our children our stories, our facts, our faith and so forth, we also want them to develop the ability to question our stories, our facts, and our formulations, perhaps even our faith statements so that they will come to have a faith of their own by which to live, by which to make sense of the world in which they live.

Earlier *Newsweek* had another special edition called “The New Teens: What Makes Them Different.” As I browsed through it I came to realize that the young people of today live in a different culture than the one I grew up in. My own children, all grown now, grew up in a world that was very different from the world in which I grew up, so different that there were times when it was difficult to know how to be helpful to them out of my own experience.

The youth of today are facing challenges and opportunities that I as a teenager knew nothing about. My heart goes out to them as they try to cope with their world and make ordered sense out of it. We must give them all the help we can out of our own understanding of the Christian faith. At the same time we must have the confidence that they too will find their way through to a solid and sure foundation, not in spite of their critical questioning but because of it. Someone has said that there is no such thing as a second hand faith nor are there second generation Christians, only first generation Christians.

The Christian faith not only permits critical reflection; it requires it. An unexamined faith, someone has said, is no faith at all. This calls for teachers of youth who themselves have a mature faith, one that has been examined and made one's own. It requires teachers who are not threatened by the questionings of our youth and by their own attempts to state their faith understandings in terms of their own experience and comprehension of God, of the world and of their place in the world. I believe that if we have confidence in them and believe in them and are willing to listen to them that they will return the favor and that in the process they will come to have an owned faith and that our faith, being challenged, will grow as well.

In 1990, a report was issued of a research project entitled "Effective Christian Education: A National Case Study of Protestant Congregations". The study report states, "The primary aim of congregational life is to nurture—among children, youth and adults—a vibrant, life-changing faith, the kind of faith that shapes one's way of being, thinking and acting." They concluded that of all the factors that move us toward this goal (they identified six such factors), the most powerful one is an effective Christian education program which includes Sunday school classes, Bible studies, adult forums, family events, music and drama programs and new member classes.

When they speak of mature faith, they are speaking of "a way of living, not just of an adherence to doctrine and dogma. Secondly, mature faith is life-transforming and has a dramatic, lasting impact on the believer."

To achieve such a goal, the nurturing of a mature faith in children, youth and adults, a vibrant, life-changing faith, the kind of faith that shapes one's way of being, thinking and acting is a demanding and challenging task not only for us teachers, but for everyone: pastors, parents, teachers, children, youth and adults. Perhaps it is too much to ask of one agency to which we give only one hour a week. But it is at least a place to begin and now is as good a time as any to make a new beginning. Could any work be more important?

2

Nurture: Passing on the Faith

Recently, a Denver newspaper and television station conducted a poll among local high school students assessing their academic mastery in a variety of basic subjects. The results were not encouraging. The schools have not done a good job in combating ignorance and illiteracy and preparing these young men and women to become good citizens.

This has caused me to reflect on the quality of our preparation as a church of our children and youth for citizenship in the kingdom of God. I am unaware of any recent research into this matter to give us answers to this question. I am aware, however, that many thoughtful observers are concerned that we may be losing ground. The impact of our culture on our children and youth is not supportive of our concerns and efforts in this regard. Are we in danger of biblical illiteracy and lack of moral clarity when it comes to our young people to say nothing of the adult generation? How long can we continue to neglect serious Bible study and still claim to be a church that is founded on the teachings of the Bible?

These are two areas that need increased attention: a) knowledge and b) values. What are the instruments which the church has created to pass on the needed information to become an informed Christian in today's world? Do we really believe that one hour a week of biblical instruction is enough to do the job? Have we adequately prepared the teachers and given them sufficient resources for this task? Do all of us have a sufficient awareness that teaching is a high and holy calling deserving of our best efforts?

Here are some practical things that can be done even now:

1. Be sure that the church library has a number of Bible study aids such as Bible dictionaries, commentaries, maps, encyclopedias and the like.

2. Conduct workshops for teachers to acquaint them with these resources as well as to teach them new methods of teaching.

3. Conduct in-depth Bible study classes for the teachers. Since they cannot attend the adult Sunday school classes they miss out on regular Bible study with other adults.

4. Help to pay the way to Christian education conferences and workshops that are sponsored by the denomination.

5. Provide the teachers and children with the best curriculum available. Herald Press and Faith and Life Press curriculum materials are prepared by experienced Mennonite educators who are committed to the church and its theology. Independent publishers may provide materials with good educational approaches but are usually committed to a different theology.

6. Find ways to help teachers to become aware of their students, the ways they learn and grow, and the world in which they live. That world is very different from the one that most adults grew up in. Our children need all the help we can offer them when it comes to responsible sexuality, saying no to drugs and steroids and the like.

What has been said so far assumes pretty much the status quo in terms of our existing Christian education programs, the Sunday school hour supplemented with Venture Club and Life Planning programs and, in a decreasing number of congregations, a summer Bible school. However, it seems less and less likely to me that such a limited approach to such an important need will be adequate for our day. Therefore, I am suggesting that we find additional strategies to supplement what we are already doing while at the same time increasing our present efforts to make them more effective.

In some areas of the church, children are able to attend church- or parent-sponsored schools with Christian teachers and a curriculum that is Christ-centered, where the Bible and the Christian faith are an integral part of the program. Not only is the Bible itself a vital part of the subject matter that is taught, its principles are applied to other subjects as well. It is time for the Mennonite church to consider developing such schools from the elementary through secondary levels on a wider basis.

There may be some areas of the church which cannot provide such a comprehensive educational program for children. A lesser alternative which should be seriously considered is the development of a home-based program of biblical studies, developmentally graded. This is the day of the computer and children have demonstrated their capacity to utilize this technology in their learning. Someone should be commissioned to develop such a computer-based learning program, one which combines fun with solid learning. It should be a program that invites parents to learn with their children.

Another piece of modern technology that is becoming increasingly available is the VCR. Video-cassettes are an effective instrument to provide information and to teach values; what is needed now is effective programming to harness its usefulness.

Until the late 50s or early 60s, the winter Bible schools provided much-needed and widely appreciated instruction in biblical and related studies. Then, for the most part, they disappeared with nothing to replace them. The Keystone Bible Institute is a creative exception. This program is a series of one-week seminars and classes held in various parts of the Keystone State, Pennsylvania. It is surprising that this program has not caught on in other parts of the church. While this program is primarily for adults, it is after all the adults who are the parents and teachers of our children and youth. It is one way of providing them the resources they need to carry out their task.

Finally, I want to mention the most difficult, yet most basic part of my proposed strategy. It has to do with the role of parents and the home. Long before there were synagogue schools, the faith was passed on from parent to child in the homes of ancient Israel. It was passed on in the midst of daily living.

> "When you sit in your house, when you lie down and when you rise up, and when you walk by the way, you shall teach these things diligently to your children." (Deut. 6:7)

Among the duties that parents have toward their children, for example, were these:

a) teaching them Torah (the Law);
b) giving them moral instruction;

"Hear, my son your father's instruction and reject not your mother's teaching: for they are a fair garland for your head and pendants for your neck. My son if sinners entice you do not consent." Proverbs 1:8-10.

c) teaching them the oral tradition;
"I will open my mouth in a parable: I will utter dark sayings from of old, things that we have heard and known that our fathers have told us. We will not hide them from our children but tell to the coming generation the glorious deeds of the Lord and his might and the wonders which he has wrought." Psalm 78:2-4.

Teaching and learning in the family included such rituals as the lighting of the Sabbath lamp, sweeping in the corners in preparation for the Passover, and rituals surrounding the birth of a child. Also included were the observance of special feasts and fasts such as the Passover Seder. During this meal the children would ask questions concerning the meaning of certain parts of the meal, for example, the unleavened bread and the bitter herbs. As the descendants of the slaves who had been delivered from bondage in Egypt settled down in the land of promise one generation of children after another would ask their parents about these events and the symbols and ceremonies and images which were born out of them. Then the parents would tell them what they had heard from their parents and what the grandparents had heard from their parents as one generation told the next and the tradition was passed on.

For such a model to become effective in our time would require two things:

1. parents would have to be intentional about this dimension of their parenting responsibility and take the necessary time to be with their children and to teach them the faith in the midst of living;
2. parents would have to have a vital faith by which to live, a faith to share with and model for their children.

Without these two things there can be no effective Christian nurture.

The Mennonite Church has a long and honored tradition of utilizing the services of lay teachers. It is a practice we will wish to retain. To do so effectively we must equip these persons as fully as possible in such ways as have been mentioned above. I would like to see the seminaries and colleges offer week-long modules of Christian education courses in

January and June upon whose completion a certificate or degree would be offered. Some of our lay teachers would be able to come to the campus for short blocks of time without having to move their families or interrupt their work schedules unduly.

In addition I would like to see every congregation or cluster of congregations employ a trained Christian educator whose task is to equip the lay teachers and the parents for the fulfillment of their ministry. This person, in addition to mentoring each teacher on an individual basis, would offer courses in Bible, church history, theology, ethics, the arts, personal development, how persons learn, lesson planning, and methods of teaching and learning. A very important part of the resources offered by the Christian educator would be help to the parents on parenting and ways of passing on the Christian faith to their children since parents are the primary teachers of their children.

One final proposal is that every congregation calling a pastor check the candidate's resume to see if there is evidence that the candidate has the gift of teaching and a commitment to the teaching ministry of the church. If not, this would be adequate grounds to consider another candidate. In many cases the pastor is the only person in the congregation who has college or seminary training in biblical and related studies. This training should be made available to the congregation through the sermon and in other settings as well. The pastor can offer insights not only into the content of particular books of the Bible but also into methods of Bible study. Resources such as commentaries, dictionaries, Bible handbooks, etc. will help the Bible to come alive. An additional resource which the congregation has a right to expect from its pastor who is supposed to be "apt to teach" is insight into how to become an effective teacher.

Perhaps little or none of what I have proposed is new to many of my readers. But then, I am assuming that my task is not to convince you but to remind you that passing on the faith is a task that dare not be taken lightly.

3

The Family: A Setting for Education

I think it was in the late 1950's that it first occurred to me that the family plays a vital role in shaping the person and equipping him for life in the world. I was at that time principal of a Mennonite secondary school and I remember engaging in conversations with my colleagues about the good job we were doing in educating these youngsters. Then we would point with pride to Doug and Don and Doreen and Bill and Janet and Dave and Nick. When other names would come up, names which for some reason I can't remember, we would say with a sigh of resignation, "Well, what can **we** do considering the kind of homes from which they come?" After a time of engaging in this kind of self-deception, it began to dawn on me that if we were doing well as a school with children from good homes, and not so well with children from other kinds of homes, it might well be that we were a lesser educational influence than the families—good or otherwise—who sent us their children to educate.

Now all of us know that there were families before there were schools, and that families were significant settings for education before formal educational institutions (schools) were set up. In ancient Israel, the faith was passed on from one generation to the next in the midst of daily living: "when you sit in your house or when you walk by the way, when you lie down and when you rise up..." Long before the advent of synagogue schools, the sons were asking the fathers, "What is the meaning of these stones?" and the fathers would reply, "Once we were slaves in Egypt, and God brought us out over the sea and to the mountain where he made us a people. Then through the wilderness and over the river into the land which is our home." What a tremendous lesson in history, or if you please, in theology, or geography, or sociology, and all of this material is so vital to the son's sense of identity! It tells him who he is, who his people are, where he came from. It helps him to locate himself in terms of his history, his geography, his social context, his religious privilege and obligation and destiny.

I was the youngest in a family of 4 sons and 1 daughter. I grew up on a farm in southwestern Ontario. Among my early recollections are the depression of the early 30's, the kidnapping of the Lindbergh baby, the abdication of the man who had been Prince of Wales and was to become Duke of Windsor after a few months as King of England and the Commonwealth in order to marry the woman he loved. I remember the rise of Hitler and the declaration of war in September 1939. I remember the stirring speeches of Winston Churchill and the solemn tolling of Big Ben late each night just before the BBC News direct from London. I also remember the majestic way Lorne Greene would read the news on the Canadian Broadcasting Corporation years before he became Ben Cartwright on the Bonanza show.

I have homier recollections too—of the warm puppy I received for my 6th birthday and of the cold winter when he was lost for several months and I thought he would never come back

—of homemade ice cream, and Sunday dinners shared with uncles, aunts and cousins

—of the excitement and strange sounds and smells that accompanied butchering day on the farm

—of the morning we were awakened before sunup to embark on a trip to relatives in Michigan in the Model T Ford and the ride on the ferryboat from Sarnia to Port Huron before the Bluewater Bridge was built

—of the day we spent watching the fishing boats return to the harbor in Goderich and the lady (my parent's friend but not mine) whom we visited on the way home who mistook my boyish bangs for something else and gushed "and is this your little girl?"

—of the conversation I overheard in the kitchen of a friend's home when we were visiting as my friend was deciding with his mother which of us would get the bigger of two bananas

—of Christmas when we would have oranges and grapefruit and candy and nuts (though we rarely sampled these goodies at any other time of the year) and the year I received as a gift a tin drummer you could wind up and watch him play

—of the prayers I would recite at meals and at bedtime, of my father reading the Scriptures and leading in morning prayer before breakfast

—of my mother's quiet faith, less expressive than my father's but equally profound.

Although lacking the formal opportunities for a higher education, all the members of my family were intellectually curious. My father had accumulated a modest library of his own and we subscribed to the National Geographic. We made active use of the school and public libraries. We also subscribed to a newspaper and listened avidly to the news broadcasts on the radio. In fact we had a battery radio before we had electricity on our farm. In addition we entertained visitors to our community like foreign missionaries and others and in ways like these there were opened to us larger windows on the world. While we did not travel more than several hundred miles from our home, our minds and spirits roamed the continent and circled the globe with whatever vehicles we had at hand.

My grandmother (on my father's side) was conflict-oriented, a very powerful and dominant member in our home. She had been widowed early in life and buried her husband and her two little boys just a few months before giving birth to my father. This, no doubt, affected her outlook on life and the way she related to other people.

One childhood experience which made a profound impact on me was the visit of her only sister to our community. Her sister lived in Tucson, Arizona, and although they stayed in touch by correspondence they were not really friends. Apparently there had been a conflict over inheritance matters many years earlier which had never been resolved. In any case, her sister Elizabeth refused to come to visit my grandmother (whom she hadn't seen for 20 or 30 years) but stayed with her husband's relatives in a neighboring community. My grandmother for her part refused to go the 15 miles to see her sister in spite of my father's urgent pleas. And so Elizabeth and Anna went to their graves unreconciled.

My grandmother on my mother's side was a very quiet and gentle woman. My earliest recollection of her was being held on her lap while she rocked and sang me a lullaby. She too had been widowed at an early age but had married a second time a widower with a family of his own. There was neither enough room nor enough money for two families—three in fact—since this new marriage resulted in the birth of several additional children. As a result, one of the children (my mother) was given to an uncle and an aunt to raise and grew up in their home almost as one of their own children. My mother was not without a family but actually had four families to claim as her own—her cousins (who considered her their sister), her full brothers and sisters, her half brothers, and her step brothers and sisters—a very confusing set of circumstances for me to comprehend. As a small boy, I remember feeling both resentment at her being the one who had to leave home and deep gratitude and affection for her adoptive family.

My mother was not a strong person and I remember that she was often sick in bed. Her younger sister, my aunt Mary, would come to care for her within a few minutes of a phone call and stay at her bedside until she was able to manage by herself. Since my only sister was the second child in our family and was married by the time I was 9 or 10, I learned early to help around the house—making beds, dusting, vacuuming, scrubbing and waxing floors, setting the table, washing dishes, even some elementary cooking. Little did I realize then how fortunate I was for I was being prepared for life at a time when traditional male-female roles are being significantly redefined.

These few examples are both by way of introducing myself to you and of illustrating the way in which the family educates the person and prepares him/her for life. If it be objected that none of these has to do with the transmission of knowledge, my response is that transmitting knowledge is only one dimension of education and that the areas of values and relationships are of equal educational significance. The family environment is second to none in shaping the personality and in passing on values that are deeply held and lived by.

Education is not limited to the three R's; it is not restricted to the classroom and the 9 to 4 or 8 to 3 schedule. Now I do not want to be understood as depreciating in any sense that form of education that is organized around schools and teachers and classes and formal curriculum materials. I am not anti-school. It is just that my vision is that school and education are not the same thing. That is to say, education goes on outside the formal educational structures and it's too easy to forget what I said at the beginning, that there were families before there were schools and that the family carried an educational function. It still does though obviously with the explosion of knowledge and technology the school is a vital part of our social order.

The family's educational function is a less formal one, i.e., it is one context where learning goes on in the midst of living. Informal education is a little girl helping her mother set the table or assisting her father repair a leaky faucet. Informal education is a boy helping Dad prune a rosebush or watching Mother knitting or crocheting or painting a picture or doing a flower arrangement. It's participation in a family decision or a discussion of a controversial TV program or political issue. It has to do with how the family views its neighbors and gets along with them. It involves grace at meals and table talk. Among the learnings which are of special importance in the family today are these:

1) developing a sense of security
2) developing a sense of belonging
3) developing a sense of personal worth
4) developing a sense of the dignity and worth of other persons
5) appreciating the mystery, wonder and sacredness of life
6) developing the capacity for gratitude
7) developing the capacity for relationships
8) developing the capacity to forgive and receive forgiveness
9) developing the capacity to value animals and things
10) developing the capacity to decide
11) learning a language
12) learning gender identity

All of these have to do with the person in his/her relationships and it is precisely in this area—the shaping of the personality, the formation of one's personhood—that the family's primary educational function resides. What do these things have to do with Christian faith? Much in every way! The spiritual and the emotional and the relational are all woven together in a growing person's experience. Faith must not be separated from life. I believe that teaching the doctrine and history of our faith are more the responsibility of the teaching church through the

Sunday school and the other settings where teaching and learning take place. However, integrating these lessons from our history and our doctrine into the personality, into one's life is more the responsibility of the Christian family where life is lived and personality is shaped, but in the end, of course, these things (doctrine and life) belong together.

These years of growing up within the family are the time when a person learns to love (if ever he learns it) by being loved.

She learns to care for others (if ever she learns it) by looking out for their interests and needs and not just for her own.

He learns a sense of responsibility, that he must carry his share of the family chores so that everyone's needs are provided for and no one is taken advantage of.

She learns what it is to make mistakes, to hurt others through neglect or deliberately. She learns to forgive and to be forgiven.

There was an oft-quoted line in the movie, *Love Story*. "Love is never having to say you're sorry." I strongly disagree. Love carries with it the ability to say, even on the part of parents to their children, "I'm sorry. I made a mistake. Please forgive me."

Learning the lessons of forgiveness, one of the most important lessons of the Christian life, happens right in the texture of daily living. The Lord's Prayer teaches us that!

> "Give us this day our daily bread
> And forgive us our debts
> As we forgive our debtors."

The meaning of a word can be grasped only as we experience its lived meaning; otherwise it is only a sound. For example, take the word "trust". Trust cannot be taught apart from a trusting relationship; it must be awakened in the course of living with persons who can be trusted. Only then does the verbal symbol take on any meaning for a person. The Spirit of God sanctifies human relationships and through them makes communication possible between persons and between persons and God. The language of relationships and the language of words must fit together, flow together if meaningful communication is to take place.

The home initiates the growing child into the use of the church's language primarily at the point of the experiences in relationship out of which words grow. In addition to the word trust, all other basic words in the Christian vocabulary such as **love, faith, forgiveness, hope, reconciliation, grace, joy, peace, patience, kindness, goodness, gentleness, self-control** grow out of relationships in the Christian home. They must be experienced before they can be meaningfully verbalized. These are, for the most part, words of relationship. Love and acceptance, so crucial to every human being, are needs from the moment of birth until the moment of death. These needs are first satisfied in the relationship with parents; if they are not adequately met in that relationship and in subsequent relationships in the family, the person may find it difficult to show love and acceptance to others in later years.

It is in the family setting that the capacity for speech and language is nurtured as the mother and father lovingly coax those first inarticulate grunts and squeals from the young child and through a process which all of us have experienced at firsthand but none can adequately describe, the transformation from mere noise to intelligible words takes place. The rudiments of a language are learned in a family long before they are learned in a school. The school can only build upon the solid foundation which has been laid down in the family. The school picks up the task in a more formal, systematic way teaching the child the meaning of new words, how to spell words, how to put words together so they express a larger complex of ideas and how words and ideas arise out of the world in which they live. Words help them to make ordered sense out of their experience.

So it is with the Sunday school. Our faith has its own distinctive vocabulary, the language of faith, and it must be learned, just as any language is learned. In a more formal and systematic way, the Sunday school helps children to organize their vocabulary, enlarge and extend it, put new content into it, relate it to their widening religious world and thus to make ordered sense out of it. In this way, growing children begin to lay hold on the **tradition**, the **culture**, the **history** and the **literary treasures** to which they are the heirs. This task includes telling them the fascinating stories of the Bible, introducing them to the biblical characters, reliving with them the biblical drama, helping them discover the covenant structure of the Bible, and aiding them in their grasp of the essentials of the biblical message. The well-known example of Timothy as reported in 2 Timothy 3:14-15 serves as a pattern and points to the goal of this acquaintance "with the sacred writings which are able to instruct you for salvation through faith in Christ Jesus."

Learning in the family is more like learning to drive a car than like learning arithmetic or chemistry. We saw earlier how a small child learns a complex set of skills called language long before he goes to school simply by living in the family. This happens not by sitting down with a book and a teacher but by responding in various ways to the people who talk with the child. Much encouragement and reinforcement of effort are given in response to the child's efforts but there is a built-in motivation to learn to communicate as well. Communication is a fundamental part of any relationship and the growing child thrives and grows on relationships.

The complex of interpersonal relationships we call the family not only uses language to communicate, it is itself a language. Rueul Howe calls this, "the language of relationships." It is in our relationships that we experience both life's greatest joys and its greatest problems. Our relationships reflect both the agony and the ecstasy of our being.

> When we communicate with others,
>   talk and listen,
>   hear and understand,
> when we come out of our aloneness,
> when we love and are loved
>   we are most truly happy.
>
> When we cannot get through to others or they cannot reach us,
> when we are ignored or misunderstood,
> when we hate or are hated,
>   we are truly most miserable.

Nor can a person who is alienated and isolated from other persons find consolation in withdrawing from others into fellowship with God alone. "If anyone says, I love God and hates his brother, he is a liar for he who does not love his brother whom he has seen cannot love God whom he has not seen. And this commandment we have from him that he who loves God should love his brother also." 1 John 4:20-21.

The task of the family in Christian nurture includes helping persons learn

> to communicate with each other, to hear and be heard,
> to love and be loved,
> to forgive and to be forgiven,
> to accept and to be accepted,
> in short, to belong.

One cannot be a person all alone. I need you in order to be and in order to become. It is in our relationships that we exist at all. This is, I believe, the profoundest theological meaning of family and one of the reasons that family images are to be found among the images which illumine the nature of life together in the household of faith.

Another of the tasks of the home in the Christian nurture of children is helping children learn to make decisions. Perhaps the first visible evidence of its emergence is to be seen in the baby sitting in a high chair. Picture, if you will, mother spooning in the food with baby swallowing every mouthful obediently and unthinkingly. But if mother were a careful observer she would notice that after a time baby's cheeks are filling up with food and she would be less surprised when it comes spewing back out in the form of a small volcano. That is baby's first articulate "no" and it is followed by many others. Note the toddler's delight with the very sound of the word "no" and the power that goes with it to control other people's responses and limit their pleasures. "Come sit on my knee." "No!" "Will you help me with the dishes?" "Do I have to?" "Do your homework first, then watch TV." "Oh mother!" "Will you carry out the garbage for me?" "Later!" "Please make your bed and tidy up your room." "It's not important!" "Hurry with your shower and let some others use the bathroom." "I have to shampoo my hair." "Will you go to the ball game with me tomorrow night?" "I'd love to!" It's at about that point in the developmental process when Susie is beginning to say "yes", when you thought she knew only how to say "no", that mother begins reinforcing her ability to say no. On one occasion, my wife and I attended a meeting of the American Association for Marriage and Family Therapy; one of the speakers, now a professional therapist as well as a mother, said her mother's letters to her when she was in college always ended with the words, "maintain your character", and she always knew precisely what was intended. It was the only form of sex education she received.

I have focused primarily on the "no" but the capacity to decide involves also the ability to say "yes", to make an affirmation. The developing person must learn how to discriminate, to assess a situation and understand what it's all about and what is going on, what are the implications and consequences of this response or that one (of a yes, a no, or a maybe). The curriculum of living and growing up is filled with all manner of such decisions so that it could be said without exaggeration that living is deciding and education is learning to decide wisely.

I am impressed with the wide range of decisions to be made—both their scope and the measure of importance attached to them. I am also impressed with the fact that as a parent it has been very difficult to give my children the amount of free space they need to make their **own** decisions as they get older. I am also impressed that my experience could be very valuable to them and could save them a lot of pain if they chose to profit by it. But I have become reconciled (almost) to the reality that wisdom can't be told. Each person and each generation, it seems, must learn wisdom for itself rather than primarily through the experience of the preceding generation. The social environment (both within our family and beyond it in the church, the school, the community, the nation, the world) is far different for my children than the one in which their mother and I grew up.

You can without effort think of many such occasions at each step in the developmental process from deciding which toys I want to play with to whether I will share them, what dress to wear, what I want for Christmas, who my friends will be, whether to drop piano lessons and go out for cheerleading instead, whom to date and where to go, should I go to college and on and on and on. A major decision has to do with the matter of personal faith and membership in the body of Christ and what discipleship calls for.

I should like to say a word before I conclude lest I be misunderstood. I have not been assuming a family situation that is perfect—parents who are always loving and understanding, who never make mistakes or lose their tempers, brothers and sisters who never fight and quarrel and so forth. We are not perfect in our families even in what are sometimes called "the best of families," far from it. This realization may lead us to despair, especially when we realize how far short of the mark we really fall. But let me point this out to you, if we **were** perfect, we would have no need for God in our families. We would have no occasion to learn grace and forgiveness. God can use our feeble faltering efforts as parents and children living together and out of these accomplish his own good purposes for us.

At a certain point both parent and child must recognize their limitations and look to God who alone can love them perfectly and accept them fully. The ultimate source of love, acceptance and forgiveness is in God. As parents we can lead our children toward God by loving them even in fragmentary ways and by acknowledging to them that God is the source of our loving. Of course, our children do not automatically become members of God's family of faith simply by growing up in a human family, not even in a Christian family. Just as we are born by physical birth into a human family, so we must be born by spiritual birth into God's family.

The Christian family cannot guarantee that this will happen. It can, however, be a place where God is experienced. The Christian family points beyond itself to a larger family, the family of faith. But it not only **points**, it also **prepares** the growing person for living in the family of faith. It becomes a training ground for true spiritual community since the lessons it teaches are so basic for the life of faith.

Finally, the Christian family not only **points** to and not only **prepares** for, but it also **participates** in that larger spiritual family toward which it **points** and for which it **prepares**. The presence of Christ, if he is truly the head of this house as our wall mottoes proclaim, makes all the difference and transforms even the humblest cottage into a little bit of heaven on earth.

4

The Teacher: Example, Revealer, Change Agent

The ministry of teaching finds its model in the ministry of Jesus who was himself a teacher and its mandate in the commission he gave his followers to make disciples, baptize and teach them (Mt. 28:19-20). The gift of teaching is included in each of the lists of spiritual gifts given by Christ to the members of his body (Rom. 12:7; 1 Cor. 12:28; Eph. 4:11). It is essential both to the mission of the church in the world in evangelizing and discipling persons as well as to its inner life in building up the body of Christ and equipping its members for their ministry. The aim of teaching, like that of all the spiritual gifts, is "to prepare God's people for works of service, so that the body of Christ may be built up until we all reach unity in the faith and in the knowledge of the Son of God and become mature, attaining to the whole measure of the fullness of Christ" (Eph. 4:12-13 NIV).

L. J. Sherrill notes that Jesus is called Teacher (or an equivalent form of address) sixty-one times in the gospels. Forty-seven additional times he is spoken of as teaching.[1] Jesus did not simply go about telling people how to get along with their neighbors and that they shouldn't steal. By his words and by his actions, he was announcing that what the prophets had looked forward to was now coming into fulfillment. In his suffering, death and resurrection, he made it possible for people to enter into the kingdom of God which he proclaimed and interpreted. His life was an example of what kingdom living was all about, his teaching revealed and interpreted the nature of the kingdom, and his total ministry including his prophetic deeds were oriented toward the goal of inaugurating God's rule in the hearts and lives of the people.

Obviously teaching was an important part of Jesus' total ministry. He was recognized as a teacher and called master or rabbi by his disciples, by the crowds and even by those who opposed him. His followers were known as disciples, i.e., learners or pupils, those who attached themselves to a rabbi and formed his school. Of course, Jesus was also seen as a prophet, a miracle worker, a healer, a revolutionary, a reformer, a charismatic figure, a preacher, a Savior from sin. And he was all of these. Nor was his teaching something other than these; it was woven into the texture of his total ministry and gave it cohesiveness.

Matthew, very early in his gospel, reports on Jesus' ministries of teaching and preaching that are so closely intertwined that it is well-nigh impossible to separate them. "From that time on Jesus began to preach, 'Repent, for the kingdom of heaven is near.'" (Mt. 4:17) Then follows the calling of the first disciples (Mt. 4:18-22) and then in Mt. 4:23, he begins his ministry in earnest.

> "Jesus went throughout Galilee,
> teaching in their synagogues,
> preaching the good news of the kingdom,
> and healing every disease and sickness among the people."

A great surge of excitement swept across the countryside as the news of this proclaimer-healer-teacher spread and large crowds started to follow him around. When he saw the crowds, he withdrew a little distance from them and gathering his disciples around him in an inner circle, he began to **teach** them. This is sometimes referred to as the Sermon on the Mount, a **sermon** that is **taught**.

Harold Lindsell's note on Mt. 5:1 in the R.S.V. study text states,

> The impression is usually given that the Sermon on the Mount was spoken on a single occasion during the early ministry of our Lord. Many hold that these three chapters contain teachings of Jesus which were given on many different occasions. Undoubtedly, much that Jesus said has not been recorded and many of his utterances were probably repeated in different places and on various occasions.

At the conclusion of the Sermon, Matthew reports in 7:28-29 that "when Jesus had finished saying these things, the crowd was amazed at his teaching because he taught as one who had authority and not as their teachers of the law." Apparently the crowd had pressed in closer upon Jesus and his circle of disciples to hear what he was teaching them. We shall return to this text a little later to reflect on why the crowd was amazed but first let us examine the content of his teaching as well as his style or method.

Jesus begins with what we have come to call the Beatitudes, Blessed are you __________; blessed are you __________." It is a text reminiscent of Deuteronomy 28:1-6. The context in Deuteronomy is the covenant making between God and his people. The law has been set forth. There are curses for disobedience; there is blessing for obedience.

It is not an accident that Matthew places this material on Jesus' teaching about the law so early in his account because he is appealing to Jewish hearers. Note the strong, keen interest of the people in what Jesus has to say about the law. Then in 5:17ff, Matthew sets forth explicitly Jesus' interpretation of the law.

> Do not think that I have come to abolish the law or the prophets; I have not come to abolish them but to fulfill them. (Mt. 5:17)

It is not surprising that this would be an early theme in Jesus' teaching and in Matthew's gospel considering how central *Torah*—the law—was in Jewish teaching. The people would want to know at once where this new teacher stood in relation to *Torah.*

5:21 - "You have heard that it was said to the people long ago…but I say unto you"
5:21 - Do not murder
5:27 - Do not commit adultery
5:33 - Do not break your oath
5:38 - Eye for eye and tooth for tooth
5:43 - Love your neighbor and hate your enemy

In each case, Jesus did a reinterpretation of the meaning and application of the commandment which involved going back behind the interpretations and applications with which the people were familiar. He went right back to first principles, to the heart and core of the law as God first intended it and sent it forth. Jesus said, "Don't even be angry with your brother and never call him a fool"; "Don't even look at another person lustfully"; "Do not swear at all but simply let your yes be yes and your no be no"; "Do not resist an evil person"; "Love your enemies and pray for those who persecute you".

Jesus then went on to reinterpret various religious rituals and observances—alms, prayer and fasting. He taught them about basic values, attitudes and relationships by setting up contrasts between

- treasures on earth and treasures in heaven
- light and darkness
- God and mammon
- trust and anxiety
- being judgmental of others vs. being self-critical
- narrow and wide gates
- true and false prophets
- true and false confessions
- the wise man and the foolish man

These materials in chapters 5-7 of Matthew's gospel are followed by more healing, miracles, confrontation and conflict and by a long section in which Jesus teaches in parables. Finally come the passion materials, Jesus' death and resurrection and the commission to his disciples to carry on the ministry he had begun and taught them to do:

> "Therefore go and make disciples of all nations, baptizing them in the name of the Father and of the Son and of the Holy Spirit, and teaching them to obey everything I have commanded you. And surely I will be with you always to the very end of the age." Mt. 28:19-20.

The material in chapters 5-7 is one example of a major **discourse** in which a number of people gather around him to hear what he had to say. Sometimes he gave his discourses on the side of the mountain, sometimes in a level place, sometimes in a synagogue, sometimes in a boat, sometimes in a private home, once while walking through a grainfield, once on the shore of the lake, in short, wherever he came into contact with persons who were ready to listen to him.

But the discourse or lecture or sermon was only one medium of interpretation or teaching. A second major medium was the **story** and particularly the **parable** which is a special kind of story. A parable is a story which draws its characters, its plot, its scene from the everyday world which was part of everyone's experience. It engages the listener with things he is familiar with and uses them as a bridge to help him walk into a new and unfamiliar world with some degree of understanding. It moves the hearer

- from the known to the unknown
- from the physical world to the spiritual world
- from the earthly to the heavenly.

It is based on analogy. "The kingdom of heaven is like..." Jesus drew his parables from incidents his hearers could easily identify with: a farmer going out to sow, weeds growing up with the wheat, sheep that are lost, being in debt, two sons who took a different course in life, one faithful and loyal—the other a runaway and a spendthrift, a wedding feast and on and on.

Notice how effective parables are for teaching a simple truth:

a) they are interesting
b) they are easily grasped
c) they are easily remembered
d) they are like a joke. "Did you get the point?"
e) there is in them an explosive quality. On the face of it, they are harmless enough, but they are capable of penetrating the barriers to spiritual truth and of doing their work in the interiority of the listener.

A third method of teaching employed by Jesus was the use of **images**, **symbols** and **figures of speech** such as analogies. In fact some of the parables are simply analogies, not extended stories. Examples are the parable of the leaven (Mt. 13:33); the grain of mustard seed (13:31-32); the hidden treasure (13:44); the pearl (13:45); the fishing net (13:47-48). Other images (metaphors) which he used effectively are fishers of men, the narrow way, the straight gate, the door, the shepherd, the harvest, light, salt, candle, temple. He also employed symbols to illumine kingdom realities, both symbolic objects and symbolic acts: washing the disciple's feet, the child in the midst, the bread and the wine, the cup, the cross, the wind, the vine and its branches.

A fourth method that Jesus employed was his frequent use of **short sayings**. They were pregnant with meaning, intended for pondering, vivid, often quoted, easily remembered.

Mt. 9:37 "The harvest is plentiful; the laborers are few."

Mt. 10:24-25 "A disciple is not above his teacher, nor a servant above his master; it is enough for the disciple to be like his teacher and the servant like his master."

Mt. 10:34 "Do not think that I have come to bring peace on earth; I have not come to bring peace but a sword."

Besides the short sayings of Jesus, there are the **hard sayings**. These are challenges which confronted a person and required a decisive response. They were easy enough to understand but not at all easy to practice.

Mt. 10:37-38 "He who loves father or mother more than me is not worthy of me; and he who loves son or daughter more than me is not worthy of me; and he who does not take his cross and follow me is not worthy of me."

Mt. 10:39 "He who finds his life will lose it and he who loses his life for my sake will find it."

Mt. 8:19-20 "Teacher, I will follow you wherever you go." And Jesus said to him, "Foxes have holes and birds of the air have nests; but the Son of man has nowhere to lay his head."

Mt. 8:21-22 "Lord, let me first go and bury my father." But Jesus said to him, "Follow me and leave the dead to bury their own dead."

Questions and answers were yet another way in which Jesus got across his message of the kingdom of God. Sometimes the question was rhetorical; sometimes he used it to lead up to a point he was making; sometimes he answered a question with a question; sometimes it was a call for decision.

Mt. 7:9-10 "What man of you, if his son asks him for bread will give him a stone? Or if he asks for a fish will give him a serpent?"

Mt. 7:3 "Why do you see the speck that is in your brother's eye, but do not notice the log that is in your own eye?"

Mt. 22:15-22, esp. v. 20 "Whose likeness and inscription is this?"

The **critical incident** became yet another occasion for interpreting the kingdom. One such incident is recorded in Mt. 26:6-13. It was the occasion when a woman poured a jar of expensive perfume on his head and the disciples at that very moment developed a conscience about the plight of the poor. It is from this incident that we have those oft-quoted and misquoted words of Jesus, "The poor you will always have with you." Jesus was commending her not for her profligacy but for her spiritual sensitivity. "When she poured this perfume on my body, she did it to prepare me for burial." (Mt. 26:12)

Another critical incident occurred when Mrs. Zebedee, the mother of two of Jesus' disciples, James and John, came to Jesus with a request that her boys be permitted to sit on his immediate right and left in his kingdom. "You don't know what you are asking," said Jesus. "Can you drink the cup I am going to drink?" (Mt. 20:22) This became the occasion for teaching about the nature of power in the upside-down kingdom where "whoever wants to become great among you must be your servant and whoever wants to be first must be your slave." (Mt. 20:26-27) The impact of these lessons at such times of dramatic encounter and heightened awareness was very powerful. These were truly teachable moments.

Another interesting point to be made is the **copious use of Scripture** which Jesus made indicating both a wide and deep acquaintance with the Hebrew Scriptures. It would make an interesting research project to note the sources that he drew upon most frequently and how he interpreted these texts. It is quite natural that Jesus would make *Torah* (the law) the subject matter of his teaching for that would have been the subject matter he had been taught as a boy and as a young man. We noted that he began with *Torah* and his reinterpretation of it in the first major teaching setting recorded in the gospel of Matthew. As we saw, Matthew places it first in order to underscore its central significance in Jesus' teaching. Matthew, writing to a Jewish audience, knew that the issue of how Jesus interpreted the law would be one of central importance to them.

But an even more important theme that dominates many or most of the teachings of Jesus is the kingdom of God. In one sense this is a new theme but in another sense, it is simply another way of interpreting an old theme, **law**. Both **law** and **kingdom** speak of God's authority, God's rule in the hearts and lives of his people. Jesus announced the immediate inbreak of the kingdom of God with a sense of urgency. Law for some had become an impersonal code, a heavy and burdensome set of regulations. But the announcement of the imminent arrival of the King to be with his subjects brings with it a renewed sense of excitement and enthusiasm. It calls for a living response, not merely passive conformity.

Moreover, Jesus was not only proclaiming or heralding the coming of the kingdom; he saw his ministry of healing and forgiving sins and calling on people to repent as actually inaugurating the kingdom.

> The Spirit of the Lord is on me,
> because he has anointed me to preach good news to the poor.
> He has sent me to proclaim freedom for the prisoners
> and recovery of sight for the blind,
> to release the oppressed,
> to proclaim the year of the Lord's favor.
> --
> Today this Scripture is fulfilled in your hearing. (Luke 4:18-19, 21)

Jesus had a sense of destiny and authority which gave the note of integrity and authenticity to what he did and what he taught. He could not be evaded; he could not be ignored. The kingdom of God was his basic theme; the "sermon" on the mount was the promulgation of the constitution of the kingdom. He went beyond and behind the traditional interpretations and applications of the law; he sliced through the layers and layers which had accumulated over the years to the heart of TORAH, to the original intention of God. His interpretation was even more demanding and exacting than that of the Pharisees for he insisted on examining not only the act but also the motive, not only the deed but what was hidden in the heart. The scribes worked with secondary sources; Jesus worked with the primary source, the law as it came forth from the heart of God. Small wonder that the "crowds were amazed at his teaching because he taught as one who had authority and not as their teachers of the law." (Mt. 7:28-29) He knew at first hand whereof he spoke and there was a total congruence between who he was, what he said, what he did and how he lived. He embodied in his own person a full obedience to the will of God for he was obedient—even unto death.

The commission Jesus gave his disciples at the end of his earthly ministry was essentially that of carrying on what he had begun—making disciples, baptizing them and teaching them to observe all that he had commanded. Teaching is an integral part of that commission. What does it mean to teach as Jesus taught? Our teaching ministry, if it is to resemble his, must be set within the context of our participation in his mission today. Bible study in the living context of our involvement in mission is Bible study that is alive and fruitful. The questions and issues that emerge from our encounter with the world as we go out on the front lines to do spiritual battle will be authentic ones, life and death ones. The answers will be found only through a serious search of the Word of God with a view both to knowing and to doing the will of God.

Those teachers who pattern their teaching after the example of the Master Teacher will have a vision of the kingdom of God guiding them. They will see the sinfulness and brokenness of the world, the poverty, disease, illiteracy, malnutrition, exploitation, discrimination, prejudice, injustice, violence, and misplaced priorities so widespread in our society. But they will neither ignore these realities nor despair. They will be sustained by the vision that God is moving and acting in history, that his reign will ultimately triumph over the forces of sin and death which separate, alienate and destroy people. They will hear the echo of the words of the prophet Isaiah as they reverberated like thunder in the synagogue at Nazareth the day that Jesus read them out loud. (Luke 4:18-19, 21; quoting Isaiah 61:1-2)

Those teachers who pattern their teaching after the example of the Master Teacher will have both a heightened awareness of the brokenness of the world and a vision of what the world can become as people submit themselves to the rule of God.

After a period of following Jesus around, observing his ministry of preaching, teaching and healing, the twelve disciples of Jesus were sent out by him to carry out that same ministry under his authority and following his example. It was in that setting as he was giving them their final orientation that he said to them, "A disciple is not above his teacher, nor a servant above his master; it is enough for the disciple to be like his teacher, and the servant like his master." (Mt. 10:24)

Paul made much of the idea of the **teacher as example**, as guide, as mentor, even invoking the image of the teacher as parent.

> For though you have countless guides in Christ, you do not have many fathers. For I became your father in Christ Jesus through the gospel. I urge you, then, be imitators of me. (I Cor. 4:15-17)

This admonition is repeated and qualified in 1 Corinthians 11:1, "Be imitators of me, as I am of Christ."

Following that eloquent statement in Philippians 3:4-16 in which he talks about his central goal in life as being "the prize of the upward call of God in Christ Jesus," Paul calls on his readers to "join in imitating me, and mark those who so live as you have an example in us." (Phil. 3:17) Several times in his letters to the Thessalonian believers, Paul refers to the fact that they "became imitators of us and of the Lord...so that you became an example to all the believers in Macedonia and in Achaia." (1 Thess. 1:6-7) In the second letter, he refers to an example he set for them in his conduct which they were to imitate. (2 Thess. 3:7-9) In his admonition to Timothy, Paul emphasized how important it is for the teacher to set an example.

> Command and teach these things. Let no one despise your youth, but set the believers an example in speech and conduct, in love, in faith, in purity. Till I come, attend to the public reading of Scripture, to preaching, to teaching. Do not neglect the gift you have, which was given you by prophetic utterance when the elders laid their hands upon you. Practice these duties, devote yourself to them, so that all may see your progress. Take heed to yourself and to your teaching; hold to that, for by so doing you will save both yourself and your hearers. (1 Tim. 4:11-16)

The Teacher-Disciple or Paul-Timothy programs are good illustrations of teaching programs in which being an example is a central feature of the teaching-learning model. Other developments which make heavy use of this element are the Life Planning Program of the Office of Youth Ministries of the Mennonite Board of Congregational Ministries and, more recently, a number of mentoring programs. The key to the success of these programs is **the quality of the relationship between an adult**

and a youth. Among other roles, the adult serves as mentor, guide, counselor, role model.

Formally, the term **advocate** has been selected to describe these multiple functions, a term which is defined as an adult who is willing to care deeply about a young person, one who is willing to give time to a youth, one who wants more than anything else that youth to become all that he or she was created by God to be. While this role is built centrally into the design of these programs, I believe it is implicit in all effective teaching in the church at every age level. It is a high view of teaching which calls for complete integrity between the teacher's life and the teacher's words. It was this total congruity between his words and his actions that gave the ring of authority to Jesus' teaching and caused the crowd to marvel.

A second way in which we may pattern our teaching after that of Jesus is that of the **teacher as revealer**. Is it not presumptuous, we may ask, to think of our teaching as revelation? Revelation is the self-disclosure of God, his nature, his person, his will. In centering his teaching on the kingdom of God, Jesus was doing precisely this, revealing the Father, his person, his will. What a high calling to follow in his footsteps entering into that very task! What a demanding challenge! How might we go about it?

One way of thinking about this task which commends itself to me is to think of the Bible as recording various conversations between God and his people in which God discloses himself, his person, his will. I am interested in those conversations. I want to listen in on them, in fact, I want to participate in them. I want to hear God speaking and I want to join in the conversation with him. As a Bible teacher, I want the members of my class to tune in on those conversations and eventually to become part of them for without response there is no revelation. Revelation and response belong together.

Conversation is not an easy thing, at least conversation in which there is clear communication is not easy. I agree with that saying that goes as follows: "I know you believe you understand what you think I said, but I am not sure you realize that what you heard is not what I meant." No, conversation is not easy even at best when both parties are physically present in the same place at the same time speaking the same language.

Let's make it even more difficult; let's make it a letter or a written document. The reader receives it some time after it has been written. He puzzles over the meaning of certain phrases. He cannot be sure if the writer is making a joke or if the writer was angry. He cannot look into the writer's face to search for clues, a dimple or a glint in the eye or the firm set of the jaw. He cannot ask for clarification.

Let's make it even more difficult; the letter is written in a foreign language. Perhaps it has been translated but something is lost in the translation, some subtle nuance of meaning. Several translations appear but they do not agree with each other. The additional factors to take into account are the fact that the documents were written hundreds of years ago, several thousand in some cases. In fact we don't even have the originals, just copies of copies of copies and there have been little changes here and there along the way. The people who participated in these early conversations lived in a world far different from ours and faced situations very different from ours in many respects.

Now who is going to fan the embers of these ancient conversations to get them to burst into flame, to come alive again for us in our situation today so that we can hear God speaking and actually join in that conversation? The teacher of the Bible, that's who. The teacher operates on the assumption that the Scriptures are a living, contemporary document and that by studying them we will be able to hear the living Lord of the text speaking to his people again. The task of teaching has as its goal the revival of that original conversation. The task of reconstructing the ancient text and deciphering its meaning in its original setting is not the end of the process but one of the means to the end, a living conversation. We reconstruct the original conversation so that we may participate in it.

We may be helped in visualizing this process by imagining a group of people sitting around a fire deeply engaged in conversation. We first see them from a distance and the earnestness of their talk attracts our curiosity. We move in closer so that we can overhear what it is that causes them to speak in such an animated manner. The more we hear the more interested we become, the closer we move in to the edge of the circle. Our excitement about the subject mounts until finally we can keep silent no longer and we break in with our comments. The people in the circle move closer together in order to make room for us to join them. Now we are no longer conscious of the differences in years, in situations, in language. Now we are contemporaries with Jesus and his disciples so that if our desire for power and prominence get out of hand and are betrayed in the way we speak and jostle for position we see him turn to us and hear him say to us, "Whoever would be great among you must be your servant." (Mark 10:43)

One of the most effective methods of joining the original conversations is one that Jesus employed, the story, especially the parable. I once employed this method in a Keystone Bible Institute. Several people sat around an imaginary bonfire retelling the Biblical parables in their own words or telling parables of the kingdom of their own composition drawing on familiar events of our time. Gradually, one by one other members of the group drew near and joined the circle, interrupting with the words, "That reminds me of a story," and proceeded to tell it. At the end of the evening, there were no spectators outside the circle; we had all been drawn in as participants. It was an exciting evening.

Our final reflections are on the **teacher as change agent**. When teaching becomes revelation in fact, there is response. Without response, there is no self-disclosure of God's person or his purpose. Response involves change on the part of those responding. If the response is a "no", there is a hardening of the heart and further separation and alienation. If the response is a "yes", the response of faith, there is new life. There is repentance, there is healing, there is a closing of the gap which separates us from God. We gain new awareness of ourselves and of our true condition. We begin to see the world from God's point of view. God's purposes begin to pulse in our lives and motivate our desires and actions.

This change in our inner beings leads to change in our relationships. We are bound together into a community of those who belong to him. The New Testament speaks of this community in various ways including the people of God, the body of Christ, the fellowship of the Holy Spirit. It is this transformation from individualism to life together in Christ that is the most radical difference between those whose response is "yes" and those whose response is "no". This is the watershed which determines how persons respond to every significant issue which faces humankind in our world today, economic, social, ideological, political. Individualism and self-realization, the twin gods of secular society, represent the most virile challenge to life in the kingdom of God that we face today.

Change in the inner being which leads to change in relationships also calls for change in the way we confront our world. Earlier we noted that to pattern our teaching after that of Jesus is to have a heightened awareness of both the brokenness of the world and of the transformation of that world when the kingdom of God has fully come. When Jesus called on people to "repent, for the kingdom of heaven is at hand," (Mt. 3:2) it is clear that he was calling not only for a change of heart but for a radical change in human relationships and for the way people who repented were to live in the world.

It is sadly true that all too often we fail to discern the larger implications and applications of the good news of the kingdom. We fail to see, as one person recently put it, that the gospel isn't good news for everybody. It is good news indeed to the poor, to the captives, to the blind and to the oppressed. But is it good news to the oppressor, to the captors, to the rich and to the overprivileged?

How may we sort out whether the gospel is good news or bad news for us? How may we discover what God requires of us? How shall we respond to God's selfdisclosure? These questions raise more than educational issues but they do have some educational implications. One method of teaching-learning that can be helpful in this respect is known as action-reflection. Whether one begins with action or reflection is not the most important; what is important is that both be included in the process of study and that they interact with each other.

Numerous examples of the action-reflection method may be cited from Jesus' teaching ministry. In Matthew 12 there is a record of Jesus going through the grainfields on the sabbath and of his disciples plucking the grain and eating it. This became the occasion for an important lesson on the meaning of sabbath. This incident is followed by another one in the synagogue where Jesus healed a man with a withered hand. Luke's account (Luke 10:25-37) of Jesus' encounter with the lawyer who inquired about how he might inherit eternal life is twice punctuated with the admonition to try out the theory under discussion in actual life. "You have answered right; do this and you will live" (Luke 10:28). "Go and do likewise" (Luke 10:37). The lesson Jesus was teaching here could not be learned through abstractions alone; it had to be lived in order to be mastered.

In this lies a necessary corrective to so much of the teaching and learning which goes on in the church. Perhaps it is because we are bound too closely into a building (time and place) that we are bound too closely into a strategy which emphasizes reflection to the exclusion of decision and action. Only when we recover the rhythm of action-reflection will learning take place in its fullest and deepest measure.

Conclusion

We have looked at the teacher in terms of three roles: example, revealer, and change agent. Each of these provides a pattern for Christian teachers in our time. As example, Jesus models a life that is totally submissive to the will of God. As a result, his words and his life are congruent with each other and both serve as an interpretation of the kingdom of God. As revealer, Jesus illumined in many different ways what the kingdom of God is like. He employed such effective methods as discourse, story, images, symbols, figures of speech, short sayings, hard sayings, questions and answers, the critical incident, and copious use of Scripture. As change agent, he not only announced the kingdom but set about inaugurating it and calling upon people to repent and live transformed lives in the kingdom. Such transformation called for conversion, for life together in the body of Christ as well as for confrontation of the principalities and powers to acknowledge God's sovereignty in every area of life.

Such is the commission we have received, to carry on the ministry Jesus began. Is this task too large for us? Yes and no! It is if we attempt to carry it out in our own strength, even if we copy his model as carefully as we can. But we need not go in our own strength. We teach under the mandate of him to whom has been given all authority in heaven and on earth and with the assurance that "lo, I am with you always, to the close of the age." (Mt. 28:20)

---

[1] L.J. Sherrill, *The Rise of Christian Education* (New York: The Macmillan Company, 1994), 86.

II

Congregational Education

Because my people had a long memory in which the biblical world was as real as the modern world (or more so), I came to share that memory, that tradition, that history and claim it as my own.

5

The Teaching Ministry of the Church

One of the most vigorous debates in New Testament theology of the past several decades centered on the distinction between *kerygma* and *didache*, a distinction first made popular in English-speaking theological circles by C.H. Dodd. His brief work *The Apostolic Preaching and Its Developments* has proven to be extremely influential and some scholars have accepted this distinction. At the same time, a reaction on the part of other scholars has set in against this distinction as being unduly arbitrary and as doing violence to the true nature of the biblical revelation. This distinction has significant implications for the educational ministry of the church and it is from this perspective that we shall attempt to discern the central issues in the debate.

The distinction drawn by Dodd is not alone that of content, but extends also to the activity appropriate to the communication of a particular type of content. Thus, according to this point of view, there is material in the New Testament whose communication is properly the task of preaching (*kerygma*), distinct from that New Testament material whose communication is properly the task of teaching (*didache*). The content of Christian teaching, it is held, is largely ethical instruction, though it includes to some extent the "reasoned commendation of Christianity to persons interested but not yet convinced. Sometimes, especially in the Johannine writings, it includes the exposition of theological doctrine."[1] The *kerygma*, on the other hand, represents the core of the preaching of the earliest church, the proclamation to the world at large of their gospel.

Dodd examines with care two major N.T. sources in order to discover the essential elements of the *kerygma* proclaimed by the apostles. These sources are the epistles of Paul and the Acts of the Apostles. The Pauline epistles themselves, says Dodd, while they are primarily *didache* and not *kerygma* (that is, they are addressed to believers and deal with problems of the Christian life) do yield by inference valid data concerning the original *kerygma* out of which they arose. Those passages which give evidence of being common formulary statements (e.g., I Cor. 15: lff.;

Rom. 8:31-34) are particularly fertile for yielding information concerning the original *kerygma* for in them the oral tradition of the earliest church has been set down in written form.

The second major source is to be found in the accounts of the apostolic sermons in the first chapters of the Acts of the Apostles. While there are several points in the Pauline *kerygma* omitted in the Jerusalem *kerygma* of Acts, yet, Dodd concludes, all the essential points of the latter appear in Paul. The Pauline *kerygma* is outlined as follows:

> The prophecies are fulfilled, and the new age is inaugurated by the coming of Christ.
> He was born of the seed of David.
> He died according to the Scriptures, to deliver us out of the present evil age.
> He was buried.
> He rose on the third day according to the Scriptures.
> He is exalted at the right hand of God, as Son of God and Lord of the quick and dead.
> He will come again as Judge and Savior of men.[2]

Dodd summarizes the *kerygma* of Acts as gleaned particularly from the sermons attributed to Peter and asserts that these two sources "supplement one another and taken together they afford a comprehensive view of the content of the early *kergyma*." The main points in the summary are:

> (a) The age of fulfillment has dawned.
> (b) This has taken place through the ministry, death, and resurrection of Jesus, of which a brief account is given, with proof from the Scriptures that all took place through 'the determinate counsel and foreknowledge of God'. This is what is known as the 'historical section' of the *kerygma* and includes references to Jesus' Davidic descent, his earthly ministry, his death and resurrection.
> (c) By virtue of the resurrection, Jesus has been exalted at the right hand of God, as Messianic head of the new Israel.
> (d) The Holy Spirit in the Church is the sign of Christ's present power and glory.
> (e) The Messianic age will shortly reach its consummation in the return of Christ.

(f) The *kerygma* always closes with an appeal for repentance, the offer of forgiveness and of the Holy Spirit, and the promise of 'salvation', that is, of 'the life of the age to come', to those who enter the elect community.[3]

There are three distinct aspects in Dodd's summary of the *kerygma*: the conviction that prophecy has passed into fulfillment, the historical section which reviews the life, death, resurrection and ascension of Christ, and the call to repentance. This provides the structure for the Gospel of Mark which, it is suggested, is simply an expanded form of the historical section. The Gospel of Matthew puts less proportionate emphasis on the historical facts of the passion, death, and resurrection and makes much of the theme "born of the seed of David" and the fulfillment of prophecy. It is in Matthew, moreover, that a new kind of material appears, "a large collection of sayings of Jesus arranged so as to form a fairly systematic account of his teaching. It is presented as a new Law given by the Messianic King."[4] Dodd holds that Matthew is a combination of *kerygma* and *didache* with *didache* predominating.

T.W. Manson has done a major piece of research into the teaching work of Jesus.[5] He limits his study to the Synoptic Gospels and their sources. He holds that one must see Jesus' teaching in the context of his earthly life and ministry, so that part of the task is a reconstruction of the life of Jesus. "The life interprets the teaching and the teaching the life."[6] Through this methodological procedure, he arrives at a number of significant conclusions. One such conclusion is that the confession of Peter marks a turning point in the life of Jesus and that this significantly affected the character of his teaching and occasioned the emergence of new keywords into his vocabulary. One such term which reflects a new self-consciousness is "Son of Man" with its Messianic implications. Manson further observes that it is possible to demonstrate that the character of the teaching varied according to the audience involved: "Jesus has one way of dealing with the Scribes and Pharisees, another for the multitudes and yet another for his intimate disciples."[7] These variations in his teaching involve not only its content but extend also to the method which he employed.

The primary contribution of Manson to the discussion is that his work demonstrates that the teaching of Jesus profoundly influenced the theological understanding of the earliest church and that it is a gross misrepresentation of it to categorize it as merely ethical instruction. His teaching about the kingdom of God, which he declared was now at hand, reflected a unique understanding of the Old Testament doctrine of God's kingship and provided the basis for the New Testament interpretation of the kingdom. Jesus' teaching, his use of such terms as 'Son of Man', and certain crucial experiences in his life (e.g., baptism, temptation) point significantly to Jesus' self-understanding in terms of his role in the coming kingdom. He did not simply go about telling people how to get along with their neighbors and that they shouldn't steal. By his words and by his life he was announcing that what the prophets had looked forward to was now coming into fulfillment. And in his death and resurrection he made it possible for men and women to enter into the new order which he both proclaimed and taught. The *kerygma* which the church proclaimed after his resurrection was essentially implicit in the teachings of Jesus concerning the kingdom prior to his death.

L.J. Sherill notes that Jesus is called Teacher (or an equivalent form of address) sixty-one times in the gospels. Forty-seven times he is spoken of as teaching. The content of his teaching is referred to as *didache* ten times.[8] These statistics alone give a strong impression that teaching was an important aspect of his ministry. Manson's study of the content of Jesus' teaching, to which we have just referred, demonstrates even more conclusively that his teaching ministry was by no means a peripheral matter. But what of his preaching? What role did this play in his ministry and how was it related to his teaching? Sherrill observes that while there is evidence that Jesus' ministry was characterized by teaching from beginning to end, his preaching was confined to the time prior to Peter's confession and that it ceased entirely at that point. The conclusion he draws from this is that Jesus felt it necessary to teach others about the nature of the kingdom he was proclaiming in order that they would not misconceive it. This accounts for the accompaniment of teaching with his preaching. However with Peter's confession, Jesus was officially recognized as Messiah and "his own proclaiming of the glad tidings that the kingdom is at hand disappear for the perfectly natural reason that what he had been proclaiming had now come to pass and was beginning to be acknowledged."[9]

Jesus turned his attention from this point on to the task of instructing those who acknowledged him as the Messiah, revealing himself more fully, elaborating the implications of their discipleship, and moving with them into deeper levels of understanding of the kingdom of God. The time was rapidly approaching when his teaching too would be over and he would move into the events of his passion and inaugurate the kingdom he had proclaimed and taught. The task of proclamation would fall to the disciples of Jesus. These conclusions of Sherrill's are similar to those of Manson noted earlier. Manson also concluded that Peter's confession, "Thou art the Christ" marked a turning point in the character of Jesus' teaching ministry.

We have yet to consider in a more detailed fashion the interrelationship between Jesus' preaching and teaching. Before we proceed further, however, we must clarify the problem as we face it in the churches today and trace the alleged influence of Dodd's work upon it. James Smart and Stanley Glen have been leading voices objecting to too sharp a distinction between *kerygma* and *didache*, between preaching and teaching, and hold that it has resulted in the subordination of the teaching ministry, a subordination sketched vividly by Glen in his book *The Recovery of the Teaching Ministry.*[10] A survey conducted by S.W. Blizzard and reported in *The Christian Century*, April 25, 1956 showed that Protestant ministers tend to place teaching at the bottom of their list of priorities. There are other evidences as well that the church as a whole does not fully appreciate the importance of teaching in its ministry.

Smart welcomes Dodd's discussion of *kerygma* as the content of preaching in that it represents "a protest against the insipid moralism of a pulpit that has forgotten the *kerygma* that was the indispensable essence of the Church's original preaching";[11] however, he vigorously rejects the definition of the *didache* as ethical instruction for this has

> validated what is actually one of the chief sicknesses of education in the Church, that it has been so consistently moralistic in its character and has lacked the depth and power of the *kerygma.* He (Dodd) has done nothing less than detach the work of teaching from all essential relation to the *kerygma.*[12]

Smart believes that some distinction between *kerygma* and *didache* must be maintained but that it must be better understood and that it is equally important to understand and maintain their unity. Teaching which is not related to the *kerygma* runs the risk of becoming moralistic and legalistic. Preaching that does not include teaching runs the risk of becoming irrelevant because the proclaimed Word is not really heard and understood by the congregation and as a result it cannot fulfill that for which it is sent forth.

Smart holds that the unity of preaching and teaching lies in the fact that both are "the service of the Word of God. It is the same Jesus Christ who is to be taught and who is to be preached. The content of preaching and teaching is the same."[13] Preaching is the proclamation of that Word to a person in his unbelief whether that person is a Christian or not. For even the believer in Christ needs that Word to root out the traces of sin and unfaith. Teaching, when it is addressed to the believer, is a channel for God's work of grace in his life, claiming and sanctifying the whole of it for God. When addressed to the nonbeliever, "teaching" simply refers to the informal rabbinic approach used by Jesus and Paul as over against the formal proclamation of the preacher. What is being said is no different, however, from what would be said in preaching.

J. Stanley Glen puts forth a rather strange and totally unacceptable argument for the unity that exists between preaching and teaching. He holds that

> ...whereas preaching has reference to God making himself known through and in spite of the preacher to the heart of the believer, teaching has reference to the interpretation and communication of the message by human means. Both are inseparably united in one act, in that the Word of God is heard through the word of man. That is to say, preaching is to teaching what the Word of God is to the word of man.[14]

Behind this conclusion lies the premise that "preaching stands closer to revelation while teaching stands closer to reason."[15] The unity of preaching and teaching can thus be more clearly discerned when one sees the essential unity that obtains between revelation and reason, a unity which, Glen believes, may be perceived analogously in the incarnation. Moreover, he sees it as the same unity which exists between grace and truth "inasmuch as the *kerygma* is representative of the grace of God and the *didache* representative of the truth *of* God."[16]

We may well conclude, when we have examined Glen's analogies, that the problem he attempts to resolve is still with us, that he has indeed merely underscored the original problem. It is no satisfactory resolution of the problem to state as he does that on the one hand we have the Word of God (revelation, grace) and on the other hand a human word (reason, interpretation, truth). It may be granted that revelation does occur through preaching, but on the basis of his argument he is bound to conclude that it also occurs through teaching.

More impressive and conclusive for his argument is his reference to the way in which the Synoptic writers incorporate Jesus' teaching into the gospel narrative as providing the clue to the integral relationship between *didache* and *kerygma*. This clue is investigated and elaborated in an article by John J. Vincent in the *Scottish Journal of Theology*.[17] The key concept which points to the solution is the phrase *"didactic kerygma"* (i.e., a gospel that is taught). Let me attempt briefly to summarize his argument.

The starting-point is a distinction made originally by Krister Stendahl that *kerygmatic* preaching need not necessarily have *kerygma* (as defined by Dodd) as its content.[18] It may indeed be a summary of the events of salvation, but on the other hand it may just well be "*kerygmatisch*", that is, concrete exhortation or teaching. One illustration is to be found in Romans 2:21—"You then who teach others, why don't you teach yourself? You who preach that a man should not steal, do you steal?" Here it is clear that preaching and teaching are for all practical purposes synonymous and that the content of the preacher's preaching is good, solid ethical *didache*. The argument maintains that the distinction between preaching and teaching **in terms of the content involved** is an unnatural separation.

Vincent then examines the conclusion of Gerhard Friedrich who also holds that this distinction is false in terms of the *activity* of proclaiming and the *content* of the proclamation. Friedrich finds that in the New Testament, and especially in the Synoptics, *kerússein* (to preach) and *didáskein* (to teach) often stand side by side (Mt. 4:23; 9:35; 11:1; Acts 28:31; Rom. 2:21). The only distinction he can find is in that of the audience to which the message is addressed and the appropriate adaptation of the *one* message to the particular audience, in one case geared to edification and in another case geared to the demand for decision. This is the same position held by James Smart to which reference was made earlier.

Vincent goes on to make a firsthand study of the use of the verb *kerússo* (to preach) and its object in the Synoptics and concludes from it that no definitive observations can be made concerning the content of the preaching, certainly one cannot derive from it the points established by Dodd. He concludes, moreover, that the term *didache* and its correlates *didáskalos* (a teacher), *didaskalía* (instruction or teaching) and *didásko* (to teach, to be a teacher) occur more frequently in the Synoptics than do the cognates of *kerygma*. The term, *didásko* itself occurs 95 times in the New Testament, and two-thirds of these usages occur in the Gospels and in Acts 1-5, a fact which has caused one scholar, K.H. Rengstorf, to comment, "It is already clearly seen where the center of gravity of New Testament *didáskein* (teaching) lies—in the circle of Jesus and the earliest church, and not in the Gentile Christian churches of Asia Minor or the Greek church."[19]

Vincent now narrows down his study of *didache* to Mark which is "popularly thought to be the 'most *kerygma*tic' and the 'least *didactic*'" and makes the surprising discovery that Mark uses the term, *to teach*, at least as frequently as he uses the term, *to preach*, and that the content of the teaching turns out to be the *kerygma* itself. For this reason, the only *kerygma* of which we can speak on the basis of the Synoptics is a *didactic kerygma*, a *kerygma* which is the content of Jesus' teaching.[20]

It is true, as we have already seen, that there is abundant evidence to show that Jesus was a teacher. We fail, however, to capture the full significance of his teaching if we do not also observe that his teaching was accompanied by a corresponding activity. He was not only teaching about the kingdom; he was actually inaugurating it. And it is in this fact that we discover the real basis for the unity of *kerygma* and *didache*.

> The whole of the *didache* of Jesus is the description of the event, the demands, the circumstances, and the implications of the good news—that is, of Himself. He is the one described in the beatitudes; He is the judge, the master, the shepherd, the householder, the messenger; He is the physician, the Good Samaritan, and the Lord. The sermon, the parables, and the sayings are the only *kerygma* of which the Synoptics know. They are not 'mere' teachings; they are *didactic kerygma*, and the disciple is not merely one who responds to 'good news' (saying 'Lord, Lord'), but throws in his lot with the one who first gave up all and takes up his cross with the one who

> first bears it for all. ... The content of *didactic kerygma* is, then, the whole person and mission of Jesus as presented to and imposed upon the crowds, and as surrendered to by those who become disciples, who then themselves pass it on.[21]

The integral interrelationship between *kerygma* and *didache* which we discern in the Synoptics is characteristic also of the rest of the New Testament literature. This is the only adequate safeguard against both the subordination of teaching and its perversion into shallow moralism. Teaching must be securely anchored in the *kerygma* if it is to be Christian teaching based on the New Testament and if it is effectively to fulfill the important role to which it has been assigned.

But to anchor the teaching ministry of the church in the *kerygma* is to do more than to include the content about the life, death, resurrection and ascension of Christ in the curriculum of study. Jesus' teaching ministry was set within the context of what he was doing in the world. Our teaching ministry, if it is to resemble his and bear within it the marks of authenticity, must be set within the context of involvement and participation in his mission today. James Smart's diagnosis concerning the chief sickness of the teaching program of the church was that it had descended into a shallow moralism because it was not related to the *kerygma*. My own diagnosis is that the chief sickness of the church's teaching ministry lies in the fact that our Sunday school classes stop short of true Christian learning in that they consist primarily of discussion, even though the discussion may consist of reviewing the facts of the *kerygma*. True Christian learning involves decision-making and action as well as study and discussion. Without this, Christian learning and teaching are cut off from the living *kerygma* which is to be discerned in the present work and mission of Christ in the world.

Let me illustrate what I have in mind by drawing an analogy. Picture a group of military officers—a general and his field staff—getting together once a week to discuss military strategy. They consult their manuals and maps. They study the location and strength of the enemy and try to anticipate his movements and his strategy. After an hour of this, they get up, shake hands all around and congratulate themselves on having had a good discussion, and agree to meet again the following week. Can you imagine this going on week in and week out for years? Obviously not, because there's a real war going on and these men have to do something more than sit around and discuss the war. They have to get in there and fight or they and their armies will be destroyed and their territory overrun by the enemy.

Obviously, the chain linking thought and discussion with decision making and action is so essential that we cannot seriously entertain the thought of breaking it. The consequences are too disastrous. Only in the congregation do we tolerate the armchair general mentality. This is the thing that is lacking in many Sunday school classes. We consider and discuss the issues with greater or lesser degrees of insight. But do we make decisions? Are we aware that we're on the spot and must make up our minds and do something about it?

We are living in a world that won't hold still. The world is changing rapidly; things are going on around us; crucial problems are staring us in the face demanding to be reckoned with and resolved. As our economy is beginning to shift from a rural to an urban one, Mennonites are finding themselves in the city. Let us rejoice that God is giving our church another opportunity to participate in his work of reconciliation and healing the sick in body and mind and the estranged in spirit. As we take the gospel to the city we will face the problems of poverty, of slums, of illiteracy and illegitimacy, of disease, of malnutrition, of an exploding population, of inadequate housing, of racial discrimination and prejudice, of restless underprivileged people who are easily incited to violence on the streets and exploited by those who have unworthy ends in view. We can ignore these issues and problems; we can refuse to make up our minds about them and act upon them, but we cannot do so and be the obedient church in mission. To talk about the biblical imperative for mission apart from actually being involved in mission is unprofitable. No wonder we are tired of it; it lacks authenticity.

But Bible study in the living context of involvement in mission is Bible study that is alive and fruitful. The questions that emerge from our encounter with the world as we go out in mission will be authentic questions. The answers will be found only through a serious search of the Word of God with a view both to knowing and to doing the will of God.

[1] C.H. Dodd, *The Apostolic Preaching and its Developments* (London: Harper and Brothers, 1954), 7.
[2] *Ibid.*, 17.
[3] *Ibid.*, 21-24.
[4] *Ibid.*, 53. Dodd points out that this didactic material in Matthew bears a close resemblance to the document known as the *Didache*, or *Teaching of the Twelve Apostles*. This is a document which was discovered at Constantinople in 1873 and whose discovery created a flurry of scholarly excitement and research. It is generally accepted to have come from the late first century church and to be based on the sayings of our Lord. It is thought to have been drawn up for the purpose of catechising pagan converts in preparation for baptism.
[5] T.W. Manson, *The Teaching of Jesus* (Cambridge: University Press, 1945).
[6] *Ibid.*, 13.
[7] *Ibid.*, 17.
[8] L.J. Sherrill, *The Rise of Christian Education* (New York: The Macmillan Company, 1944), 86.
[9] *Ibid.*, 83.
[10] J. Stanley Glen, *The Recovery of the Teaching Ministry* (Philadelphia: Westminster Press, 1960).
[11] James D. Smart, *The Teaching Ministry of the Church* (Philadelphia: Westminster Press, 1954), 21.
[12] *Ibid.*, 22.
[13] *Ibid.*, 19.
[14] Glen, 87.
[15] *Ibid.*, 86.
[16] *Ibid.*, 93.
[17] John J. Vincent, "Didactic Kerygma in the Synoptic Gospels", *Scottish Journal of Theology*, Vol. Ten (Edinburgh: Oliver and Boyd, 1957), 262-273.
[18] *Ibid.*, 265.
[19] *Ibid.*, 270.
[20] *Ibid.*, 270-271.
[21] *Ibid.*, 272-273.

6

Teaching the Bible in the Congregation

"All Scripture is inspired by God and profitable for teaching, for reproof, for correction, and for training in righteousness, that the man of God may be complete, equipped for every good work." 2 Timothy 3:16-17

This is a text which I heard frequently as a boy in church and it left an indelible impression on my mind. I do not recall hearing a great deal of discussion about the nature of the Scriptures and the meaning of inspiration. Our little country church lived far from the theological controversies and debates that were going on elsewhere in the early part of this century. Though I cannot recall ever hearing the phrase, "the authority of the Scriptures", there was never any doubt in my mind that they carried authority. That was axiomatic and unquestioned. We turned to them for guidance for daily living and we found it.

Nor do I recall ever hearing the ministers speak of *heilsgeschichte*. At this time of the year, each year, our aged bishop would review the entire history of salvation in German, an undertaking which took several hours. The most dramatic parts were rendered with quivering chin and tears in his eyes. And in this way, long before Jerome Bruner (*Process of Education*) laid it down as correct pedagogy that any body of knowledge can only be taught effectively when its internal structure has been grasped, I came to understand the historical frame of reference within which the first exodus and the second are part and parcel of the same event.

Yet another significant dimension of how I learned the Scriptures was the way in which the Scriptures were incarnated in the life of our congregation. I make no claims to perfection in the way my people lived out the biblical vision but I did experience authenticity then and I recognize it in retrospect. They aspired to be faithful and they understood their symbols, practices and life style to be true expressions of God's will as revealed in the Bible. That their interpretations and applications may well have been unsophisticated and naive does not set this aside. They earnestly desired to know and to do the will of God. Furthermore, I knew that I belonged in this community and in belonging to it, I was also heir to the tradition which shaped it. Because my people had a long memory in which the biblical world was as real as the modern world (or more so), I came to share that memory, that tradition, that history and claim it as my own.

It was in this kind of setting that I was taught the Bible, one in which the Bible was understood as having authority, in which the biblical history was recited regularly, and in which the community of faith understood the biblical history to be its very own history. I recall the curtained off area and the hard benches in the basement of the church building where our class met but I remember even more vividly the poster size pictures of biblical events and persons, the 3" X 5" card reproductions of those same pictures we were privileged to take home with us, and the eager enthusiasm of our teacher who explained their significance to us. I also remember being aware that he loved us .

I

H. Edward Everding, Jr., Professor of New Testament at the Iliff School of Theology in Denver wrote a stimulating article entitled "A Hermeneutical Approach to Educational Theory" in a symposium on Christian education edited by Marvin J. Taylor.[1] He states that his "thesis is that hermeneutics provides the proper frame of reference within which to develop educational theory," and focuses on "the interrelationship of biblical interpretation and teaching." He provides a brief but well-documented summary of the interpretive process in which he identifies some of the basic problems of interpreting which must be resolved, for example, the transfer of meaning between text and interpreter, the distance between them in "time, space, language and thought", the difference between the presuppositions of the interpreter and those of the text, the problem of language, and the goal of interpretation.

Everding identifies several hermeneutical approaches which include existentialist interpretation (Bultmann) in which "the original intention of the text is retrieved through a dialogic process guided by the interpreter's own questions."[2] It is a process which eventually calls for the interpreter to make a decision about his existence and to proclaim the meaning of the text and his decision in relation to that discovery in such a way that a new "event" may take place for his hearers. Additional trends are identified which Everding sees primarily as responses to this school of interpretation. One stresses the meaning of history (Pannenberg); another stresses the social context (Moltmann's "political hermeneutics"); a third is based on an analysis of language; and a fourth is interdisciplinary in character and "probes the text for the images of faith which shape human behavior."[3]

In the second part of his essay, Everding identifies several implications for educational theory. Three educational goals are set forth:

a) the student is to learn to read what the text says;
b) the student is to learn what the text means;
c) the student is to gain new self understanding in relation to the meaning of the text. This includes restructuring his way of thinking about himself and his world and shaping his life values.[4]

The achievement of these goals calls, in his judgment, for a participatory style of teaching/learning.

Everding's suggestions for educational theory leave much unsaid. His educational goals need further elaboration and greater precision as does his statement about the rationale for and the structures of participatory teaching/learning. Nonetheless I believe they are on target and point us in the right direction.

There is much in the existentialist approach to hermeneutics which he seems to prefer which is helpful. The necessity for the interpreters (teachers and students) to be aware of their presuppositions; the process of entering into vigorous conversation with the text and of being addressed by it as well as bringing their questions; the demand that is laid on the interpreter for decision; and the proclamation of one's discovery/decision in which the former event becomes present event are all examples. Everding is aware of the tendencies of existentialist hermeneutics toward individualism and relativism but does not, in my judgment, provide adequate safeguards and controls. Nor does he criticize its anti-historical bias.

II

I believe there are clues to an authentic model of biblical teaching in the congregation in the experience of the early Anabaptists. Perhaps it is not too far from the mark to call what they were doing "Anabaptist existentialism" (in spite of the obvious anachronism) in which the triple threats to true biblical faith of individualism, relativism and anti-historicism were overcome.

There were among the early Anabaptists a number of Bible Schools, as they were called, in St. Gall and in Zurich where one Andrew Castelberger held Bible meetings teaching from the book of Romans. Later on Grebel and Manz also taught in Zurich; Grebel taught the Gospel of Matthew from the original Greek and Manz taught from the Hebrew Old Testament.[5] One has to marvel at the seriousness of purpose with which these people came to their study of the Word of God in spite of great difficulties: no lesson books, unable to read the Scriptures in their own tongue, and after a time forbidden under the threat of punishment by the law to gather in this way.

Their study of the Word of God was a serious matter. They wanted to hear its message; they wanted to know the will of God; they were diligent in searching it out. Those first Bible Schools were not only a time for knowing the Word of God; they were also times for making decisions to do the will of God. They began to ask questions about their beliefs and their customs, questions that had slumbered for a long time but which like burning coals that have been almost extinguished burst into flame when a gust of fresh air uncovers them.

What was the meaning of church membership? What did it mean to be a Christian? to be born from above? to be buried with Christ in baptism? to rise with him in newness of life and to walk with him in resurrection life? What actually takes place at the table of the Lord? How does one make ready for going to the table? How should one live when one has broken bread there and leaves the table to go out into the world again? How should one live as a Christian in society? What is the relation of the church to the government? What is the Christian attitude to war and military service? Who is my neighbor and how should I relate to him? What about suing at law or swearing an oath in court? These are only a few of the large and difficult questions that began to burst into flame, questions that had been settled for years for which the old answers would no longer do.

This kind of Bible study is dangerous. A safer approach is simply to examine the Bible as though it were some ancient document far removed from life today, or to look for the answers to the questions we bring to the text rather than to open ourselves to the questions which are placed upon us by the text and by the Lord of the text. The kind of Bible study in which they engaged was the kind in which the questioner became the questioned. They were willing to have their questions and their answers challenged and to be faced with new questions. They were also willing to make up their minds about those questions and to answer them forthrightly. In many instances it cost them their lives.

The key to the integrity of their approach to the Scriptures lay in the context in which they studied the Scriptures and the mindset they brought to that task. It did not lie in their intellectual superiority or in their technical skills of exegesis. Though there were a few scholars among them, for the most part they, like Jesus' original disciples, were common folk. What distinguished them in their study of the Bible was their openness to hear God's word of address and their readiness to respond in obedience and faith. Their Bible study took place in the context of obedience to God's requirement as they understood it and their mission to the world into which God sent them. It was a costly obedience which did not arise out of a desire to be heroic but out of the recognition that to know God's will is to do it. This, rather than an adherence to literalistic or legalistic ways of reading the Scriptures, is the reason for their emphasis upon discipleship.

III

While I was teaching a class at AMBS called Teaching the Bible in the Congregation, I sent a request to approximately 100 pastors and teachers throughout the church asking them to reflect on some problems or issues that they had been working with in their congregation and to share those with us in the form of a question which could be included in our area examinations. It was suggested that it be the kind of issue which causes the students to reflect on their biblical, historical and theological understandings in order to work on its resolution. In addition they were asked to identify certain biblical passages which are of an unusually complex, sensitive, crucial or controversial nature in the life of the congregation. These were to be passages which they had used as a basis for their preaching/teaching in recent times. They were asked to indicate briefly how they had gone about interpreting such passages and how the congregation had responded to this interpretation.

The class members and I combed through the responses we received looking for such things as

a) the texts that are being studied and how often they were mentioned;
b) any hermeneutical trends or principles that were evident;
c) any evidence of how the congregation responded to these texts (resistance, indifference, conflict, agreement).

What we were looking for was the hermeneutic which is at work in the congregations and how the Bible is being interpreted in relation to life. These replies provided us with current data about living congregational agenda, that is to say, the context and the mindset in which biblical interpretation is going on in these congregations.

Following is my analysis of the 34 replies which I received to my memorandum. Nineteen of the respondents were pastors/teachers in the Mennonite Church and fifteen in the General Conference Mennonite Church. They represented congregations in eleven states and four provinces distributed as follows: Ontario 6; Pennsylvania 5; Iowa, Kansas and Manitoba 3 each; Colorado, Ohio, Oregon and Saskatchewan, 2 each; and Alberta, Arizona, Illinois, Indiana, Nebraska and Oklahoma, 1 each.

Several reported on the use of Old Testament texts such as Genesis 1 to 11, Exodus 19-24, The Psalms, Ezekiel and Daniel. Most of the rest, however, reported on New Testament texts with a heavy concentration on Matthew (especially chapters 5 and 19, followed by chapters 18 and 28); the book of Romans (especially chapter 13); I Corinthians (especially chapters 7, 11, and 12) and Revelation (especially chapters 13 and 21). Matthew, Romans, I Corinthians and Revelation seem to represent the current Mennonite teaching canon, at least in these 34 congregations. Additional texts include Mark 10:1-12, Acts 15, Ephesians 5:21-31; Hebrews; I Peter 4:19; 3:1-7; and I John.

Issues which were repeatedly identified included the following: family life issues, baptism and church membership, the Christian's relation to government, the charismatic movement, the structuring of congregational life, the mission of the local church in its community, conflict resolution, prophecy, and various ethical and life style concerns.

In the area of family life issues, the question of marriage, divorce and remarriage was mentioned by at least 12 persons. Additional issues which surfaced in this area had to do with headship in the home, the question of singleness as over against marriage, the Christian interpretation of sexuality, premarital sexual standards, sexual infidelity, sexual ethics, abortion, marriage preparation and death and dying.

The issue of baptism and church membership included questions on how to deal with fringe, non-resident and inactive members, how to respond to persons who wish to receive baptism without becoming a member of the congregation, the need for repentance and conversion and the importance of church discipline.

The issue of the relationship to government included such matters as capital punishment, the Christian and war, the payment of war taxes, nationalism, the prophetic role of the church and the peace witness.

In connection with the charismatic movement, such questions were raised as institutionalism vs. the exercise of charismatic gifts, the ministry of the Holy Spirit, baptism in the Spirit, and speaking in tongues.

With respect to the structuring of congregational life such concerns were mentioned as the need for renewal, decision making in the congregation, leadership, authority, unity and diversity, discipline, worship, the role of women in the church, stewardship. A concern about symbolism was also evident with regard to two issues, footwashing and the wearing of the devotional veiling. Nine persons mentioned that they are struggling with the question of this latter practice.

Several persons mentioned the question of prophecy expressing concern about the impact of Hal Lindsey in their congregation as well as the Zionist view of events in the Middle East. There is, as we have noted, strong interest in studying the book of Revelation. The impact of the sects, like Armstrongism, the Jehovah's Witnesses and the Mormons on Mennonites was also identified.

In the category of various ethical and life style issues were included such concerns as gambling, lotteries, the use of alcohol, dancing, and the stewardship of our increasing wealth.

One person mentioned that he is including in his preaching/teaching such personal issues as anger, anxiety and forgiveness. A few are dealing with doctrinal themes such as the nature of man, the nature of God, sin, fall, creation.

I selected the responses of the five persons who made their hermeneutical procedures most explicit. In their responses I saw the following principles of biblical interpretation at work (not all of them in every situation, of course): 1. The assumption that the Bible speaks with authority to the issues and questions we face in our situation today; 2. the vital interaction and interpenetration of the text with the living community of faith; 3. the offering by the biblical scholar (the teacher) of his insights and his scholarship to the congregation for testing rather than as the final word; 4. the assumption that the Holy Spirit plays a crucial role in the illumination of the meaning of the text and its application to our situation; 5. the recognition that the Word, the Spirit and the church must agree as to the meaning of the text for us; 6. the expectation that there must be decision and response to what we discern together, i.e., the recognition that the Bible touches life; 7. the recognition that our culture affects the way we hear and respond to the Bible; 8. the recognition that the culture of the biblical world affects the way the text is shaped and that we must understand the historical and cultural context of the text; 9. the importance of a framework of biblical history and theology within which to interpret particular texts; 10. the attention to literary forms and types as crucial to discerning the message of the text; 11. attention to the process at work within the text itself in addressing the situation at hand; 12. the recognition of some of the obstacles to hearing the word of the Lord together (lack of love, lack of commitment, polarity, defensiveness, disobedience, arrogance, individualism).

One of the respondents reported on how he handled a controversial text, I Cor. 11:2-11. His procedure included the following steps: 1) he identified the background issues; 2) he dealt with the passage as part of a series on the whole book, not in isolation; 3) he illustrated from the text itself how Paul went about discerning the mind of Christ; 4) he identified his principles of interpretation: a) What, if anything does Jesus say on the question? b) What are Paul's best insights and judgments on the question? c) What does the Spirit seem to be saying? d) What is the best counsel of the brotherhood? 5) he identified the current issues and voices on the question; 6) he looked at the larger biblical context (other texts on the same issues); 7) he examined the cultural-social context and drew comparisons between then and now (the biblical world and our world); 8) he identified the central issue; 9) with the use of an overhead projector he drew two models elaborating the central issue. These models were attempts to state the biblical pattern in current terms. He identified one as the correct view and one as an incorrect view; 10) following the sermon presentation he engaged in a discussion with members of the congregation who were interested in continuing the discussion through the second hour; 11) he stated that he offered his interpretation in a spirit of humility as one interpretation only subject to the testing of the congregation.

IV

Teaching the Bible in the congregation is like producing a drama. As learners we begin by sitting in the audience while the action unfolds on the stage. We observe God's call to Abraham, the deliverance of the slaves from Egypt, the covenant at Sinai, the exile, the promise of the deliverer, the birth of Christ and his suffering, death and resurrection. Suddenly we discover that we are no longer in the audience but up on the stage, participants in the drama surrounded by the saints of all the ages. Or to change the image, we come out of the bleachers down on the field as players in the game. Or to change the image once again, we leave the television set where the war is portrayed on the screen, enlist in the army and go to the front to fight in the real war. (Eph. 6 12)

What these images (the athlete and the soldier are biblical images) suggest to me is that learning in the biblical sense is best accomplished in the context of engagement, involvement, participation. I really don't have much to suggest by way of changing our congregational study programs. By and large we have fairly good study materials. For the most part we have teachers who are dedicated and sincere men and women of God who give marginal time in preparation and teaching as they are able. The problem as I see it is not with the **materials** or the **method**, it is not with the **content** but with the **context**. If you are studying a set of issues because you desperately need that information to help you make a decision, and if you are in a situation where you must act on the basis of that information and decision, you will be vitally engaged with that material. Where the teaching program of the congregation is weak and anemic it may be because Bible study (and congregational life generally) is taking place in an inauthentic context. That is to say, if the congregation is not involved vitally in its mission in the world there will be no real questions on that congregation's agenda. In that event their Bible study may also lack integrity.

Another reason for some of the criticism of our adult Sunday school classes may lie in the area of inappropriate expectations. The adult Sunday school class is not, nor should it be, a seminary class with the kind of academic rigor that characterizes such a school. My view is that the Sunday school is less on the academic end of the teaching/learning continuum and more on the decision/action/obedience end. The Sunday school class is a community of conversation around the Scriptures. Its task is to build a common Christian vocabulary and to clarify the Christian meanings of that vocabulary. It is a place where the members test the purpose of their lives and the implications of their decisions. It is a place where an ethical consensus is developed both in formal and informal ways. Participation in the class provides the members with a way of viewing and interpreting the world in which they live from a biblical perspective as an alternative to the other perspectives which surround their daily life. Judged by these expectations it may well be we should be prepared to give a higher grade to our Sunday schools than we have been accustomed to doing.

The task of teaching the Bible to children is essentially that of creating biblical literacy. It includes telling them the fascinating stories of the Bible, introducing them to the biblical characters, reliving with them the biblical drama, helping them discover the covenant structure of the Bible, and aiding them in their grasp of the essentials of the biblical message. The well-known example of Timothy as reported in 2 Timothy 3:14-15 serves as a pattern and points to the goal of this acquaintance "with the sacred writings which are able to instruct you for salvation through faith in Christ Jesus." It must be recognized that the process which nurtured and instructed Timothy in the faith was a family one, not a congregational one, but that does not nullify the basic point about the ultimate goal of teaching.

V

In conclusion, let us reflect once more upon the task of hermeneutics as it is expressed in teaching the Bible in the congregation.[6] The basic goal of hermeneutics, as of teaching, is to clarify communication, to facilitate a conversation. The conversation we have in mind is the conversation between God and his people today. The medium through which God is speaking is the text of the Scriptures. Conversation is not easy, even at best when both parties are physically present in the same place at the same time speaking the same language. When the conversation is not a direct verbal one but is channeled through the medium of a written document in a foreign language it becomes more difficult. When that document is an ancient text reflecting a conversation that is several thousand years old addressed to other principals than the present readers in a life situation very different in many respects from theirs, conversation becomes increasingly complex. The task of the facilitator of this conversation who stands between the parties in conversation while at the same time being a party to the conversation is well nigh impossible. Yet this is the challenge of the task of teaching.

The teacher operates on the assumption that this conversation can come alive in the congregation and that once again the living Lord of the text will speak through the text to his people now. The historical document records that original conversation. The task of interpretation has as its goal the revival of that original conversation. The task of reconstructing the ancient text and deciphering its meaning in its original setting is not the end of the process but one of the means to the end, a living conversation. We reconstruct the original conversation so that we may participate in it.

This requires not only all the cognitive skills of which we are capable in reconceptualizing the original conversation but also the rebirth of the imagination which produced the language which was the medium of that conversation. The early communities were shaped by a living response to the Lord who addressed them. The images by means of which they communicated were born out of their life together in covenant. The community of faith today shall only be able to understand those images as it participates in that same response to the living Lord and shares in that same covenant out of which the images emerged. An analysis of that language without a rebirth of the experience to which it bears witness will be somewhat empty, like form without substance.

This is why there must be some continuity between the early and the present contexts. Certainly there are discontinuities between these two worlds and we are sufficiently aware of these that no documentation is required. But there can be sufficient continuity at the point where it matters most to enable us to join in that conversation. The agenda with which the congregation wrestles today may differ in certain details from the agenda of the congregations of the first century, for example. But if our agenda arises out of our faithfulness to the Lord as we hear him speak and as we respond in faith, love and obedience, we shall be able to listen and to speak as full participants in their conversation.

---

[1]Marvin J. Taylor, ed., *Foundations for Christian Education in a Era of Change* (Nashville: Abingdon Press, 1976), 41-53

[2] *Ibid.*, 47.

[3] *Ibid.*, 49.

[4] *Ibid.*, 49-50.

[5]J.C. Wenger, *Glimpses of Mennonite History and Doctrine* (Scottdale, Pa.: Herald Press, 1949), 23-24.

[6] I have written about this in a similar vein in my paper, "The Sunday School: History and Purpose".

7

The Sunday School: History and Purpose

Teaching has always been a vital part of the life of God's people, even in Old Testament times and long before the rise of synagogue schools. (See Deuteronomy 6:4-9) Even today the privilege and responsibility of the family to provide a setting for passing on the faith from one generation to the next is widely recognized. While the ministry of teaching and nurturing children in the faith of their fathers and mothers stretches way back to the early beginnings of the people of God, the institution of the Sunday school as we know it today is a relatively modern development. Although there is some debate as to who should get the credit for founding it, there is a general consensus that the honor belongs to a newspaper publisher in Gloucester, England by the name of Robert Raikes.

Raikes' original intention was not so much religious nurture as it was social action. His schools were popularly known as "ragged" schools or "charity" schools. They took place out of doors in Gloucester's Sooty Alley. The pupils were children who idly roamed the streets in search of amusement, sometimes engaging in vandalism and petty thievery. They were illiterate children who on the other six days of the week worked long hours in the factories and sweat shops of Gloucester.

The twin impulses motivating Robert Raikes were the desire to teach these children to read and to improve their morals. The established society generally approved of the second of these goals (improving morals) since it was a way of protecting their property from vandalism and theft but frowned on the first (literacy) since it threatened their interests. Once the lower classes learned to read, it was feared, they would no longer be content with their pitiful wages and miserable lives but would aspire to higher things. They feared that these "ragged" schools would set a social revolution in motion.[1]

It was because of this mixed response that the first Sunday School Society organized in London in 1785 by a Baptist layman, William Fox, stated its purposes as follows:

> To prevent vice,
> to encourage industry and virtue,
> to dispel the ignorance of darkness,
> to diffuse the light of knowledge,
> to bring men cheerfully to submit to their stations.[2]

Fox went on to add his personal statement to give further reassurance to the threatened establishment in these words, "There is no intention of raising them [the children] above their common level; for in that case how would our manufactories be carried on, our houses erected and our tables furnished?"[3]

The first Sunday school in America was founded in 1785; by 1790 the Methodist Conference of Charleston, South Carolina had approved Sunday schools.[4] For many years, however, the Sunday school had a life of its own as a lay movement that functioned alongside and largely outside the organized church. Only later, for the most part, was it officially recognized and approved and brought into the life of the congregation.

In the early years, the public schools in colonial New England were actually religious and Protestant. They were open to all the children and they combined both sacred and secular subjects in the curriculum. England had schools only for the upper classes, hence the "ragged" schools. Luther, Calvin and Knox had promoted the idea of universal elementary education in Germany, Geneva and Scotland available to all children, combining religious instruction with general knowledge. New England adopted this pattern and for the first period of time it worked well under difficult pioneer conditions.

However, by the turn of the 19th century, new forces were at work which undermined this arrangement. The religious monopoly of the Puritans broke down with the coming of Baptists, Quakers and Episcopalians. How can you teach religion when you cannot agree on how it is to be interpreted? Second, the doctrine of the separation of church and state was written into the federal Constitution. This led to the loss of influence by the church in public affairs, including public education. Third, there was a growing secularization in all areas of society.

In 1827, Massachusetts passed a law forbidding the teaching of sectarian religion in the public schools. This resulted in the withdrawal of religious content from the curriculum, the withdrawal of tax support from private and church schools and the elimination of religious control over public schools. This led some critics to refer to the public schools as “godless” schools.

In Virginia and the southern colonies, the earliest schools were operated by parent societies and were known as patron schools, supported by parents and friends, not by public funds. In the middle colonies (e.g., New York and Pennsylvania), the schools were church controlled, hence parochial schools. The Protestants were less effective at this than the Roman Catholics who invested deeply in their system of schools.

As the public schools became secularized and society became increasingly pluralistic, the churches had to take on the responsibility of religious education which earlier had been part and parcel of the public school curriculum. The 4th R (religion) now had to be taught apart from the 3 R’s (reading, ’riting and ’rithmetic); that task fell by and large to the Sunday school which was a ready made instrument to take on the job. By now the churches were more open to adopting the Sunday school as a member of the congregational family.

Some religious bodies were unwilling to accept an educational philosophy which divorced religious studies from secular studies and set up private school systems from elementary school right on up to colleges in which there was the possibility for an integrated approach to all knowledge. But even in these churches the Sunday school played an important educational role alongside the other schools.

The story of American higher education is filled with case after case of the denominations losing control of their colleges one by one to secularization and to the control of public or nonreligious private groups. But as these schools fell away after an initial vigorous thrust to establish a church college in every state of the Union on the part of several mainline Protestant groups (e.g., Presbyterian, Methodist,

Baptist), the Sunday school, though weakened by apathy and the loss of the original vision and fervor, continued on.

The American Sunday School Union, founded in 1815, promoted the westward expansion of the Sunday school movement in the 19th century. They sent out missionaries to go from village to village on foot to set up new schools and to sell them Bibles, lesson materials, books for their libraries and supplies of various kinds. They discouraged the use of a horse because ‘‘a horse tempts one to go too fast. Besides, the missionary is generally welcome because he can talk as well as eat. His horse is unwelcome because he eats but cannot talk.”[5]

An exception was made in the case of Stephen Paxson who named his horse, appropriately enough, Robert Raikes. Paxson, Lynn reports, “took news from one isolated settlement to another, sold his books and materials, distributed tracts and Bibles, taught, counseled, preached, gave Fourth of July orations and organized Sunday schools.”[6] He organized 1314 of them with over 83,000 pupils enrolled in Indiana, Illinois and surrounding areas. In some cases, these schools eventually grew into congregations; in other places they were the forerunner of public schools and provided a needed service until a public school system was in place.

A Manual of Public Libraries was published in 1859 which listed 50,000 libraries in the United States; 3000 were in city and town collections, 16,000 in public schools and 30,000 were in Sunday schools. The fact that they were considered public libraries is ample evidence that the Sunday schools provided a meaningful service to the total community beyond religious instruction and literacy.[7]

The story of how the Sunday school found its way into the Mennonite church has been well told by J. C. Wenger and Harold S. Bender.[8] It is a story of controversy, struggle, division and finally of victory. Already by 1840 Mennonite boys and girls were attending Sunday schools sponsored by the American Sunday School Union or local and regional associations. John F. Funk, born in 1835 and later influenced by D. L. Moody, became one of the early champions of Mennonite Sunday schools. He attended a Sunday school as a young lad in a schoolhouse near Line Lexington, Pennsylvania.

The first known Mennonite Sunday school was begun in 1840 in Waterloo County, Ontario at the Wanner Mennonite Church. However, the first permanent Mennonite Sunday school was begun by Preacher David Plank in May 1863 at the South Union Mennonite Church near West Liberty, Ohio. When he presented his proposal to the bishop, J. C. Kanagy, the bishop immediately replied, "I am in favor; I will be the principal."[9]

John F. Funk promoted the Sunday school in the Herald of Truth of which he was editor but received many critical letters opposing it. One lengthy letter began each sentence with the phrase, "We object to it because..." and went on to detail the reasons. Finally, after a dozen or more of these objections, the writer concluded with this statement, "For the sake of brevity I will add no more to this list."[10]

Another critic was less restrained and wrote an epistle entitled, "Forty-seven Reasons Why the Sunday School is of the Devil." The recurring themes of all the criticisms seemed to be a) pride and b) "we've never done it before". One critic waxed poetic with these words:

> Since man by sin has lost his God
> He seeks creation through
> And vainly strives for solid bliss
> In trying something new.[11]

As to the purpose of the Sunday school, please consider two statements, both of which apply to all age levels but in different ways and to differing degrees. The first has to do with learning the language of faith and it applies primarily, though not exclusively, to our children. The basic task is to teach each new generation the language of faith.

Our faith has its own distinctive vocabulary and it must be learned, just as any language is learned. The rudiments of a language are learned in a family long before they are learned in a school. The school can only build upon the solid foundation which has been established in the family. This points to the absolute necessity for a renewed recognition of the partnership between the family and the Sunday school.

In a more formal and systematic way, the Sunday school helps children to organize their vocabulary, enlarge and extend it, put new content into it, and relate it to their widening religious world and thus to make ordered sense out of what they see and hear. In this way, growing children begin to lay hold on the tradition, the culture, the history and the literary treasures to which they are the heirs. [12]

If a major task of the Sunday school is to teach our children the language of faith, it seems appropriate to teach them Greek and Hebrew so they can begin to read the Scriptures in the original languages. My older brothers and sister were taught the German language when they were children in Sunday school because it was then thought to be the official language of our faith. Many Jewish children are taught Hebrew in their Sabbath schools because it is recognized that you cannot adequately learn a faith unless you learn its language. Not only are you cut off from much of its literature (those texts which are not translated) but also from some of the richer, deeper nuances buried within its thought structures, nuances which even the best translations cannot convey.

The first task, then, is promoting literacy (just as Raikes' was in his "ragged" schools though the content of today's curriculum is far richer biblically and theologically). Once the basic vocabulary is in place, the task involves enlarging and extending the Christian vocabulary of children, youth and adults to clarify its deeper meanings and to build a common vocabulary so that a community of conversation around the Scriptures may be built.

The Sunday school class may become a place where its members test the purpose of their lives and the implications of their decisions. It is a place where a theological and ethical consensus is developed in both formal and informal ways. Participation in this community of conversation provides the members with a way of viewing and interpreting the world in which they live from a biblical perspective. This creates an alternative to the secular perspectives which surround their daily lives.

These are the twin tasks of the Sunday school, to teach the basic Christian vocabulary and to expand and deepen it in order to create a community of conversation. The words which we speak and the words which we live must express in the deepest possible way our life together in covenant with God and his people. It is lived meanings which we want to pass on to our children so that they may join us in our pilgrimage of faith.

This is a demanding and a challenging task, not only for the teachers but for all of us, parents, teachers, children, youth and adults. Perhaps it is too much to ask of one agency to which we give only one hour a week. But it is at least a place to begin.

---

[1] For the definitive history and interpretation of the beginnings of the Sunday school movement in England and America, see Robert W. Lynn and Elliott Wright, *The Big Little School* (Religious Education Press: Birmingham, Ala., 1980). I am indebted to Lynn and Wright for much of the material in the first part of this paper.
[2] Lynn and Wright, 6.
[3] Lynn and Wright, 6.
[4] Philip Lotz, *Studies in Religious Education* (Cokesbury Press: Nashville, 1931), 21.
[5] Lynn and Wright, 52.
[6] Lynn and Wright, 29.
[7] Lynn and Wright, 31.
[8] J.C. Wenger, *The Church Nurtures Faith* (Herald Press: Scottdale, PA, 1963) and Harold S. Bender, *Mennonite Sunday School Centennial: 1840-1940* (Mennonite Publishing House: Scottdale, 1948).
[9] Wenger, 32.
[10] Wenger, 38.
[11] Wenger, 37.
[12] I have written about this in another paper, "The Family: A Setting for Education."

8

The Relevance of Some Aspects of Piaget's Theory for the Teaching Ministry of the Church

Introduction

Who was Piaget? Jean Piaget was born in Neuchâtel, Switzerland in 1896 and died in Geneva in 1980. At age 10, he published a paper which was a description of a partly albino sparrow which he had observed. At age 15, he decided to study the biological development of knowledge. At age 18 (1915), he graduated with the baccalaureate degree from the University of Neuchâtel and three years later, at the age of twenty-one, he received the doctorate in natural science from that same university. His dissertation was a study of mollusks in the lake region around Neuchâtel. He concluded early that biological development was due not only to maturation but was also a process of adaptation to the environment which later became an important part of his theory of cognitive development.

Following his graduation, he studied experimental psychology at the University of Zurich. The next two years found him at the Sorbonne in Paris where he worked for Alfred Binet and assisted him in developing his famous intelligence tests. He became more interested in the children's wrong answers to questions than in their right answers because they gave him a glimpse into their reasoning processes. In 1921, he was appointed director of studies at the Rousseau Institute in Geneva where he continued to pursue his interest in the cognitive development of children.

In 1924 he published *The Language and Thought of the Child* and *Judgment and Reasoning of the Child,* the first of many books and articles on cognitive development which was his primary research interest throughout his life. In addition, he inspired many other scholars to do research in the field of cognitive development as well as its application to learning theory and classroom teaching. There are a number of books which outline in readily understandable form (not his gift) his basic theories. His works have been translated into English and almost thirty other languages.[1]

In 1955, he established the International Center of Genetic Epistemology at the University of Geneva with the help of a grant from the Rockefeller Foundation. Genetic epistemology is the science of how knowledge is acquired. While many people think of Piaget as a child psychologist or a learning theorist, he conceived of himself as a genetic epistemologist. As a trained biologist, his angle of approach in research was the relationship between biology and knowing.

Some psychologists held to the idea that cognitive functions are simply biological in nature, that is to say, that the thinking process is simply a biological process. In their view, there is no need for some kind of a mediating process (conscious intelligence or mind) that has a task to perform in the interaction between a subject and an object (the knower and that which is known).

Piaget had an active interest in this question and pursued it throughout his life. Although he was a biologist by training, he did not hold to the traditional biological theory of cognitive functioning but held that there were conscious mental processes at work which could be observed. He wanted to know how the mind works, not merely what it knows. He was concerned with the structures of the mind even more than with the content of its knowing. In this task, he drew upon analogies from biology rather than to conclude that knowing was strictly a biological function.

Piaget described himself as not being a nativist (innatist), nor an empiricist, but a constructionist (interactionist). In nativist theory, one's genetic program as it unfolds or develops accounts for the way one organizes one's conceptual world. In empiricist theory, behavior is determined by the environment by way of schedules of reinforcement. In constructionist (interactionist) theory, the organism (knower or learner) has the ability both to receive information from the environment (to assimilate and organize it) as well as to act upon the environment. Both abilities (to be acted upon and to act upon) have to do with adaptation. If the organism cannot adapt, it will not survive. "The organism inherits a genetic program that gradually (through a process called 'maturation') provides the biological equipment necessary for constructing a stable internal structure out of its experiences with its environment."[2]

Three Basic Concepts

While we cannot review all of Piaget's theory within the scope of this brief paper, there are three concepts which are basic to an understanding of his theory of cognitive development: assimilation, accommodation, and equilibration. Assimilation happens when "an organism utilizes something from its environment and incorporates it."[3] For example, when food is eaten, it is changed in the process but so also is the body. By analogy, in the cognitive assimilation of intellectual objects, the objects are changed but so also is the mind.

It may seem, for example, as though a ball does not change in any way when a child picks it up to explore and examine it but in reality it does change in many ways. The child may roll the ball across the floor thereby changing a stationary object into a moving object. The child may try to eat or suck the ball thereby changing a round object into one that has a chunk removed from it, or a dry ball into a wet one. Depending on how the light strikes it as it moves, the ball may be changed from a dark object into a bright and shiny one. A clean ball may be changed into a dirty one, or vice versa. A near object may be changed into a distant one, an accessible one into an inaccessible one. Furthermore, the ball may be invested with meaning. A good ball may become a bad ball if it "hits" the child on the nose. In so doing, it changes its status from being a desired object to becoming no longer desired. A similar transformation occurs when the child tries to eat the ball but discovers that it is tasteless or perhaps has an unpleasant taste.

According to Wadsworth, assimilation is "the cognitive process by which the person integrates new perceptual matter or stimulus events into existing schemata or patterns of behavior."[4] Assimilation has to do with quantity of perception (that is, the number of objects involved) and not quality of perception. The organism (knower, child) is also changed as the objects of its knowing are acted upon, initially by reflex actions such as sucking, grasping, seeing, hearing, gurgling, laughing, crying, etc. It is changed in that it develops internal schemata as part of its mental/cognitive apparatus to correspond with its external action.

Schemata are cognitive or intellectual structures "by which individuals adapt to and organize the environment."[5]

Continuing cognitive development throughout life calls for broadening and differentiating the schemata, not only for the enlargement of the number of cognitive structures (schemata) but also for reorganizing them to fit with new information. For example, when a child sees a cow for the first time, she may say, "See the big dog!" With experience, the child will create a new cognitive structure, cow, because the original one, dog, is no longer adequate.

Accommodation occurs when the child attempts to fit new data into existing schemata ("See the big dog!") only to discover that the new data no longer fit into the old schemata. There are two possible responses: a) modify existing schemata; or b) create new schemata. Both are examples of accommodation and result in new cognitive structures which make it possible to assimilate the new data. Without accommodation, the new data will be rejected or the child's perception will be distorted.

New schemata develop over time with experience. They may initially be imprecise or inaccurate. However, accommodation has to do with qualitative change, that is, the power to discriminate and differentiate, to compare and contrast, to note similarities and differences. As this happens, the repertoire of cognitive structures is differentiated and broadened in the amazing complex we know as the mind.

Equilibration has to do with the relationship between assimilation and accommodation. Assimilation without accommodation would result in a few large schemata with the ability to see only similarities, not differences. Accommodation without assimilation would result in many little schemata with the ability to see only differences, not similarities. The proper balance between them is called equilibrium.

Disequilibrium causes cognitive dissonance and discomfort; it causes the child (or the adult, for that matter) to become mentally active in order to achieve a more harmonious balance intellectually. The process of restoring equilibrium is called equilibration. All cognitive development in the child or in the adult proceeds in this way.

While the initial actions of the small child upon her environment are reflexive actions, eventually they are a) repeated habitually or intentionally and become b) generalized and c) recognitory. Through this process of acting on objects, the child is creating cognitive structures, schemata which become operational. That is, she is using them with increasing skill to act upon her environment, for example, the mother's breast, her hand, nose, ear, face, voice. In this way, she is creating an internal mental organization which both stores what she knows and enables her to engage in repeated operations which enable her to know even more. The small child does not, of course, (nor do adults, for the most part) make a theoretical distinction between what she knows and what she does.

Through the process of disequilibrium the reflex actions are mobilized (assimilation) and gradually more stable structures are set in place (accommodation). These new structures do not develop in an undifferentiated way but must be increasingly coordinated, the eye with the ear, the sucking and grasping with the seeing until an amazingly complex system ("sensori-motor") is in place. This system is the physiological basis upon which succeeding forms or levels of intelligence are built.

Four Stages of Cognitive Development

Piaget posits four stages of cognitive development. They are

a) the sensori-motor stage, 0-2 years;
b) the preoperational stage, 2-7 years;
c) the concrete operations stage, 7-11 years;
d) the formal operations stage, 11-15 years.

This is as far as Piaget takes the cognitive developmental process since he assumes that from that point onward the adolescent and the adult do not progress to a higher level of cognitive development but have all the formal cognitive structures needed to function intelligently and effectively. It becomes a matter of refining the cognitive skills already in place and putting them to work with progressively more complex content.

The sensori-motor stage extends from birth to 18-24 months, prior to articulate speech. It is a time of gathering the raw material out of which thought and speech are fashioned, a time of impressions, experiences, observations and feelings. "Sensory" refers to the active use of the five senses: hearing, seeing, smelling, touching, tasting. "Motor" refers to muscle activity which begins with random aimless movement of the arms, legs, fingers, head, etc., and moves on to purposeful activity as the child explores her body and begins to move her body around at will from place to place.

The preoperational stage extends from the end of the first stage through the entire preschool period. The child learns to use symbols and language in a preliminary way but is not yet capable of reasoning or abstract thought. He may learn to speak, to count, to identify objects such as a ball and a chair or animals such as a cat or a dog, and to recognize his written name. His world is specific, immediate, oriented around himself, his experiences, needs and wants.

The concrete operations stage extends from the beginning of the school years to the onset of puberty. The main intellectual task is the development of the child's cognitive map or framework. The child becomes able to understand his/her world and where s/he fits into it, how to cope with it as it changes and enlarges. The child learns to make sense of new experiences and to figure out where they fit into past experiences. The child's world, however, is still primarily a specific immediate world in which the five senses of present experiencing remain dominant.

The stage of formal operations extends from early adolescence through adulthood. The person learns the ability to develop and use abstractions, to think in terms of propositions, ideas and symbols as well as objects and events, to conceptualize, to solve equations, to develop and test hypotheses, to imagine possibilities beyond present experiences, to enlarge his/her vocabulary, to use language in increasingly sophisticated ways, in short, to think critically, to use logic and to reason.

"Operations" are intellectual acts or transactions, that is, functions of the mind or the intellect acting upon the world around it. Formal operations are the ability to step outside that world intellectually, to look upon it objectively, to be able to examine it, describe it and therefore to some extent to control it. The basic movement is from experiencing to exploring to acting upon or interacting with the world outside oneself.

It should be noted that each of the above stages may be subdivided into smaller substages and that the stages must be constructed, they do not come fully formed. For example, Piaget divides the sensori-motor stage into six clearly identifiable substages.

Four Factors in Intellectual Development

How does the knower move from one stage to the next? or for that matter, make progress within a given stage? According to Herbert Ginsburg and Sylvia Opper, the development of the intellect depends on four factors:

1. organic growth (biological maturation);
2. experience, both physical and logical;
3. social transmission;
4. equilibration.[6]

Organic growth refers simply to the physical growth of the child. The maturation of the child's body is essential to the development of cognition. The coordination of hand and eye, for example, is a necessary precondition for grasping objects which in turn is a necessary part of the learning process. The entire sensori-motor stage upon which later stages of knowing are built could not fall into place without the biological maturation of the young child.

Physical experience involves interaction with the physical world, gaining familiarity with it through the five senses. Logical experience involves being able to think about physical experience at one or several steps removed from it, to reflect on it using memory, abstraction, symbols, language, etc.

Social transmission involves human feedback (smile, frown, word, touch, etc.), language, reading and the like. It is at this point that formal education finds its distinctive place in the process of cognitive development.

Equilibration, as we have seen earlier, takes place when new experiences throw the equilibrium into disarray and create cognitive dissonance. The "new" that the learner experiences no longer fits with what he already knows. This excites curiosity and promotes exploration. However, the new experience may be so far removed from present knowing that no connection is made. This happens when there is no cognitive structure corresponding even roughly to the external reality upon which to build.

Equilibration is the process of exploring the new and rearranging the old so that the new can fit into it and make sense. It is an active process in which the learner is not simply a passive receiver of new stimuli or data nor a responder to them. The learner is also an active initiator of experience, one who constructs knowledge by acting upon objects of knowing and creating structures of knowledge, that is, cognitive structures.

This is not all there is to know about Piaget, of course; however, it is hoped that for the reader who has not met Piaget before this will provide the necessary background for understanding the main body of this paper and that for the informed Piagetian it will be a helpful review.

Piaget arrived at his formulations by observing his own children, a methodology which was severely criticized by other scholars. His early books are filled with example after example of observations of his children's actions on rattles, balls and other objects. His methods were criticized because of a) the lack of an adequate size population; b) the lack of objective distance (he was emotionally involved with his objects of study); and c) the fact that they involved observation only, there was no controlled laboratory environment. However, further studies by others have basically confirmed his conclusions and cross-cultural studies have demonstrated that cognitive development in every culture follows the same sequence although there is a time lag in primitive cultures.

In recent years, Piaget's conceptualization of stages has come under critical review. Piaget was aware of this before his death in 1980 and was himself engaged in rethinking his stage theory. The concept of a spiral, rather than a ladder, was one of the options he considered as being somewhat more dynamic and more descriptive of the actual process of cognitive development. However, he did not abandon what was a major element in his theory which continues to serve as an important factor in his epistemology.

For many years, Piaget was largely ignored by North American psychologists and learning theorists who were oriented around different assumptions and different methods. However, beginning in the 1960s, favorable references to Piaget's work began to appear in many American textbooks on educational psychology as an alternative to behaviorist theories of learning. Piaget and B.F. Skinner (with their sharply contrasting points of view) appear to be the major figures in learning theory today.

And yet, as we noted earlier, Piaget did not think of himself as a psychologist or a learning theorist but as an epistemologist. His preoccupation was with the question of how persons come to know something, what are the mental processes by means of which the knower assimilates and organizes knowledge and what is the contribution of biology to this process. He made the assumption that the knower is not only acted upon by the environment (the empiricist view) but that the knower is an active initiating center in the process of knowing.

Because the person is active, makes choices and decisions and is subject to error, we have the basis for moral development and responsibility as well as cognitive development; in fact, cognitive and moral development go hand in hand with the latter being dependent on the former. Piaget wrote a volume, *The Moral Judgment of the Child,*[7] based largely on his observation of Genevan children playing the game of marbles. While he did not pursue the subject much farther, others, including especially Lawrence Kohlberg, did and developed theories of the development of moral reasoning based also on stage theory. Skinner, on the other hand, finds no useful place in his theory for an active process called mind nor for a stage theory for either cognitive or moral development.

Learning Theory and Classroom Practice

The task of translating Piaget's theories of cognitive development into learning theory and classroom practice was left to his disciples of whom there are many in the United States, Canada and the United Kingdom as well as in other parts of the world.[8] For example, Constance Kamii in the Ypsilanti (Michigan) school system is a leading example of a teacher who has tried for some years to apply Piagetian principles to early childhood education. Seymour Papert and his colleagues in the "Epistemology and Learning" Research Group at the Massachusetts Institute of Technology have also been experimenting with a Piagetian approach on the graduate school level since 1985.

In this paper, I will attempt to apply some of the findings of these educational theoreticians and practitioners to the teaching ministry of the church.

1. Active Learning. The first and perhaps most important point to be made has to do with the critical importance of the fact that the learner (at every stage) must be an active participant in the construction of his/her own knowledge. Active learning is essential. This should hardly come as a surprise, given the strong emphasis on assimilation, accommodation and equilibration in Piaget's theory of cognitive development. These same processes are at work in learning theory and must be respected in the classroom.

One's cognitive structures are not the same thing as the content of one's knowing but are the forms within which content is contained, shaped and utilized. The content of knowledge is not simply that which we know but that which we do. It must be susceptible to being put into action. This is what Piaget means by the term, operations.

Learning has to do with the mastery of content (knowing and doing) through the exercise of the operations with successively new and complex cognitive material and experiences. And education has to do with facilitating learning, not substituting one's own learning as an educator for the learning of the student.

No one can do a learner's (child or adult) learning for her; she must do it herself in the process of creating her own cognitive structures. This seems to most of us so self-evident that it is amazing that so much education in the classroom at every level consists of telling rather than of facilitating learning, that is, of the teacher talking about what he knows rather than assisting the learner to construct her own knowledge.

Seymour Papert, head of the Epistemology and Learning Research Group at MIT, distinguishes between what he calls "constructionism" and "instructionism".

> This does not suggest that instruction is bad or useless. Instruction is not bad but overrated as the locus for significant change in education. Better learning will not come from finding better ways for the teacher to instruct but from giving the learner better opportunities to construct.[9]

Charles J. Brainerd has an excellent chapter, "Piaget on Education", in which he summarizes some of the educational implications of Piagetian theory. He states that there are two essential conditions in Piaget's view of learning. The first is that learning must be "securely grounded in spontaneous laws of cognitive development"; the second is that learning "should stress the subjects' active self-discovery because active discovery is what happens in development".[10]

Children (as well as youth and adults) play a central role in their own learning. Learning strategies should be as active as possible leading to self-discovery. This is what is meant by the term "constructivist" as used by Piaget or "constructionist" as used by Papert. Learners construct their own knowledge; it cannot be constructed for them by others and passed on ready-made. That kind of "knowledge" cannot be assimilated.

> You cannot further understanding in a child simply by talking to him. Good pedagogy must involve presenting the child with situations in which he himself experiments, in the broadest sense of the term—trying things out to see what happens, manipulating symbols, posing questions and seeking his own answers, reconciling what he finds one time with what he finds at another, comparing his findings with those of other children.[11]

Brainerd cites an example of a learning situation in which children were to learn conservation. The apparatus was set up and the children manipulated it by pouring water from one glass into another of a different size and shape. The teacher gave general instructions and asked questions but did not confirm nor invalidate the students' answers. Three learning conditions which were observed were:

a) learning was active rather than passive; the children, not the teacher, manipulated the apparatus;
b) the teacher did not lead the students to a predetermined answer;
c) the teacher provided no reinforcement.[12]

However, the teacher did adopt pedagogical strategies which set up cognitive dissonance or disequilibrium which created curiosity about what the children were observing and the desire to go beyond their initial conclusions. The conflict was not between the child's views and the teacher's views but between conflicting views which the child himself/herself held as well as conflicting views between children.

> A major thrust of a teaching strategy is to confront the child with the illogical nature of his point of view. The reason for

> confrontation is that it is a necessary and sufficient requirement for cognitive growth. The shift from egocentric to sociocentric thought comes about through confrontation with the animate and inanimate environment. These forces impinge on the child, inducing disequilibrium. The child strives to reconcile the discrepancies and evolve new processes by which to adapt to the new situations.[13]

Do these principles and perspectives apply also to the teaching ministry of the church? In my opinion, yes! Knowledge about the Christian faith, as it develops throughout the various stages, must be constructed by the child, the youth, and the adult. It cannot be handed over by the teacher (or by the parent) to the child. We as teachers and parents must trust children to be able to construct their own faith knowledge, facilitating that process without taking it over and thereby sabotaging it.

What is at stake here is no less than the making of a theologian, a person who at every age and stage of cognitive development is able to think her own thoughts about Christianity and increasingly able (as appropriate to her stage of development) to think critically, to comprehend religious symbols, to speak the language of the faith community, to share in its memories, to participate intelligently in its rituals and activities, to imagine alternative possibilities, to solve theological problems, to understand her world and her place in it, to think about God and God's purposes in the world, to reflect meaningfully about ethical dilemmas, to make moral decisions and the like.

This will not come about if the teaching/learning strategies are basically passive and the process primarily involves telling the child what the teacher knows or reinforcing the right answers. Piaget does, it is true, make some room for receptive learning in the mastery of some types of content and recognizes that Skinner's teaching machines may indeed have a rightful place if only, he notes wryly, to help the teacher see that he is dispensable.

How would such an approach work in an actual classroom in Sunday school with preoperational children? This is the stage where language is beginning to form in a preliminary way. The emphasis is on immediate experience, the here and now. Stories are important, especially those stories to which the children can relate from their own everyday life at home. Stories bring pleasure but they also are capable of advancing insight especially if the children are encouraged to talk about them as well as to tell their own stories. Acting out these stories or drawing pictures about them are also useful ways of telling their own stories.

Some years ago, many Sunday school and daily vacation Bible school classes had a sand table. I have no personal experience or memories of how teachers utilized this learning device but I can think of creative ways in which children could be allowed to act out and tell their stories and to intermingle their stories with the ones told by the teacher. The stories told by the teacher will include stories from the faith tradition (the Bible, church history and the church of today) within which the child is being nurtured. An important feature of storytelling by the teacher and by the children is giving the children practice in explaining how the stories from the tradition remind them of their own stories as well as the other way round and sharing what understandings they derive from these stories.

Two things to be avoided are a) moralizing and b) taking up all the time with the teacher's story and not allowing time for the stories of the children. The preoperational child is a good storyteller if he finds a good listener. A good listener will ask questions of the storytelling child which will advance the process of cognitive development. The teacher should avoid leading the child on to draw the "right" conclusions which are implicit in her story but may appropriately find out from the child what conclusions or inferences, if any, she is in fact making and engage in conversation with her to elicit further reflection about them.

At the formal operational level (high school and beyond) an illustration comes to mind. Recently, a high school student in Elkhart, Indiana was accidentally shot and killed. A Mennonite pastor participated in the funeral and seeing the pain in the eyes of the dead boy's friends as they walked past his coffin suggested a therapeutic way in which they might respond to this tragedy. Out of it, at the young people's initiative, came a project called "Drop Your Guns". They raised money to buy back the guns which people kept in their homes. Many people responded and plans are under way to melt them down and create a monument in memory of their dead friend. The pastor could have told them the lesson of the senseless death of their friend but they figured it out for themselves as well as how to respond to it. They made good use of their cognitive skills of thinking critically, using logic and reason. They imagined an alternative to guns and violence and made it a reality.

In ways like these, the theologians, ethicists and practitioners of today and tomorrow are being formed as they construct their knowledge. The construction of knowledge is a process, an active process, in which the learner is an active participant. The structures of knowledge are not a store of information and beliefs but operations with which one can act on the environment.

2. Learning Readiness. Learning readiness is an important issue in the developmental perspective. Skinner minimizes the significance of the developmental stages and has no place for them in his theory. His focus is on the critical role of the environment; "if only we do things right we can teach children of just about any age just about any material we wish. Piaget would tend to say that no matter what we do, we cannot teach children anything until they are ready to learn it."[14]

Brainerd suggests four principles which arise as a result:

a) Do not try to teach children material that is beyond their level of cognitive development.
b) Avoid acceleration; thorough mastery is to be preferred.
c) Curriculum should be developmentally based, that is, new concepts should be introduced "in the same order that these concepts emerge during spontaneous cognitive development, for example, classification, relationships, seriation, conservation, etc."
d) The teacher must know the cognitive level of each child before an appropriate sequence of instruction can be developed.

How might these principles be applied in the case of concrete operational children in the Sunday school setting? Children at this stage of development require specific concrete experience rather than lengthy verbal explanations. Teachers should supplement their words with demonstrations or experiments; better still, their experiments should be supplemented with words. "According to Piaget, concrete-operational children will learn far more from a few simple demonstrations than from hours of lecturing."[15]

It is preferable to begin with something specific and concrete than with abstractions and generalizations. It should be something in which the children have an active interest and in which they can participate. Although the experience may involve physical activity with a concrete object, it need not be limited to that. It might be an event, a problem, an experiment, a decision or even an idea to which they can relate out of their own experiences. The main point to be emphasized is that they must be participants, not observers, in the educational event.

The event may be physical or not, but it must be concrete. It must be sufficiently close to previously gained knowledge that it can be assimilated into already existing cognitive structures and accommodated by the learner. It must be appropriate to the level of cognitive development achieved by the child.

I once observed a lesson on the coming of the Holy Spirit on the day of Pentecost taught to a class of kindergarten children. The teacher tried valiantly to interpret this event to the children but it seemed a vain effort. I have mused about where such a lesson might best be introduced. Certainly at the level of formal operations it is appropriate. But is it possible to present it to children at the level of concrete operations?

If I were to do so, I would begin by asking them about their own experiences of the presence of God. I would lift out such elements as joy in the presence of God's people and emphasize the fact that this was the birthday of the church. We would discuss the church of which their families are a part, who makes up the church and whether there are people in it from various cultures and backgrounds. This could lead to an awareness that the church is universal and that people from every culture and nation can be a part of it. I would tell stories coming from the church in other cultures. I would also invite them to reflect on the symbols of the dove and the tongues of flame since children at this stage are beginning to think in terms of symbols although I would not expect them to have total insight in these matters.

One of the significant cognitive developments in the concrete operations stage is the ability to classify.[16] When children are given a pile of objects of different geometric shapes (circles, squares, triangles, etc.) and asked to create piles of similar objects, they are usually able to do so during the later part of this stage. If an additional variable is added, for example, color, the task becomes more complex. The solution to this task calls for the ability to create a hierarchy with different levels; at the higher level is the shape and at the next lower level is the color. That is to say, triangles, squares and circles are at the top and red, green and blue are one step lower.

The ability to think in terms of class inclusion calls for the child to identify all the triangles, no matter what color, as belonging to the class known as triangles. If the child is asked whether there are more triangles or more green triangles, he will answer that there are more triangles if he has mastered the concept of class inclusion. In other words, things can be different from each other but still belong to the same class.

This cognitive structure is essential if one is to understand the nature of the church. From the story of the first Pentecost we learn that people of different nationalities, cultures, languages and gender were called into one body, they belonged together. Concrete operational children are able to grasp this truth whereas preoperational children are not. I would invite these children (concrete operational) to consider various differences among Christians (national, language, denominational, gender, age, etc.) and ask whether they can all be members of the same body, the body of Christ.

3. The Role of the Peer Group. A third important educational implication of Piaget's theory has to do with the role of the peer group in learning. Ginsburg and Opper state that social interaction is vital to learning, that "children should have the opportunity to talk with one another in school, to argue and debate. Social interaction, particularly when it is centered around relevant physical experience, promotes intellectual growth."[17]

Piaget speaks of the egocentrism of early childhood, referring to its "epistemological meaning (difficulty in understanding differences in points of view between the speakers and therefore in decentration) rather than its popular or 'moral' meaning."[18] He notes that from the beginning the child sees everything (people, objects and events) only with reference to himself and his own experience. He further observes that in the case of "conversation" among young children, everyone talks and nobody listens.

> The fact is that the speech of subjects between four and six (observed in situations in which children work, play and speak freely) is not intended to provide information, ask questions, etc., (that is, it is not socialized language), but consists rather of monologues or "collective monologues" in the course of which everyone talks to himself without listening to the others (that is, egocentric language).[19]

This description is more true of child to child conversations than it is of child to adult conversations due partly to the active role of the parents or teachers in guiding the interaction. However, in both instances,

> one sees the systematic difficulty children have in taking the point of view of the other, in making him grasp the desired information, and in modifying his initial comprehension. It is only after long training that the child reaches the point (at the operatory stage) where he speaks no longer for himself but from the point of view of the other.[20]

The concept of decentration (moving from egocentrism to sociocentrism) is an important one in the cognitive and moral development of the child in Piagetian theory. In the sensori-motor period, the infant learns (slowly) to decenter behavior, that is, he learns to take a playmate into account and to play with his friend, not simply alongside his friend. In the preoperational period the child learns to decenter thought, that is, he learns to speak to the other and to listen to the other, to have a genuine conversation. In the concrete operational period, the child develops the ability to focus on several dimensions of a situation simultaneously and is able to see their relationship to each other, that is, he is able to take into account more than one perspective or point of view at the same time.

The concrete-operational child is able to take into account not only the static states of a situation but also the dynamic transformations which may occur. For example, he is able to take into account the transformation of water into ice and ice into water or the changing shape of water poured from a tall thin container into a low and wide container and back again into a tall thin container. These transformations back into the original state also demonstrate the capacity for reversibility of thought in that the child is able to visualize the original state without actually having it demonstrated.

In infancy the child is centered around the self and does not distinguish the self from other persons or objects. The mother, for example, is not seen as an autonomous being with needs and desires of her own but as an extension of the child's own ego. Her function is solely to pleasure the infant and meet the infant's needs. The child sees himself as the cause of all events. When the child cries the mother drops everything and comes running. His egocentricity is seen in that he experiences everything in terms of the self or in terms of one dimension only.

As the child grows in social experience, he comes to differentiate (an important cognitive achievement) between self and others, self and objects, others and objects (people and things). As differentiation occurs, a greater sense of self also develops and the child learns to make the distinction between "me" and "not me". This process of differentiation begins in the sensori-motor period and continues throughout the developmental process.

Maturity is the ability to distinguish self from others (clear ego boundaries), to take the other person into account and to value the other person and his/her needs and thoughts, to have a sense of worth (one's own and the other person's) and to be able to distinguish between persons and things. In Piagetian terms, this calls for decentering and differentiation. There follow cognitive, social and moral consequences.

Ginsburg and Opper observe that the young child's egocentrism (or that of an egocentric adult, for that matter) is a major barrier to gaining an objective view of reality. It is only as he gains in social experience, as he learns to hear and understand another's point of view and as he learns to take into account two or more variables which may at times be in conflict with each other, that cognitive development is enhanced.

> One method which promotes the relinquishment of egocentrism is social interaction. When one child talks to another, he comes to realize that his way of viewing things is not the only perspective. The child sees that other people do not necessarily share his opinions. Social interaction inevitably leads to arguments and discussion. The child's views are questioned, and he must defend and justify his opinions. This action forces the child to clarify his

> thoughts, for if he wants to convince others of the validity of his own views, the child must present them clearly and logically. In addition, other people may not be as tolerant of his inconsistencies as is the child himself and they do not hesitate to point them out.[21]

The teacher of preoperational children will create plenty of opportunities for social interaction for children to move beyond their cognitive, social and moral egocentrism. There should be occasions when children play together, work together and talk together. Differences should be lifted up, not ignored or brushed aside, to bring children into dialogue with each other.

The emphasis on peer interaction was most clearly stated in Piaget, *The Language and Thought of the Child*. He argued that peer interaction was essential to help a child make the transition from one stage to the next, for example, helping the child to decenter through encountering conflicts between his point of view and that of others.

> Piaget believed strongly that for intellectual development, the cooperation among children is as important as the child's cooperation with adults. Without the opportunity to see the relativity of perspectives, the child remains prisoner of his own naturally egocentric point of view. A clash of convictions among children can readily cause an awareness of different points of view. Other children at similar cognitive levels can often help the child more than the adult can to move out of his egocentricity.[22]

Differences in points of view may be on the level not only of ideas but also in terms of preferences for food, music, games or toys. They may be cultural or ethnic if the class is fortunate enough to contain some cultural diversity. It can be as simple as discussing different family customs or rituals. The biblical stories can be a source of broadening cultural perspectives as differences between the biblical situations in life and that of the present day are highlighted. It is important in this regard that we stress not only the continuities between the biblical world and the modern world but also the discontinuities.

One lesson which I remember from my early childhood Sunday school days can be summed up in the song we were taught that

Jesus loves the little children,
All the children of the world.
Red, brown, yellow, black and white,
They are precious in his sight,
Jesus loves the little children of the world.

Of course, the lesson would have sunk in more powerfully had our experience been less monochromatic but nonetheless we were vaccinated against racism when that virulent disease attacked us later in life. We were also made aware, albeit in a very limited way, that there was a wider world out there (that it was God's world) and that it was different in many respects from the familiar one in which we lived. In modest ways like this we were nudged to move beyond our egocentricity to a broader perspective. Some writers refer to this as a personal Copernican revolution.

4. Moral Development. A fourth implication of Piaget's theory has to do with the moral development of the child; it involves knowing the difference between right and wrong and the reasons for the difference. As we noted earlier, moral development and cognitive development take place simultaneously with the former being dependent on the latter. Moral development is dependent on such cognitive skills as the ability to differentiate (e.g., between self and others, objects and things, etc.), to see the relationship between cause and effect, to see things in terms of time and space, to make ordered sense out of isolated bits and pieces within a larger framework of meaning, the ability to decenter, that is, to take into account more than one variable in a given situation with some of these variables being in apparent conflict with each other, and the ability to move beyond egocentrism.

Piaget's seminal research into the area of the child's moral reasoning (see, for example, *The Moral Judgment of the Child*) provided the impetus for scholars like Lawrence Kohlberg of Harvard University to build upon and even move beyond the work of Piaget. Kohlberg, however, continued to use Piaget's methodology which was to tell stories which pose moral dilemmas as a way of eliciting the response of the child in order to observe the kind of moral reasoning that the child engages in. The responses are then analyzed according to the level of moral awareness that they represent. He also believed in stage theory although he developed his own taxonomy of moral development.

Kohlberg posited three levels or six stages of moral reasoning.[23] The first level is known as the pre-conventional level in which cultural rules of what is good and bad, right and wrong, are accepted uncritically and unquestioningly. Stage one of this level is the punishment and obedience stage, that is to say, right and wrong are determined by what gets punished and what is approved.

Stage two of the first level is the stage of instrumental relativism. Right is what is fair. The criterion of fairness that is applied is a very egocentric one, that is to say, what is fair for me.

The second level is known as the conventional level. Whereas in the preconventional level the rules that apply are someone else's rules, but rules to which I submit, on the conventional level the cultural rules become my rules. I identify with them, am loyal to them and support them. The rules are our rules, the rules of our group or our society. Stage three is known as the good boy-nice girl stage in which there is unquestioning conformity to social expectations. Stage four is the law and order stage in which there is respect for authority, fixed rules, and an emphasis on doing one's duty.

The third level is described as the post-conventional level in which moral values are defined in terms of principles or ideals which exist apart from any particular society, group or nation. Stage five is described as social contract legalism in which there is respect for law. Stage six is defined as the stage of universal ethical principles such as justice, human rights and concern for the oppressed with an emphasis on freedom, autonomy and individual conscience.

There has been some debate as to whether stage six is in fact an organic stage developing out of and moving beyond the first five stages or whether it is of a different order. Kohlberg himself has shown some hesitation in recent years about stage six simply because he cannot find enough people to provide any demonstrable evidence that such a stage in fact exists except as a theoretical construct. While there are individual ethical heroes such as Ghandi and King, they appear to be exceptions to the rule rather than the inevitable endpoint of moral development for all.

While strong concern for ethical sensitivity is a valid part of learning to think Christianly, there is always the danger of moralism, legalism and creating guilt. When we emphasize achieving the higher levels of moral development (stages five and six) we are undertaking to realize levels of moral maturity which few people achieve. It is also important to recognize that younger children need to master moral concepts on their own level of cognitive development before we seek to inculcate moral reasoning on a higher level. (Values Clarification is one approach to inculcating moral reasoning which many educators find helpful.)

It should be noted that the research of Piaget and Kohlberg had to do with moral reasoning, not moral behavior. While one would expect a high degree of correlation between the two we cannot take for granted that persons who reason morally in a certain way necessarily manifest that kind of moral behavior.

A high school class in Goshen, Indiana studied the ethics of abortion as public policy. The teacher decided not to present his point of view as the "right" one but encouraged the students to study the issue for themselves. He suggested that they interview their parents, their ministers, social workers, counselors, political representatives and other community leaders and that they read books and articles on the subject. He encouraged them to discuss the issues among each other and to articulate their own personal convictions. He also scheduled a classroom debate. This learning event was written up in the local newspaper and received editorial and community commendation. Students at this age of cognitive and moral development reserve the right in any case to make up their own minds on subjects such as these. Drawing upon Piagetian principles and methods, the teacher assisted the students in moving (or at the least to make the effort to do so) from level two to level three of moral reasoning.

Moral reasoning is simply one aspect of cognition, of logical thought. There is a high degree of correlation between the way in which youth, for example, engage in moral reasoning and in their patterns of thinking generally. Ginsburg and Opper in summarizing the general characteristics of adolescent thought note the following:

1. a strong emotional attachment to the ideals of freedom, courage, loyalty, and justice;
2. the ability to imagine both the possible and the ideal;
3. a powerful social vision;
4. flexibility and reversibility of thought;

5. reality is secondary to possibility; possibility dominates reality;
6. the ability to anticipate a course of action; they are not easily confused;
7. the ability to take into account all the variables of a situation in all possible combinations;
8. the ability to deal not only with concrete situations but to engage in abstract and theoretical discussions of potential situations.[24]

These are the qualities of thought which make moral reasoning possible. The question of the content and direction of that thought is another matter, however. In my view, Piaget does not deal adequately with the importance of the social context nor the values of the community within which persons do their moral thinking and behaving.

Conclusion

We have briefly explored four elements in Piaget's theory of cognitive development in terms of their application to learning theory and educational practice, namely, active learning, learning readiness, role of the peer group and moral development. Each of these concepts makes a significant contribution to the way Christian educators go about their task in the teaching ministry of the church.

There are some limitations, however, in Piaget's theory which must also be taken into account. Sherry Turkle and Seymour Papert in an essay, "Epistemological Pluralism: Styles and Voices Within the Computer Culture" identify two cognitive styles, hard and soft, and observe that our culture, dominated as it is by the scientific enterprise, values the hard cognitive style more highly than the other.

> The ideal typical hard and soft approaches are each characterized by a cluster of attributes. Some involve organization of work (the hards prefer abstract thinking and systematic planning, the softs prefer a negotiational approach and concrete forms of reasoning); other attributes concern the kind of relationship that the subject forms with computational objects. Hard mastery is characterized by a distanced stance, soft mastery by a closeness to objects.... Hard mastery is resonant with the logical and hierarchical elements of the traditional construction of 'scientific method'.[25]

Papert and Turkle take issue with their mentor, Piaget, at this very point. As we have seen earlier, the mature stage of cognitive development in Piaget's theory is characterized by logicomathematical reasoning. The classroom applications of his learning theory have been primarily in the areas of science and mathematics. Turkle and Papert state that

> Piaget sees a progression from egocentric beginnings to a final "formal stage" when propositional logic and the hypothetico-deductive method "liberate" intelligence from the need for concrete situations to mediate thinking. In this vision, mature thinking is abstract thinking. We disagree: for us, formal reasoning is not a stage, but a style.[26]

They also deplore the "cultural elitism" and "privileged status" of this approach to cognition in our society and believe that hard approaches to knowing (e.g., logico-mathematical reasoning) should be "on tap", not "on top".

This touches on a basic point at issue in the search for the relevance of Piaget's work for the ministry of Christian education. We would not deny that critical reasoning has a valued place in the development of thinking our way into the heritage of the Christian faith. We would, however, insist that it takes us only part of the way into a fuller comprehension of the gospel, what is described in Ephesians 4:13 as attaining "to the unity of the faith and of the knowledge of the Son of God, to maturity, to the measure of the full stature of Christ." (NRSV)

Further, while the curricular content of Christian education is susceptible to logical analysis, it lends itself equally well to symbolism and metaphor, to contemplation and meditation, to art and poetry, to the love of God and neighbor and to the doing which lies at the heart of Christian discipleship as faith is translated into practice.

James W. Fowler makes this very point even as he acknowledges his indebtedness to Piaget for his own work on faith development, particularly the concept of stages. Fowler postulates six stages of faith development. However, he states that "stages of faith deal with different domains of knowing than either the cognitive stages of Piaget or the moral stages of Kohlberg."[27]

> The research on faith development owes a great debt of gratitude to Piaget, Kohlberg and many of their associates. We shall continue to acknowledge and build on that indebtedness. But the structural-developmental perspective, as they have shaped it, also has some serious limitations that must be faced and dealt with in the effort to treat faith in structural-developmental terms. The first such difficulty arises out of the way Piaget, and Kohlberg following him, have conceptually separated cognition or knowing from emotion or affection.[28]

Fowler makes a distinction between two kinds of reasoning, both of which are essential to faith development. The first he calls "the logic of rational certainty" which "describes the relatively narrow understanding of cognition with which Piaget works"; the second which he calls "the logic of conviction" characterizes "the necessary combination of rationality and passionality that faith involves".[29]

Thomas Groome addresses this issue in a similar vein as he revives an ancient concept called "conation" which involves not only information but also formation and transformation. Conation is not intended by him to be an alternative nor a supplement to cognition; "it includes and yet is more than what is typically meant by cognition, even in the richest sense of the term." It refers to persons' appropriation of information "in a way that shapes their identity and agency in the world—their cognition, their affections, and their behavior."[30] For this to happen, the educational event must take place in the context of a Christian community which surrounds the learners as they seek their Christian "identity and agency".

> What now does it mean to propose 'conation in Christian faith' as the desired learning outcome of Christian religious education? Clearly it engages a person's whole 'being'; it subsumes cognition, affection, and volition in synthesis as a self-in-community who reflects and realizes Christian identity and agency. Christian conation means 'being' and becoming Christian. Pedagogically this poses the task of informing, forming and transforming people in the pattern of lived Christian faith—to know, desire and do with others what is ingredient to being Christian in right relationship with God, self, others and creation after the way of Jesus. It means educating people's 'character' to realize the believing, trusting and doing that is constitutive of lived Christian faith in the world....The unity of

> knowing, loving and serving God by knowing, loving and serving one's neighbor as oneself after the way of Jesus makes for specifically Christian faith conation. To educate people's 'being' in such discipleship should permeate the whole curriculum—its dynamics, content and environment.[31]

These criticisms notwithstanding, the work of Piaget makes an invaluable contribution to Christian education theory and practice of which these four examples are only beginning illustrations. Further work is required to mine the fuller richness of Piaget's theories, especially in comprehending the implications of stage theory for learning readiness and educational practice.

---

[1]The interested reader may consult one or several of Piaget's own writings such as Jean Piaget, *The Language and Thought of the Child*, translated by M. Gabain, 2d edition (New York: Harcourt, Brace and Company, 1932); or Jean Piaget, *The Origins of Intelligence in Children*, translated by Margaret Cook (New York: W. W. Norton and Company, Inc., 1952); or Jean Piaget and Barbel Inhelder, *The Psychology of the Child*, translated by Helen Weaver (New York: Basic Books, Inc., 1969). Several secondary works are John L. Phillips, Jr., *The Origins of Intellect in Piaget's Theory*, 2d edition (San Francisco: W. H. Freeman and Company, 1975); or Herbert Ginsburg and Sylvia Opper, *Piaget's Theory of Intellectual Development*, 2d edition (Englewood Cliffs, New Jersey: Prentice Hall, Inc., 1979); or Barry J. Wadsworth, *Piaget's Theory of Cognitive Development* (New York: McKay, 1971); or Charles J. Brainerd, *Piaget's Theory of Intelligence* (Englewood Cliffs, New Jersey: Prentice Hall, Inc., 1978).

[2] Phillips, 7.

[3] Phillips, 10.

[4] Wadsworth, 14.

[5] Wadsworth, 10.

[6] Ginsburg and Opper, 206-218.

[7] Jean Piaget, *The Moral Judgment of the Child*, translated by M. Gabain (New York: Harcourt, Brace and World, Inc., 1932).

[8] Two of Piaget's books did, however, address the issue of educational practice. They are *The Science of Education and the Psychology of the Child*, translated by D. Coltman (New York: Orion Press, 1970) and *To Understand Is to Invent: The Future of Education*, translated by G. and A. Roberts (New York: Grossman, 1973).

[9] Seymour Papert, "Introduction", *Constructionist Learning*, ed. by Idit Harel (Cambridge, MA: MIT Media Laboratory, 1990), 3.

[10] Brainerd, 280.
[11] Eleanor Duckworth, in *Piaget Rediscovered*, edited by R. E. Ripple and V. N. Rockcastle (Ithaca, New York: Cornell University Press, 1964), 2.
[12] Brainerd, 281.
[13] Brainerd, 282. Quoted from Irving Sigel, "The Piagetian System and the World of Education", *Studies in Cognitive Development*, edited by D. Elkind and J. H. Flavell (New York: Oxford University Press, 1969), 473.
[14] Brainerd, 273.
[15] Brainerd, 278-9.
[16] Ginsburg and Opper, 115-131.
[17] Ginsburg and Opper, 237.
[18] Piaget and Inhelder, 118
[19] Piaget and Inhelder, 120-21.
[20] Piaget and Inhelder, 121-22.
[21] Ginsburg and Opper, 229-30.
[22] Brainerd, 283. Quoted from Constance Kamii in *Piaget in the Classroom*, edited by M. Schwebel and J. Raph (New York: Basic Books, Inc., 1973), 200.
[23] Lawrence Kohlberg's unpublished doctoral dissertation at the University of Chicago in 1958 was titled *The Development of Modes of Moral Thinking and Choice in the Years Two to Sixteen*. See also Ronald Duska and Mariellen Whelan, *Moral Development: A Guide to Piaget and Kohlberg* (New York: Paulist Press, 1975).
[24] Ginsburg and Opper, 198-204.
[25] Sherry Turkle and Seymour Papert, ''Epistemological Pluralism: Styles and Voices Within the Computer Culture'', *Constructionist Learning*, ed. by Idit Harel, 350.
[26] Turkle and Papert, 358.
[27] James W. Fowler, *Stages of Faith* (San Francisco: Harper and Row, 1981), 99.
[28] Fowler, 101.
[29] Fowler, 102.
[30] Thomas H. Groome, *Sharing Faith* (San Francisco: Harper and Row, 1991), 26.
[31] Groome, 30.

III

Educational Theory: Goals and Process

Conversion is a reorientation of one's life; as such it speaks to the motivation and direction of the educational experience. Moreover, it involves a receptivity to a new power of life and growth coming not from within a person but from God.

9

The Aims of Education

The following sections are a summary of the aims of education as articulated by six philosophers who have significantly influenced educational theory and practice in the western world: Plato, Aristotle, Rousseau, Kant, Dewey, and Whitehead. Few of them (Dewey is an exception) saw their theories translated into actual practice but all of them made an impact on the educational enterprise at some stage of its history. No systematic attempt is here made to present and interpret the larger philosophical position of these men. We limit our attention to their statement of educational aims as these become explicit in their writings.

Plato

The educational question posed by Plato in the Meno, Can virtue be taught?, raises at once the issue of what is involved in teaching, learning, and knowing. Plato opposes two sharply contrasting sets of opinions with regard to these issues. Meno, reflecting a characteristic Sophist view, is of the opinion that teaching is passing on factual data, that learning is memorizing it, and that knowing is remembering what one has been told by his teacher. To this view, Plato opposes a process of shared inquiry in which both teacher and learner participate, and the resultant knowledge is the insight at which they arrive together. This knowledge is something which the learner discovers—something he has not been told by his teacher.

This kind of teaching-learning procedure calls for a different kind of involvement on the part of the learner, one in which he moves from passive receptivity to active and direct participation, thereby assuming a significant measure of personal responsibility and initiative for what he learns. Motivation for learning assumes a new character under these circumstances, becoming integral to the process itself and not external in the form of rewards and punishments. The learner must genuinely want to know, if this sort of engagement is indeed requisite for true learning.

Socrates demonstrates how to achieve this kind of motivation in his experiment with the slave boy; the challenge is built right into the pursuit of knowledge by showing up the inadequacy of the initial response. Each subsequent response is subjected to the test of critical examination, shown to be tentative and thus the springboard for further exploration. The effect is to induce dissatisfaction with the present opinion and by breaking down the intellectual equilibrium to inject into the inquiry a spirit of anticipation and excitement. Only when there is a real desire to know will there be sufficient internal impetus to seek the truth; apart from this it is impossible to teach a person anything.

The "Socratic method" practiced by Plato has proven its excellence as a teaching instrument through the years and is highly regarded even today. The metaphysical basis upon which Plato rested it has, however, been rejected by contemporary advocates of the method. Plato held that the soul of man is immortal, that having existed from all time it has seen and learned all things. Knowledge, then, is merely recollection of what the soul already knows but may have forgotten in its incorporation into a finite human body. Thus, one should not be surprised that the learner should be able to discover, i.e., to remember, something which no one has told him. The enduring excellence of the method is not, of course, this obsolescent metaphysical dogma but the quality of the intellectual engagement inherent in it.

To return to the original question, the Meno gives no conclusive answer as to whether virtue can be taught, mainly because Socrates and Meno have been unable to arrive at a conclusive definition of virtue. If virtue is knowledge, and knowledge is defined as factual data, then obviously virtue can be taught. But in failing to demonstrate the validity of this equation, the question remained an open one.

With regard to knowledge, Plato distinguished four levels of perceiving it: conjecture, belief, understanding and science (knowledge by reason). This latter level, representing the top segment of his diagram of the "divided line" (Republic, Book 6), is the level of immediate perception of the ideal forms, and at the top point of the line is the recognition of the form of the good. Plato held that not all persons had the innate capacity to reach the top level of the line of knowledge. In the state, however, there were some who could be educated to this point and these, he felt, should be trained to serve the state as its philosopher kings. He developed a curriculum which was designed through the course of many years to bring those capable of it to a vision of the good. His curriculum presupposed a social structure in which there are three classes: the rulers, the protectors, and the producers. The factor which determined one's social class was to be this intellectual capacity; this likewise determined the education one would receive. Each class had its appropriate curriculum outlined for it in Plato's visionary scheme, a curriculum which would lead the learner to his relative level on the scale of knowledge.

We need not, for the purposes of this paper, sketch in detail the structure of this utopian society and the elements in the curriculum except to underscore the importance of mathematical training and the stress on formal discipline in order to achieve the vision of the good, the beautiful, and the true. Another point of real significance to note is Plato's recognition of the close relationship between the structure of a given society and its educational institutions. This insight is an integral part of John Dewey's educational philosophy and its fuller implications will be traced in our consideration of his work. A third point of real significance is Plato's recognition of differences among individuals in intellectual capacity and his provision for curricula appropriate to these capacities. Both these latter points found an important place and further development in Dewey's scheme. At the same time, he presented a valid critique of Plato's theory at these points which we shall examine in due course.

Aristotle

To understand Aristotle's views in education, we must understand his views concerning human nature and conduct. Two underlying convictions modify to some extent his optimism in the power of education. They are that human conduct cannot be anticipated as can events in natural science and that education being a social, not a natural affair, one should not be too hopeful that the application of scientific method to the process of education will invariably yield the desired results. This caution is well founded and it underscores the fact that education, as a human affair, must allow for the complexities and dynamics which characterize human life and growth. At the same time one should not despair (and indeed Aristotle did not) of accomplishing something by way of human development, for in asserting that education is a human affair, Aristotle was being revolutionary.

Aristotle's views conflicted sharply with the theology of his time in that he regarded happiness (eudimonia) not as the result of the work and favors of external deities, but as the product of internal factors active within the human soul. Virtue (arete), for Aristotle, meant **excellence** or **perfection**, not limited to any one area of life such as morality but inclusive of all. Virtue depends on knowledge. Education, then, becomes a matter of cultivating or encouraging this inner activity in terms of the pursuit of knowledge for one's virtue and happiness quite apart from any consideration of the activity of the gods. The principle of change is **within** a person; the task of education is the perfection of human potentialities.[1] This perfecting does not consist of introducing factors external to the self but of drawing out and developing what is latent within it. The more one believes that one is capable of shaping his life and destiny, the more significant becomes the task of education.

Contemporary Christian theology is a far cry from the fatalistic attitude toward the gods and their arbitrary intervention in the everyday life of individuals. Christianity while holding to the importance of our relationship with God nevertheless does not presume upon God's concern for human welfare in order to release us from responsibility in human affairs and growth. Consequently Aristotle's educational views are quite compatible with Christian thought; in fact, the Thomistic system which underlies Roman Catholic education is avowedly Aristotelian.

A second significant factor is Aristotle's definition of a human being as a rational animal. This implies a two-fold nature: one's animality involves the biological activities of the body—eating, breathing, reproducing, etc. One's capacities for pain and pleasure, imagination, sensation, and habit formation likewise belong to his animal nature and are shared in common with the more complex animals. The animal part is non-rational but it can be held in check in a measure by one's rationality. A human being like the higher animals forms habits by which his body is controlled, but unlike the animals "there is no necessity that he (man) form one rather than another complete set of habits. Aristotle plainly thinks that by taking thought men can add to their stature."[2]

Another significant difference between persons and the other animals is that while sensation is common to both, it is only in humans that sensation gives rise to abstraction, discursive thinking, and intellectual intuition.[3] Sensation becomes the link between one's animal and rational nature. One's *raison d'être* is to develop one's rationality to its highest perfection, both in practical and theoretical matters. One's greatest happiness, the highest development of one's virtue, lies in this. One's innate curiosity, one's desire to know, must be satisfied if one is to achieve perfect happiness.

It is in the development of the practical rationality (ethics) that one determines his habits and thus exercises through reason a control over his animal nature, over the appetites and passions of the body. Aristotle does not, of course, hold out for the complete repression and denial of the body's legitimate claims. His "golden mean" determined by the rationality lies between denying them completely and giving them free course. While habits may be formed on the basis of

> ...a reasoned desire for self-improvement...neither reasoning nor wishing, but only repeated deliberate action becoming habitual will change a man's character. And without self-realization in his domain, happiness is beyond a man's grasp. Classroom instruction can thus contribute little to the moral education which makes other education possible.[4]

Thus we see that for Aristotle it is not only a matter of "taking thought" in order to "add to one's stature"; it is a matter of giving practical expression to the thought in the forming of proper habits. He does, however, assert that reason does have the ability to discern and to achieve that which makes for perfection and happiness.

One final observation is that to be human is to be a social being. One's development, morally and intellectually (as well as the meeting of one's physical needs) is dependent on other people, the family and the community. One can achieve self-realization only in society; therefore we can say that to be human is to be a "political animal".[5] One's education is not a private affair, then; it is a matter of community concern.

Aristotle's insistence that the highest end of being human is to be a person whose powers have been developed to their highest excellence is a proper emphasis. It seems to me self-evident and incontrovertible that happiness lies in one's highest intellectual and moral development. Aristotle's frank recognition of the importance of habit, i.e., of translating what one knows intellectually into effective daily practice, is also well taken.

To say that the end of education is the achievement of one's highest perfection, and thus his happiness, is to state the goal in general terms. A more specific statement of the objectives of education is to classify them as civic, vocational, and liberal.[6] Aristotle believed it was possible to build a curriculum which would meet all these goals. His curriculum, as outlined in his *Politics, Book 8*, consists of reading and writing, gymnastics, music and drawing. Reading, writing, and drawing are taught as the useful arts necessary to practical living; gymnastics develops courage. These contribute then to the development of the good citizen and to his vocational pursuits.

There is in *Politics, Book 8* an extended discussion of the liberal goal in education and the place of music in the curriculum. The liberal pursuits are those which are foundational for more advanced intellectual activity. One's highest end, his virtue, consists in rational perfection; liberal pursuits contribute most significantly to the achievement of this end. However, even liberal pursuits, if overdone, may become vulgar and thus defeat the chief end of virtue. Those pursuits are vulgar which threaten the capacity of the body, soul, and mind for the pursuit of virtue. We should note, however, that a greater tendency toward rendering one vulgar lies in the illiberal pursuits, i.e., the useful arts which are focused upon preparing one for one's vocation in life. Aristotle holds as vulgar the "industries that earn wages, for they make the mind preoccupied and degraded."[7] The pursuit of the useful arts is not, however, intrinsically vulgar; one must be both selective and moderate in his choice and the extent of his involvement. Drawing, for example, while included in the curriculum primarily for its practical value may lead to an appreciation of bodily beauty and thus prove to be a liberal pursuit. One should not, Aristotle believed, seek for utility in everything; this is not suited to those who are "great-souled and free."[8] In this respect, Aristotle differs from Dewey who insists that one important criterion for the inclusion of a thing in his curriculum is its pragmatic value. However, there are points of correspondence between the two men, as Brumbaugh and Lawrence point out, a correspondence which we shall examine more carefully in another context.

As to the place of music in the curriculum, Aristotle justifies it on the grounds that music is a pleasurable leisure experience and the virtuous person must be able to occupy leisure nobly. Moreover, he is convinced that music has an effect on the moral quality of the soul, either for good or bad depending on the quality of the music. The harmony of the music can effect a corresponding harmony in the soul. Therefore music should be included in the education of the young. Care must be exercised in the choice of music and instruments; moreover, care must be taken not to place too much emphasis on music to the exclusion of other aspects of the individual's development. In either case, the possibility is present of making an illiberal pursuit. The three criteria he sets up for the selection of music in the curriculum are: moderation, possibility, and suitability.[9] He shows a preference for the Dorian mode and a strong aversion for the flute based upon their respective conduciveness to virtue.

The question of method in teaching music also turns out to be an important one. Aristotle holds that a learner must actually learn to play an instrument if he is to achieve a genuine appreciation of music. Indeed, it is extremely difficult, if not impossible to become a judge of musical performance if one has not performed oneself. The purpose is not to make one a professional performer (which tends toward vulgarity), but simply to increase the capacity for enjoyment. It is in this respect that Aristotle corresponds with Dewey; learning by doing was not Dewey's innovation—it is at least as old as Aristotle. There is, admittedly, real validity to the argument that the awareness of technique which comes through direct handling of it increases the learner's understanding of and appreciation for music. On the other hand the discipline of continued drill may merely produce a mechanical technician and a sense of drudgery. The pleasurable sensation experienced by the musical layman may be different in quality from the aesthetic awareness of the artist when both are listening to a symphony, but each is "appreciating" the music in his own way.

Rousseau

Rousseau's educational theories embodied in *Emile* were greeted by a great storm of official protest. In spite of this (perhaps because of this, considering the public interest the protest stirred up) many of his views found favor in educational practice, particularly in the systems of Basedow, Pestalozzi, and Froebel. Some of his views were patently absurd; some however had an enduring validity and it is largely with these latter that we will here concern ourselves.

He finds the fundamental principles of his system not in society, but in nature. In this respect, he differs significantly from Plato, Aristotle, and notably from Dewey for whom education is a social affair. Rousseau, in typically Romantic fashion, believes in getting back to nature; society is a corruption and perversion of nature and education is merely an instrument of this perversion. Therefore, he takes Emile out of his social environment, isolating him from contact with it as much as possible and using "natural" pedagogical principles in his education. His thesis is false; obviously Rousseau has a naive view of human nature and of human society. In spite of this, there is something to be said for viewing society with a critical eye and being selective of the social patterns which are impressed upon those being educated. However Dewey is right in his insistence that since education must prepare one to live in a social situation, it must take place in a social context.

Rousseau had a salutary effect on educational theory and practice in his insistence on the importance of discovering the natural capacities of the child and the natural laws by which he grows. The disproportionate emphasis on the tradition to be communicated had made of the learner a forgotten entity. Rousseau insisted that the child is not an adult in miniature and that his education should be appropriate to his age. The learning process ought to unfold the powers of the child in due proportion to his present stage of development. Moreover, education should have an immediate relevance and not be oriented primarily toward adulthood, for since there is no guarantee of tomorrow such education would have been wasted upon those who die young. Childhood has its own rightful place in human life just as adulthood has. The former is not to be made subservient to the latter.

Rosseau's insistence that the task of the educator is to arouse in the learner the sense of the observer and the pioneer underscores again the importance of motivation for education. The child should be helped to become a discoverer and not a mere imitator, to assume personal responsibility for learning and to eschew slavish dependence upon what others say. This reminds us of Plato's protest against the methods of the Sophists. The practical implication for Rousseau is that the educator should address himself more to the will than to custom, more to the reason than to memory. However, since reason is one of the latest faculties to unfold, one should not appeal primarily to reason at too early a stage. To do this is to treat the child as an adult and to make an instrument of a result.[10] In this early stage, it is well to allow the child to discover for himself the limitations his environment places upon his actions. Within these limitations, he must be allowed the greatest measure of freedom he desires.

Rousseau differs significantly from Aristotle in his view of the role of habit in a person's growth. For Aristotle, habit occupies a crucial role in confirming and incorporating into one's life what the intellect perceives. Without the weight of the repeated act, the intellect is powerless to effect change. For Rousseau, the only habit a child should learn is to contract no habits, for habits only serve to add wants to those already provided by nature.[11] In this way, Rousseau is again flying in the face of the child's true nature and is losing a powerful ally for human growth and development as well.

There is one significant respect in which Rousseau and Dewey correspond, and that is the importance both attach to the idea of learning by doing. Rousseau provides Emile with direct sense experience of the things he is to learn rather than to conduct verbal recitations about them. He holds that this is the natural way a child learns even from earliest infancy where his first impressions are those of sensation. From sensation the child goes on to learn the connection between an object and himself—extension. Still later comes the understanding of the relationship between the object and himself; it may be a thing to be desired, avoided, used, ignored, etc. Rousseau carries this dogma to the point where he would postpone the learning of reading and access to books to a much later point in the child's life than other educators. For Dewey, reading becomes "useful" much earlier than for Rousseau.

One final point which we will consider is his dictum to proceed slowly. In this way we will find the point of readiness which is most appropriate to teaching a given thing; we will also discover that some things do not need to be taught. Rousseau's philosophy here presupposes a leisurely and somewhat irresponsible approach to education which ignores the pressures and demands of society. In his hypothetical system he could afford to do so; in our existential situation we cannot.

Kant

Kant's greatest contribution to educational theory is in the area of the understanding of what it means to be human. He has a dichotomous view of human nature, making a distinction between one's noumenal self and his phenomenal self. The latter is an observable, material entity involved in the sequence of historical causes and processes. The former lies outside the phenomenal order with power to influence the causal sequences in which one is involved. This is the basis of his idea of human freedom—the conviction that our wills can introduce new efficient causes into the chain of historical sequences. And it is this possibility of personal freedom which gives the individual his dignity and worth and entitles him to our respect. But this idea of freedom also involves a moral responsibility, a feeling of "oughtness" which distinguishes one from the world of other animals and of things. A person may reject his freedom and choose to live on the phenomenal level as a thing, but he does not thus lose his moral responsibility or his intrinsic value as a person. He does, however, so long as he has abdicated his responsibility (or better, tried to evade it), lose his right to be treated as a person of dignity and to be regarded with respect.

This moral responsibility is defined by Kant as a "categorical imperative,"[12] an imperative to action which is self-evident, compelling and inescapable. It may even, on occasion, deny one's natural impulses. It is the "overriding demand to act as a rational being." It indicates what rational and responsible behavior requires but gives no specific content. This arises from every immediate situation which calls for decision. This sense of duty or reverence for law is an expression of the influence of the noumenal self over the phenomenal self. Only as that influence is effective does one realize his true end as a rational and moral being.

The educational implications from these considerations are clear. Each learner is to be treated as a person of dignity and worthy of the teacher's respect. He is to be treated as an end and not as a means. His will and his personal moral responsibility give him an intrinsic value. His freedom is not to be violated. Of course this does not mean he is free to do as he chooses. His duty to act as a rational being is clear; his "categorical imperative" is inescapable. He may need to be reminded of his ultimate goal, but the motive for striving toward it comes not externally from the teacher but from his clear sense of duty. To the extent that he attempts to abdicate from his responsibility, he loses his dignity and his right to the teacher's respect and reverts to another form of discipline.

We find in this brief sketch of Kantian thought educational relevance in the areas of motivation, discipline, teacher-student relations, and the ultimate goal of human development.

Dewey

At the heart of John Dewey's educational system is his attempt to synthesize the dualisms which characterized the education of his day; the dualism between school and society, theory and practice, pupil and teacher impeded true education, in his opinion. Before we examine how he replaced these dualisms, it will be helpful to examine an important foundational principle of his thought. Frequently, Dewey's system is referred to as "progressive education", a view of education opposed to conservative education. It may serve to sharpen the contrast by recalling that Plato considered that a necessary prerequisite to the institution of his educational program was a political revolution to create the Republic. That is, his system presupposed a democratic society which was to be brought about not through the gradual process of education but through the powerful political influence of enlightened rulers. Thus Plato recognized the close connection between the character of a given society and the nature of the education appropriate to and possible in it. However, he did not envisage that education should have any creative effect upon that society except to maintain it and facilitate its orderly function. In this sense, Plato's view of education in society was conservative.

Dewey's view, on the other hand, was progressive in that education was to serve as a powerful agent in social evolution as over against being pressed into the service of perpetuating established custom. The emphasis for him does not fall on the heritage of the past as embodied in the oral and literary tradition, but on the utilization of present experience for the modification and improvement of personal and social existence, to root out social evils and replace them with better habits and conditions. His own summary statement of his educational viewpoint is that it is "the idea of continuous reconstruction of experience, an idea which is marked off from education as preparation for a remote future, as unfolding, as external formation, and as recapitulation of the past."[13] This reconstruction of experience adds to the meaning and quality of experience, and in addition it enables one to predict with greater certainty the course of continuing experience as well as to increase the power of controlling or directing that subsequent experience.

Such a view of education holds it to be vital to the very life of society. In fact Dewey states that "what nutrition and reproduction are to physiological life, education is to the social life."[14] This is true in any society, and more pressingly the case in a complex highly developed society. In this latter instance, education has to be more formally and studiously taken in hand to militate against the increasing danger of disruptive and disintegrative tendencies. However, this increasingly formal character of the educational enterprise makes for a divorce between direct social experience and experience in school. This divorce both modifies the quality of the formal school experience and the extent of education's impact upon society.

To counteract this unfortunate tendency, the formal school situation must approximate as closely as possible the social situation outside its walls. However, it must always remain a specialized environment whose important functions are

> simplifying and ordering the factors of the disposition it is wished to develop; purifying and idealizing the existing social customs; creating a wider and better balanced environment than that by which the young would be likely, if left to themselves, to be influenced.[15]

A second dualism he attempted to break down was that of theory and practice. To lead to theory by way of art was not something original with Dewey as we have seen, but in Dewey it acquired a new importance. He is strongly opposed to that approach which merely seeks to transmit knowledge by way of verbal or literary communication. This does not lead to a creative reconstruction of present experience, nor does it give unified insight into the reality of the matter. History, for example, tends to be but a hodge podge of facts, dates and figures which are not seen clearly in relation to each other and whose relevance for the contemporary situation is lost. To begin with the present and immediate historical situation, to enter actively and directly into it insofar as possible, is to come to a much deeper awareness of historical problems and to provide the vantage point for a larger perspective within which to view the total sequence of historical events. For Dewey, first hand experience is essential to learning. Theory is to a great extent determined, not only discerned, by its consequences in practice; thus it is impossible to arrive at it through pure abstraction.

Throughout this review, we have been aware of a tendency toward recognizing the importance of the individual in education. This was already evident in Plato's concern for an educational system which would give the appropriate kind of education to each individual in order that he might find and fill his appropriate station in life. This tendency is heightened by Dewey who grounds his educational system upon a democratic social ideal in which all individuals have a right to equal participation and in which there will be the fullest possible interaction by all in the social enterprise of learning. In this way the highest personal fulfillment of each learner will be enhanced, but it will always be with a view to responsible social involvement. While lauding this insight of Plato, Dewey correctly contends that Plato's classification of all persons into three intellectual levels falls far short of doing justice to the wide range of individual differences modern psychology has discovered. For this, of course, Plato is not to be censured, not having had access to the findings of twentieth century science; in fact, his insight was remarkably advanced for his day.

Along with this emphasis on the unique capacities and interests of each individual learner has come a renewed respect for the child. This respect is reflected not only in giving him ample opportunity for the development of his powers and a rightful place in the social learning situation, but also in the method of teaching and in the teacher-pupil relationship. The authority of the teacher to guide and control the learning process is no longer expressed in a direct personal way, as was the case, for example, in the formal recitation period when the emphasis was upon the memorization of the data (woe betide the child with the faulty memory). The control does not consist in commands and prohibitions, rewards and punishments, but "in centering the impulses acting at any one time upon some specific end and in introducing an order of continuity into the sequence of acts."[16] By and large, this is a natural result of joint activity where each individual adjusts his activities and interests, subordinating them to the group in its attempt to define and achieve its goal. The resulting common understanding of the goal and the means necessary to achieve it are the essential factors in social control.

Whitehead

We begin our consideration of Whitehead's contribution to educational thought with several of his educational dicta which will lead us directly into his more involved philosophical position. "Do not teach too many subjects" is his first commandment, and the second is "What you teach, teach thoroughly."[17] He deplores the dead weight of inert ideas which have burdened countless numbers of students and have proven intellectually thwarting. Ideas should be absorbed at once into the mind and their implications for the present circumstances of the learner's life understood and experienced. In this emphasis on the necessity for education to be primarily relevant and useful for the present rather than for the future, Whitehead is not alone, as we have seen. "Education is the art of the utilization of knowledge."[18] The main problem in education is to keep knowledge alive, to prevent it from becoming inert.

He further denounces the notion that the mind is an instrument which requires sharpening. The mind, he insists, is not a passive entity; it is

> a perpetual activity, delicate, receptive, responsive to stimulus. You cannot postpone its life until you have sharpened it. Whatever interest attaches to your subject matter must be evoked here and now; whatever powers you are strengthening in the pupil must be exercised here and now; whatever possibilities of mental life your teaching should impart must be exhibited here and now.[19]

One solution he proposes to make learning vital and immediate is to wipe out the lack of connection between the various subjects and to unify the curriculum. There is, after all, he insists, only one subject matter in the curriculum and that is Life—life in all its manifestations. Mathematics, for example, should not be presented as an autonomous set of facts, as an abstract science, but as a way of rendering clear the quantitative aspect of the world.

Professor Brumbaugh has shown in his monograph *Whitehead as a Philosopher of Education* the further educational implications of Whitehead's critique of abstraction. The focus of Aristotle's thought upon formal typed categories led to a selective attention which finally prevented recognition of other equally significant aspects of reality which lay unnoticed simply because of the knower's preoccupation with his abstractions. The instrumentalists, likewise, in their preoccupation with **doing** things and discerning their pragmatic value also limited their grasp of reality by too narrow a frame of attention. Their abstractions failed to disclose the individuality of people and things, and again the limiting categories, primarily functional (what is it for?) which reflect a partial view of reality, appear. Neither approach was able to realize the "depth of individuality" which is the ultimate goal of education and of human life. A view of reality that does away with abstractions which isolate some aspects of reality to the exclusion of others is what is designated by Whitehead's phrase "aesthetic insight." By this is meant a view of any given thing in the wholeness of its existence, an insight which reveals it as it really is.

This aesthetic awareness corresponds to the final stage of the cyclic process which constitutes for Whitehead the rhythm of education. Learning, he insists, does not take place in an unbroken gradual continuum. Rather there are three stages which correspond roughly to Hegel's three stages characterizing any progress. The first stage is that of romance when the learner is fascinated by the novelty of the situation he is encountering. All sorts of open-ended questions arise and tantalizing relationships begin to manifest themselves and invite further exploration. The excitement of discovery constitutes the emotional atmosphere in this initial stage of learning.

The intellectual ferment created by this prior and necessary stage leads naturally to the second stage which is an attempt to locate the connections and define the relationships and set everything in systematic order. It is the stage of exacting analysis and definitive formulation. It is a necessary stage, but without the prior stage of romance it will not be productive of intellectual endeavor unless it is buttressed by external motivation and discipline.

The final stage is that of generalization. "It is a return to romanticism with the added advantage of classified ideas and relevant technique. It is the fruition which has been the goal of the precise training. It is the final success."[20] This is the stage of mastery, of satisfaction. Whitehead warns against allowing the learner to leave the learning situation without achieving the satisfaction which concludes the cycle. Without this satisfaction which comes through mastery, real learning has not taken place.

In some cases a cycle may be very brief—a part of one lesson; or again it may encompass the whole unit or the course. Education consists in the continual repetition of these cycles, with one cycle stimulating a new one in ever widening circles. One satisfaction achieved gives a sense both of completeness and of the kind of incompleteness which serves as a springboard for further learning. The motivation for learning comes from the stimuli thus provided which is inherent in the rhythmic patterns. Motivation need not be external to the process.

This rhythm is also operative in the mutual tension exerted between freedom and discipline in the normal dynamics of learning. In real learning there must be both. The stage of romance is really characterized by freedom—freedom to explore, to investigate, to ask questions. The subsequent stage is characterized by discipline (expressed in its highest form as self-discipline) through which systematic order and precision are brought about. But the final stage is again characterized by freedom of the highest sort—a disciplined freedom. The learning process may be characterized as a "creative advance"—that is, the learner moves through his lessons fully aware of the formal harmony which characterizes the learning situation and the material, but with a sense of freedom and adventure withal. His learning task is to bring about a creative synthesis in which the end result will be something entirely original. Such a result is difficult both to measure and to achieve. But it is a marvelous ideal which transforms the task of education both for the learner and for the teacher for whom all too frequently it has become a menial drudgery.

CONCLUSION

In summary, the aim of education for Plato is to assist the soul to "remember" what it already knows, to discover what no one has told him. This takes place through a process of critical questioning of preliminary conclusions (the Socratic method) thereby creating intellectual disequilibrium. In this way, the learner proceeds through four levels of perception: conjecture, belief, understanding and finally, science which is knowledge through reason.

For Aristotle, the aim of education is virtue, excellence, perfection. The method involves drawing out, cultivating what is latent within. It requires the development of the learner's rationality to its highest perfection both in theoretical and practical matters which leads to perfect happiness.

For Rousseau, the aim is the unfolding of the natural powers of the developing child like a flower unfolds. To achieve this, the child must be removed from society which tends to pressure and corrupt with its artificial constraints and expectations. Only in this way can nature take over the process allowing the child to become a discoverer instead of a slavish imitator.

For Kant, the aim of education is for the learner to become a rational and moral being, that is, to be capable of rational thinking and moral responsibility. The educational process is one which respects the freedom and dignity of the learner while at the same time reminding the learner of the "categorical imperative" which is inescapable.

For Dewey, the aim of education is the "creative reconstruction of experience" rather than a recapitulation of the past. Education is seen by him as a powerful agent in social evolution rather than as an instrument of society for socializing the learner into society's norms and values. Through direct experience, that is, through entering directly and immediately into the present historical situation, each learner participates in the process of creating knowledge. To achieve this, the artificial walls which have been created to separate schools from society must come down.

For Whitehead, the aim of education is for the learner to comprehend the present significance of the ideas presented to him and to grasp the unity and interconnectedness of all these ideas, that is to say, the unity of knowledge. There are three stages of knowledge: a) romance, the excitement of discovery; b) systematization, exacting analysis and definitive formulation; and c) generalization, the stage of mastery and of satisfaction.

[1] This insight into Aristotle's thought as well as the subsequent paragraphs dealing with the nature of man are based on R.S. Brumbaugh and N.M. Lawrence, Jr., *Aristotle's Philosophy of Education* (reprinted from *Educational Theory*, Vol. IX, No. 1, January, 1959), 1.
[2] Brumbaugh and Lawrence, 7.
[3] *Ibid.*, 8.
[4] Brumbaugh and Lawrence, 10.
[5] Brumbaugh and Lawrence, 12.
[6] *Ibid.*, 12.
[7] Aristotle, *Politics, Book 8*, Chapter 2.
[8] Aristotle, *Politics, Book 8*, Chapter 3.
[9] Aristotle, *Politics, Book 8*, Chapter 7.
[10] Jean Jacques Rousseau, *Emile*, trans. by Barbara Foxley (London: J.M. Dent and Sons, Ltd., 1957), 53.
[11] *Ibid.*, 30.
[12] Immanuel Kant, *Fundamental Principles of the Metaphysics of Ethics*, trans. by T.K. Abbott (London: Longmans, Green, and Company, 1923), 37.
[13] John Dewey, *Democracy and Education* (New York: The Macmillan Company, 1936), 93.
[14] *Ibid.*
[15] *Ibid.*, 27.
[16] *Ibid.*, 47.
[17] Alfred North Whitehead, *The Aims of Education* (New York: The Macmillan Company, 1955), 14.
[18] *Ibid.*, 16.
[19] *Ibid.*, 18.
[20] *Ibid.*, 30.

10

On Being and Becoming a Person

A few years ago an unknown author under the nom de plum Vercors produced a novel entitled *You Shall Know Them.* The plot centers around the discovery of a tribe of creatures (dubbed tropis) in the wilds of New Guinea which appeared to be half-human and half-animal. Through a series of fantastic events including the artificial insemination of a female tropi by a human male and the subsequent deliberate killing of the resulting offspring, the question was raised before a British court whether murder had been committed. Before a verdict can be reached, of course, it must be decided whether or not the victim was human. And in this intriguing way Vercors dramatically raises the question of what constitutes a human being. The question is raised much more effectively than it is answered, for indeed how is such a definition to be made? Is it determined on legal grounds? on biological grounds? on psychological grounds? or on philosophical and theological grounds? No matter how one goes about it, the enormous difficulties involved in such a definition immediately become apparent.

Yet no educators can avoid the question for long if they are to deserve the name of educator. This is a question of first importance in any philosophy of education and it has been variously answered in the traditional philosophies. Since education is largely a human affair, it must be fully aware of the nature and possibilities of the subject with which it has to do. Only then can it determine the character of the educational process, the methods appropriate to it and the ends toward which it strives.

Our exploration of the meaning of human existence involves also an exploration of the environment in which we live. The several main features of that environment which are here included for consideration are the natural realm, the animal kingdom, the social order, and the cultural stream. While it is not theologically acceptable to speak of God as one aspect among others of our environment, our discussion would be seriously deficient if we were to ignore God as the all-comprehensive, all-pervasive Reality with whom we have to do within the total context of our lives. We shall consider in turn how we are related to and yet stand over against nature, the animals, society, culture, and God. Our purpose is to discover what we can about what it means to be human and what are the implications for Christian education.

A. Personhood and Nature

The Scriptures assume and affirm that to be human is to be an integral part of the natural order. "Then the Lord God formed man of dust from the ground, and breathed into his nostrils the breath of life; and man became a living being." (Genesis 2:7). "In the sweat of your face you shall eat bread till you return to the ground, for out of it you were taken; you are dust, and to dust you shall return." (Genesis 3:19). It is true that the man and the woman are given a position of authority and responsibility over the garden, over the fish, fowl, and cattle, but at the same time they share in their creaturehood. They see change and decay not only all around them but are themselves susceptible to it.

Since we are an integral part of the natural, material world, the human body is a fit subject for scientific investigation and description. There are aspects of our being which can be measured and counted with a high degree of precision. Physics measures energy, motion, temperature; chemistry measures the proportion and amount of the basic elements in the human body. Our worth in terms of material composition is pitifully small. In spite of the complexity of our physiological mechanisms, we are appropriately labeled: perishable goods, cheap. We are part and parcel of the physical and chemical world in which we exist and which exists in us. Our claim to dignity, respect and worth is not based upon the character and quality of the stuff of which we are made.

The Christian theologian has no quarrel with the scientific approach to the study of the human being as inextricably bound to the natural material order. Our quarrel is not with the scientist qua scientist; if quarrel we must, it is at the point of certain philosophical positions which are frequently associated with these investigations. Materialism, for example, is a philosophy which "holds that the [material] body alone is real, and that 'mind' is either a word without meaning or a name for certain bodily functions."[1]

Calhoun identifies two forms of materialism: mechanistic materialism and dialectical or historical materialism. The former is a view of life which holds that reality consists of atoms in motion through infinite space. Occasionally, a number of these atoms happen to come together and form bodies which we recognize as solar systems, planets, vegetation and animals, including mankind. Their motion, energy and force is determined by rigid chemical and physical laws; presently these bodies disintegrate, again in accordance with the laws of change, and the atoms are released to form yet other new bodies.

> Man is like every other part of nature—a temporary grouping of atoms into a small machine, geared into the big machine of the universe. His conduct is as completely and physically determined as that of a fine clock or a moving planet. 'Mind' is merely a certain functioning of his body, and has no power of its own. Each man is what he is irrevocably, and everything he does is fixed in advance, like clockwork.[2]

A more fluid and dynamic version of materialism is that set forth by Karl Marx. In this view, reality is not composed of atoms but of

> physical *processes* in perpetual struggle and periodic advance. Nature is not a machine, but a kind of vast growing thing—wholly impersonal and unconscious, but dynamic, fluid, and progressive. There is real progress, not merely continual reshuffling and eventual stagnation: hence, 'historical' materialism. And this progress, best seen in the pageant of animal evolution and social history, comes about through conflict: hence, 'dialectical' materialism.[3]

Both views see humanity as an integral part of nature, but they differ in their concept of nature. There is in addition in Marxism a point of view which sees mankind primarily as producer, as animal that has developed tools and exploited the material environment and taken advantage of it in a way that the lower animals have not done. "All the rest of his life, social organization, language, morals, thought systems—grow out of his economic activities."[4] Marxism holds to a very fixed economic and political view of mankind. Freedom in terms of personal choice and self-determination and the moral responsibility arising from these is a meaningless concept; morality arises from and is subordinated to the class struggle. Once the classless society has been realized, social evolution will have achieved its goal and social morality will have come of age.

Michael Polanyi provides a helpful commentary for us on this philosophical position in his book, *The Study of Man*.[5] He begins with the analogy of the machine. The chemist and the physicist study a machine only from the perspective of the physical properties of the constituent parts; they do not deal directly with questions of function and purpose for this is the interest of the engineer. The former are concerned only with questions of fact; the latter, concerned with questions of the machine's actual and potential functions, necessarily becomes involved in value judgments. Similarly, in the case of living organisms, physico-chemical investigations are meaningful (in terms of values) only insofar as they are related to the question of the function of the total physiological organism. For example, it is possible to observe the cell structure of the muscular system and describe it without making any evaluative comments; however, when we begin to describe that structure and that system in terms of locomotion we have entered the area of evaluation.

On the human level, the same holds true. Let it be granted that the human body is part of the natural order, that it is subject to its laws and processes and can be studied as such. But only insofar as one moves from such a study to the larger question of the function of the whole organism and from this to the even larger question of the meaning and value of this function does one begin to approach the distinctively human question for this is the question of responsibility. Polanyi deals with the problem of the possibility of free moral choice, insisting that it is possible even though purposeful human functioning is conditioned by the physico-chemical constitution and condition of the body just as the purposeful function of a machine is so qualified. To regard a person only from the perspective of the latter consideration, however, is to ignore the categories of purpose, value, responsibility, and choice and to fall into the error of a mechanistic materialism.[6]

To assert personal responsibility in the face of our being bound to the natural order as a part of it is to affirm that to be a person is to be a spiritual being. The question of moral responsibility can be posited only if hazard is present in the form of the possibility of error. This possibility is constituted, at least in part, by our material nature.

On the other hand, moral responsibility can be posited only if a person stands also over against nature. From a philosophical point of view there is abundant evidence that we are not only a part of but that we are distinct from, i.e., we stand over against, the natural order.

(a) A person has awareness of self, of other selves, and of things; a person is self-transcendent.
(b) A person is subject to error, hence purposive, responsive, moral.
(c) A person is capable of knowing and of making judgments, hence a thinking and valuing being who enjoys a measure of detachment from the immediate physical environment.
(d) A person is aware of both past and future as well as of the present, therefore not completely bound either by space or time, further evidence of partial detachment from the immediate environment.
(e) A person is capable of creating and using symbols, general concepts and abstract ideas. These make possible tradition, culture and communication.
(f) A person is capable of critical reflection and of constructive action. A person is capable of acting upon—exploiting and modifying—the present environment and the cultural heritage.[7]

Scientific investigation of the natural order (and of human beings as a part of it) has spawned a new optimism not only with regard to human ability to anticipate and direct the forces of nature, but also to predict and control human behavior through increasing knowledge in such areas as sociology, psychology, etc.

The new scientific understanding and description of various phenomena of human behavior hitherto not understood bring a new sense of power over the shaping of human destiny. The possession of this new knowledge about what it is to be human is at the same time the possession of a great power whose exercise will determine in great measure what we will become. Bertrand Russell is a leading optimistic apologist for this point of view.

> Man has been disciplined hitherto by his subjection to nature. Having emancipated himself from this subjection, he is showing something of the defects of slave-turned-master. A new moral outlook is called for in which submission to the powers of nature is replaced by respect for what is best in man. It is where this respect is lacking that scientific technique is dangerous. So long as it is present, science, having delivered man from bondage to nature can proceed to deliver him from bondage to the slavish part of himself.[8]

It is possible, Russell maintains, to reap the advantages of the scientific outlook and avoid the dangers if the scientist is at the same time a humanist. That is, he must have a respect for human life and subordinate his thirst for power over people to seeking the highest welfare both for individuals and for society as a whole. A science which conceives of a person as a machine and treats him accordingly, determined to make of it what it will, does violence to his nature and brings unhappiness. But a science which views a person as a tree recognizes that personality has its own particular nature and principles of growth and seeks only to enhance that development and happiness through scientific means.[9] Russell's insistence on the need for respect, sympathy, and even love is not the insistence of the scientist but that of the humanist in him.

Russell further develops the analogy of human nature as a tree and the principle of growth derived from it in his *Principles of Social Reconstruction*. The right soil and freedom from external obstructions are essential for the growth of both.[10] Modern science has opened up new possibilities for growth through its contribution in both these areas. Through the increased understanding of our psychological makeup and the development of scientific educational procedures it has fertilized the soil. Through the rise and spread of knowledge it has had its effect on tradition and social institutions, thereby clearing away many of the obstacles which have hindered human growth. The optimistic conviction that human nature is malleable and can be changed is thus undergirded and demonstrated.

We find in the above considerations a number of issues with which we must come to terms in establishing our philosophy of Christian education.

1. In what sense and to what extent does our material nature modify and determine the possibilities for self-realization?
2. In what sense and to what extent does our material nature establish or limit our freedom, personal responsibility, moral character and possibilities, values, goals and aspirations?
3. In what sense and to what extent does human effort (including education and especially Christian education) contribute to the realization of authentic human existence? Is our material nature something to be ignored, transcended, or affirmed?

Christianity is as materialistic in its view of mankind as is any current philosophy; it takes the natural order (and mankind as part of it) seriously and affirms it. Each act of creation is declared by God to be good. The dualism characteristic of much philosophical thought in Hellenism in the time of the early church was resisted by the New Testament writers. The doctrine of the resurrection of the body is sometimes cited as evidence that Christianity was and is a materialistic religion.

On the other hand, Christian faith takes issue with the position that the material universe (including mankind) requires only material factors to explain it, "that man is simply the creature of these factors and is completely destroyed by them; that his values are at best biological conveniences, entirely relative to his time and circumstance; and that every trace of his achievements will one day be annihilated."[11]

Christianity is as optimistic in its view of human nature as is any current philosophy; it takes seriously human freedom, human destiny and human possibilities. It insists, however, that our final destiny and ultimate self-realization are not to be achieved in and through our existence in a material order. Heaven is not defined as the workers' paradise, nor is it the kingdom on earth envisioned by Bertrand Russell.

But Christianity is also as pessimistic as any philosophy past or present with respect to human nature. Humanity left to its own devices inevitably seeks its own way and destroys both itself and the environment. Even our highest and noblest efforts participate in this distortion for the spirit of self-sufficiency to which they give birth prevent us from recognizing our basic dependence upon God. Our true personhood comes to us not through human striving and effort; it can only be received as a gift. Education is an appropriate activity of Christian persons but only if it is realized that one's true life must be received as a gift and that the divine gift contains a human task. Education prepares the person to enter into the task of laying hold on the gift which is offered, its function is to help us to become what we are by God's design.

B. Personhood and the Animals

Just as the physical sciences have underscored our fundamental connection with the material world, so the biological sciences have made us aware of the physical and structural continuities between human beings and the more highly developed animals. These continuities have led to a theory of the evolution of mankind from the higher primates. Though there has been considerable development and modification of Darwin's original thesis, his essential theory still enjoys wide-spread acceptance today. It was a hard-won acceptance for a number of reasons. The Copernican view of the physical universe had tended to de-emphasize the importance of mankind in the universe and thereby raised a storm of protest and controversy. The Darwinian theory tended to shrink his significance still further and was naturally resisted for this reason. In the second place, the theory was and remains just that—a theory, i.e., a proposed explanation for certain phenomena for which all the data are not in. By the very nature of the case, only a small percentage of the data is accessible although scientists continue to search diligently for the data and particularly for the missing link. In the third place, the theory of evolution has frequently been associated with an atheistic philosophy which has been quick to seize upon it as an adequate explanation of the origin of life apart from the Creator, God.

Probably the third consideration is the one which caused the church to resist the theory and brand it as heresy. In recent years, however, many Christian theologians and scholars have come to accept what scientific evidence does exist in support of the evolutionary principle while continuing to challenge and reject the anti-Christian philosophical assumptions which attend it. Christian faith finds no conflict with the fact that there are similarities between human beings and certain of the animals in terms of cellular substance, skeletal structure, respiratory system, physiological mechanisms, etc. Nor, on the other hand, is

Christianity alone in asserting that there are some significant differences between persons and animals.

How are human beings different from the animals? The answer has been sought in many ways. Some have found the difference in terms of posture, though this is much too superficial a view of the matter. Some have found it in the observation that while the animals tend to adapt themselves to the environment, mankind has reversed the order and to a considerable extent has modified the environment and adapted **it** to **himself**. Of course, even this is a relative distinction only for there are rigid limitations to human modification of the environment in which we find ourselves. There is also abundant evidence that animals, too, adapt their environment to their own peculiar habits and needs.

A more serious issue arises when one considers a major tenet of the evolutionary theory with respect to the development of mankind and of the animals. I refer to the principle of "natural selection," popularly referred to as the "survival of the fittest." Applied to animals, the theory raises no theological or philosophical concern; applied to the human race, this principle is fraught with profound significance and raises large questions with regard to social responsibility and morality. Human society has always shown itself at its best when it has exercised care and compassion for its weaker members (e.g., altruism, charity, medicine, social welfare, care for the aged). How is this to be reconciled with the evolutionary principle of natural selection? Is this not arbitrary interference with it? On what grounds? And what is the ultimate consequence of such interference?

The science of genetics has added considerably to our self-knowledge and has demonstrated that the laws of heredity apply to us as well as to the simpler organisms. The possibilities of eugenics raise a host of questions regarding morality, responsibility, and human happiness and destiny which are not properly part of the field of biological interest and concern. These are philosophical, theological and educational questions and they have far-reaching consequences. Bertrand Russell points out that if those in power were to determine which members of society are to be permitted the privilege of procreation, and further if the fetus of the unborn child can be chemically affected, a social revolution could be brought about. A superior race, or at least a superior class could be scientifically brought into existence and with scientific educational procedures their superiority would be advanced and maintained.

Another argument which has been advanced affirms that "man's capacity to think is his most outstanding attribute."[12] Speech is simply the abstract extension of the power of thought. Through the exercise of thought and speech, persons are able to communicate with others, to refine their emotions and desires, and generally to gain a significant measure of control over themselves and their environment. "Animals have no speech, and all the towering superiority of man over the animals is due almost entirely to man's gift of speech."[13]

Polanyi's discussion of the human capacity for thought and speech involves him in a consideration of the character of human knowledge. He asserts that knowledge is of two types, that which is formulated, articulate, explicit and that which is unformulated, unarticulated, tacit. The latter lacks a public, objective character; it is the most primitive form of human knowing and is "the kind of intelligence situated behind the barrier of language."[14] It is this kind of intelligence, this way of knowing, which we share in common with the animal world. "In the absence of linguistic clues man sees things, hears things, feels things, moves about, explores his surroundings and gets to know his way about, very much as animals do."[15]

Explicit knowledge is susceptible to critical reflection; it has been objectified, made external and can therefore be looked upon. Inarticulate intelligence must grope its way, plunging from one state of tacit awareness to another. "Preverbal intelligence" is acritical; it is a small spot of light surrounded by darkness. It is the uncritical acceptance of the unreasoned conclusions of the senses, yet it is essential to the highest intellectual achievements. "The explorer's fumbling progress is a much finer achievement than the well-briefed traveler's journey."[16]

This kind of knowing, primitive as it is and shared in common with the animals, is foundational to producing an articulate framework or to renewing it. Over and over again in producing, renewing, or criticizing, the thinker must go back to the data which are not themselves the product of reasoned thought but which stand prior to it, a tacit awareness of reality. Tacit **awareness** gives rise to tacit accumulation, pondering, reconsideration and reorganization of sense experience. This is the process of **understanding** and is still as such, an animal, pre-verbal process. The third stage, the language stage, adds a whole new dimension to the cognitive experience and leads to explicit, articulate knowledge. Understanding, facilitated by the process of verbal articulation, is the function of knowing what one intends, what one means, what one does; these are the acts of a person—purposive, intelligent, creative—and are the marks which distinguish a person from the animals.

This "articulate framework" which can be verbally communicated and transmitted through a wide range of community and to descending generations via symbols is the foundation of culture. Culture is the "satisfying home" of the intellect; it is both the product of the intellect and that which calls it forth in ever new attempts at reconstructing it. "All mental life by which we surpass the animals is evoked in us as we assimilate the articulate framework of our culture."[17]

Brunner is not satisfied with this answer to the question of what distinguishes mankind from the animals. He holds that the uniqueness of mankind lies not in his powers of intellect nor in his capacity to create culture; it lies, rather, in his **obligation** and his **destiny**: to be human is to be **responsible** and **personal**. As personal beings, we are in relation to God and to society. It is this relatedness which constitutes our responsibility and is the basis of morality.[18]

Calhoun's position is essentially the same. He asserts that from the point of view of Christian faith man, the animal, is a creature responsible to his Creator. He needs more room than the present in which to live. He feels a sense of obligation, a moral oughtness. "To regard such a being as completely describable in terms of phenomena is to miss the most distinctive thing about him: his being haunted by what seems a perpetual summons from beyond every present appearance."[19]

Let us consider again the questions raised at the conclusion of the first section.

1. In what sense and to what extent does our animal nature modify and determine the possibilities for self-realization?
2. In what sense and to what extent does our animal nature establish or limit our freedom, personal responsibility, moral character and possibilities, values, goals and aspirations?

C. Personhood and Society

We have already anticipated mankind's essentially social nature in our discussion of the human capacity for thought and speech. The power of speech (and the consequent intellectual powers we thus gain) is basically a social phenomenon. "Human thought grows only within language and since language can exist only in a society, all thought is rooted in society."[20] The gratification of the mental passions (as distinct from the bodily passions) "creates objects destined to gratify the same passions in others" and in so doing "enriches the mind of all humanity."[21] By the very nature of the case, therefore, Polanyi argues that the exercise of one's mental powers involves one in a social situation and makes one a responsible and moral being. Each individual is dependent upon society for most of what is known; knowledge is a matter of mutual interdependence.

Humanity's essentially social nature can be documented in other ways as well. Culture and tradition, peculiar to mankind, are social phenomena. The capacity to experience loneliness is powerful evidence of the need for others. The wide range of social institutions from the state to the Rotary Club which we have created is still further evidence. Again the biblical account of the institution of marriage which states that "it is not good that man should live alone" also corroborates this observation. There is a wholesome trend in much contemporary philosophical and theological thought which emphasizes the importance of interpersonal relationships and social involvement. Nevertheless there are serious difficulties in this position unless the corresponding truth is also recognized that not only are we integrally involved in society but also that in a real sense we stand apart from it.

> As the body takes in chemical substances, selecting from them those which tend to build up its individuality, so the mental life takes in from its social environment impressions and influences which tend to build up individual character. But the individual who becomes only a 'unit in a school,' or a 'unit in the herd,' in some great factory, city, or collectivist state, is stunted in his growth.[22]

R.L. Calhoun, in an essay entitled "The Dilemma of Humanitarian Modernism" states the question inevitably raised by a person's integral relation to society, "Does society give man his selfhood and personhood or is society the product of human selves?"[23] If we say the latter, we say that society is simply an arrangement among persons who already possess their selfhood independently of their social arrangements. This is the view characteristic of the individualist. Individualism in its extreme form denies that the community of persons is **essential** to human existence. Or, in a more subtle expression of it, the individualist is prepared to acknowledge the necessity of community and to enter into it but only on his own terms. He conceives of it not as contributing to, even constituting, his personhood but only as an impersonal arrangement by which some of the needs which he, **as a person in his own right**, must have satisfied. One well-known illustration of this point of view is the "social contract" theory of the state.

Emil Brunner is fond of characterizing modern life as a Robinson Crusoe existence; he describes the modern Robinson Crusoe as one

> who enters into community; he forms it as one who in himself is a complete man, a personality.... He unites himself to other such personalities on condition that it is he who determines whether or not the union shall exist; it is he who establishes the conditions and therefore, even in the union, remains a free lord over himself.[24]

If we were to answer the question in the other way, by asserting that it is society which gives the individual his selfhood and personhood, we would be found granting to society a power and an ultimacy which from a Christian point of view it does not possess. There are those, warns Calhoun, who hold that human society is the ultimate reality and is both responsible for and capable of directing its own affairs. Corresponding to this point of view is a confidence in social procedures such as education and technology to effect human progress. Christian faith, he goes on, denies the ultimate character to society. A person is without doubt conditioned by and to some extent a product of his society and its culture; but at the same time, he stands before God responsible as an individual. "To sin is not then simply to disobey society [which may or may not be an expression of God's will and which can never make ultimate demands] but to contradict the will of God, which is the deepest law of man's own being."[25]

If either alternative causes us to fall into the ditch, what answer shall we give? The Christian answers this question by saying that both the individual and society, personhood and community, are established by God. Brunner puts it as follows:

> Personality in the strict sense of the word...in the sense of indissoluble personality exists only where man's being is grounded in God's addressing him. There it is qualified as responsibility...I can know myself as a person only where I see my existence grounded in responsibility, and that means where I know myself to be created by and in the Word of God. This knowledge, however, is identical with that act of decision which the Christian calls faith. There alone does man acquire a truly personal existence.[26]

H. H. Farmer is just as emphatic as Brunner that "the Christian view of the essential secret of human nature, of the distinctive 'humanity of the human'....is that he is a person standing all the time in personal relationship to God. It is that relationship which constitutes him—MAN."[27] It is not that man is first of all a person, and then **as a person** enters into personal relationship with God; his very personhood is constituted by the relationship. An important clarification of this concept is made by Farmer; while not denying that the response of faith enhances one's personhood—or better still, enables him to lay hold of it in the full sense he maintains that a person is "first, last, and all the time in relation to the eternal Person, to God."[28] Our relation to God does not begin at the point where we acknowledge God; the Christian gospel declares that a person "whether he knows it or not, whether he likes it or not...stands, right down to the innermost core and essence of his being, in the profoundest possible relationship to God all the time in an order of persons."[29]

Farmer insists that a person does not stand in two distinct relationships—to God on the one hand and to other persons on the other; he stands "in one relationship which is twofold; or better still, there is one personal continuum with two poles, the infinite personal on the one hand, the finite personal on the other."[30] The individual is related to others at all times by his very existence as a person; a radical individualism or an impersonalism which turns away from and ignores this personal structure of existence not only militates against the development of true human personality but is a sin against God.

> We might express it by saying that when God created man he himself *eo facto* created an order or structure of persons in relationship with himself and with one another. This is the ultimate secret of finite personal nature, of specifically human nature. Only as a man is part of, held in, that structure is he distinctively man.... To come into existence as a man is to be incorporated in this world of the personal, to be in relation to persons—the divine person and human persons—and existence as a man is not possible on any other terms.[31]

A third issue of concern has to do with the increasing depersonalization evident in our society which vitiates genuine community and tends to distort and impair true personal existence. It is caused by a complex of factors including the tendency to regard people as objects to be exploited for selfish ends, the emphasis upon technological developments and material prosperity, and the increasing mobility of persons which militates against the possibility of establishing deep and meaningful relationships in a community.

John Macmurray, in his analysis of the impersonal relationship, distinguishes between direct and indirect relations: the former "are those which involve a personal acquaintance with one another on the part of the persons related"; the latter "are relations between persons who are not personally known to one another."[32] It is obvious that most of the relations between persons in the various natural communities are indirect. All indirect relations are impersonal. Direct relations, which obtain in the smaller natural communities such as the family, may be either personal or impersonal. The personal relationship, Macmurray holds, is its own end and requires no justification. The impersonal relationship arising from indirect relations is also legitimate; its character is instrumental to the effective functioning of the life of the larger communities. The impersonal relationship arising from direct relations, however, requires a justification; it is valid only if its character is instrumental, but if this is not the case such relationships are inappropriate and even sinful.

The impersonal is not of necessity destructive of true community, as has been shown, but becomes so only when its proper relation to the personal is distorted. The proper relation may be illustrated concretely as follows: I may meet the claim of my neighbor upon me for something—

goods or services—which I have. Our relationship is direct but impersonal; this is not in itself a violation of the community between us. Implicit within this exchange lies the possibility that on a deeper level he is not asking for or needing **something from me**, but that he is asking for **me myself**. If I am sufficiently sensitive to recognize this and over and above the something which he ostensibly asks for give him myself, our relationship moves from the area of the impersonal to the area of the personal. Our "I-It" relationship becomes an "I-Thou" relationship.[33] In the life of faith, the possibility that this may happen is ever present.

1. In what sense and to what extent does our social nature modify and determine the possibilities for realizing true personhood?

2. How does our social nature establish or limit our freedom, responsibility, morality, values, goals and aspirations?

3. What place does social effort, including Christian education, have in the process of realizing true personhood?

D. Personhood and Culture

The discussion of personhood and society closely parallels and immediately involves us in a discussion of personhood and culture, for culture is a social product, intellectual as well as material. Mankind, Polanyi states, is closely related to culture since it is not only the product of his mind and hand but also the ethos in which he lives and which brings forth the possibilities of his becoming truly personal. The creation of cultural products is basically a social affair, i.e., it creates objects to be enjoyed by all, which enrich the lives of all.

While there is a sense in which a person is created by culture (in that culture provides him with the possibility of a fuller realization of that which is distinctively human) there is a very real sense in which a person stands over against his cultural products through the exercise of his cultural activities. The creation of cultural objects is a moral and purposive activity since they are created for the enjoyment of others and for the enrichment of their lives; a person's essential dignity and right to respect are constituted on the grounds of his capacity to create intellectual and cultural products and his willingness, if need be, to sacrifice bodily pleasures for the sake of intellectual and cultural pleasures whose gratification is primarily social.

Paul Mininger, in his inaugural address as president of Goshen College, set forth a theological interpretation of culture and of its implications for Christian education. To be human, he says, is not only to be a creature, it is also to be a creator; one's personhood is realized and expressed in part through cultural activity which is the exercise of one's creative capacity. Man and woman received a divine commission for their cultural activity in Genesis 2:15, "The Lord God took the man and put him in the garden of Eden to till it and keep it." Mininger holds that this is a basic affirmation of cultural activity; it is only when this becomes ultimate and mankind turns this activity and its fruits toward the end of self-glorification, using it as a prop for his self-sufficiency before God, that it contributes to the fundamental distortion of his life. Cultural activity is a spiritual activity;

> although the Christian lives in fellowship with God in Christ, it is in the sphere of human culture where his new life becomes articulate. It is through the economic, social, domestic, political, and aesthetic activities of the disciple's life that he really bears witness to the fact that Jesus Christ is his Redeemer and Lord.[34]

The Christian witnesses to the glory and Lordship of Christ through his cultural activities.

Roger Mehl, in an essay in *The Student World* entitled, "Faith and Culture" holds a similar position. In response to the question "Why does man engage in cultural activities?" Mehl gives three replies:

1. "To construct something which will outlive him."
2. "To experience the joy of discovering the potentialities of his humanity," i.e., "to lay hold on his full humanity."
3. It may well be, and often is, an expression of man's self-confidence in his own powers and becomes a form of pride—a protest against his dependence on God.[35]

Is it not a source of profound amazement that evidence of human sinfulness is manifested not only in our baser passions but also in our noblest achievements? Cultural activity is, to be sure, spiritual activity, essential to our distinctiveness as human beings, but it is far from being spiritually neutral.

Mehl traces two streams of thought in the Christian church with regard to culture which have run parallel through the centuries and which have never been reconciled. The one affirms culture and the other regards it with suspicion. What is the true relation between faith and culture? he asks. Does it participate in God's gracious purpose for us? Does it play a role in our salvation? Is it an autonomous venture with its own norms apart from faith? Mehl holds that every interpretation of cultural activity has an implicit anthropology; but a Christian anthropology can be known only through the revelation of Jesus Christ. Through the revelation of Jesus Christ, we see the sinfulness of the pretense of self-sufficiency as rebellion against God. We see the true essence of our humanity in Jesus Christ.

What, then, is the significance of the revelation of Jesus Christ for culture?

1. In the first place it reveals that we are not made for self-sufficiency and self-determination but for a relationship with God. We can truly realize our true humanity, our full personhood, only by realizing our relationship as God's sons and daughters for which we were created. It is as the children of the Creator God that we fulfill the command "to keep and cultivate the garden." This stance determines our attitude to cultural activity and its ends.

2. In the second place, cultural activity is not in itself the work of salvation, but it is the legitimate activity and valid vocation of those who are already reconciled.

3. All of our cultural activities and products (including those of the reconciled) are and remain under the judgment of God.

4. The final and ultimate significance of our cultural activities and products escapes us.

Christian faith, therefore, summons us to our cultural task, relative and ambiguous though it is. Christian faith reminds us to maintain a critical attitude toward culture, refusing it an ultimate claim. Mininger also holds that the Christian's attitude is not one of denying culture but of recognizing its ambiguity. Every existing culture is the product of both divine and demonic forces each working through mankind to produce cultural products after their kind and put them to uses according to their own ends. This being the case, an appropriate attitude is one of discernment, discrimination, and critical involvement.

These are some of the educational implications of this view of culture:

1. Instrumental. "[we] must utilize the resources of human culture to achieve Christ's purposes for man in time and eternity."[36]
2. Transmissive. The cultural heritage forms the content of education. The church's educational program selects from it in order to build its curriculum.
3. Exploitive. The church, through its educational program, will seek to "exploit human culture for the expression, communication, and extension of the gospel of Christ."[37]
4. Prophetic. The church, through its educational program, will present an interpretation of culture as it has been given above and will seek to have its members bring their cultural activities and products under the judgment and lordship of Christ.

Mininger's definition of Christian education is as follows: "Christian education is the process by which the Christian community under a commission from Christ uses all its resources to restore man to the image of God and prepare him for expressing in all his relationships the cultural implications of the lordship of Christ."[38]

1. In what sense and to what extent does our cultural nature modify and determine our possibilities for realizing true personhood?

2. How does our cultural nature establish or limit our freedom, responsibility, morality, values, goals and aspirations?

3. What place do cultural activities and products have in the process of realizing true personhood?

E. Personhood and God

We have already referred to the account of the creation of man and woman by God which affirms their fundamental relationship with all the organic material world. An earlier creation account, however, declared that they enjoy besides a relationship of another kind which their fellow created beings do not enjoy. "So God created man in his own image, in the image of God he created him; male and female he created them." Genesis 1:27.

Emil Brunner asserts that man and woman can be finally understood only in terms of their unique relation to God. This is the **specifically human** fact which makes one a person, more than an animal or thing. The *imago dei* does not imply an absorption into the divine, a complete elimination or dissolving of human personhood but rather an "overagainstness." "Man's distinctive quality consists in the fact that God turns to him and addresses him."[39] This address is also and at the same time a call to respond. This word of address is the ground of human responsibility; responsible existence is the same thing as truly human existence. A response of No! to God's word of address is to turn away from the gift of one's true personhood. A Yes! response is one which accepts God's outgoing love and returns it in gratitude for the gift of true selfhood. In this also we find our true relation to society, for we can truly love God only as we love our brother and our sister. They are given to us both as a gift and as a responsibility for only as we love God through the brother and the sister can we lay hold on our personhood and realize authentic existence.

Christianity has a very high view of what it means to be a person; at the same time, in comparison with some other views, it is very pessimistic. For example,

> humanism as religion calls for devotion to humanity and to values that have abiding worth, but not to any divine being that has power. It views each man as himself of high worth, and capable of perfecting his life through intelligence and kindness.[40]

Its watchword is "the sufficiency and perfectibility of man." Mankind is its own god; religion is devotion to his highest values and aspirations; the goal of life is their realization; the means is education.

In comparison with Christianity, this is indeed an optimistic point of view. Christianity holds, Calhoun goes on, that the human predicament is far worse than most realize. Cleverness and intellect and education are not the final solution to the human problem, not even will power, good intent and moral striving. Intellectual and moral education do not go to the root of the problem. Nor is mankind's animal nature the basic problem; it lies rather in the attempt to exercise self-determination and freedom **in rejection of God**. As a result, a fundamental distortion has set in which is at once personal and social. Far from giving the demands of our physical and animal nature their proper due, the human race developed individual habits and social customs which reflect the fact that legitimate animal drives have run riot both in terms of excess and imbalance. Both within ourselves and within the social milieu in which we have our being there is abundant evidence of this fundamental distortion and perversion. Mankind is mired so deeply that he cannot extricate himself; he cannot even revert to the innocent level of animal existence for he is and remains a morally responsible being.

This is the meaning of the Christian doctrine of original sin. Brunner[41] describes it as a perverted state of existence in which one's true relationship to God, to others and to oneself is distorted; as a result, one's fundamental being as a responsible human person is thwarted and unfulfilled. One continues to be a responsible creature, but one's sense of responsibility, being weak, lacks clarity and one's response is ambivalent. One's existence, far from being fully human is an "existence-in-contradiction." In genuine, fulfilled human existence, there is both true personhood and true community created by God's gift of freedom to be a self and by one's responsible exercise of love.

In such a view there is room both for genuine personhood and for community. In Christ all social barriers are broken down, but true individuality stands out for all that. Each individual is loved by God as a person and is therefore a person of dignity and worthy of respect. Each individual stands personally addressed by God and is personally responsible. God calls **each one**, but he calls us into community where our true personhood is realized and experienced.

At the same time that Christianity is more pessimistic than humanism, it is also more optimistic in the hope it holds out for mankind with regard to his ultimate destiny. Christianity "sees man as at once less admirable in his present actuality and more profound in his ultimate significance than modernism takes him to be."[42] While holding that we cannot love God and the neighbor as we ought (and the full realization of human personhood depends upon it), Christian faith affirms that God loves us powerfully enough to quicken our response of obedience and love. This love, manifested in Jesus Christ, has shown itself dynamic and powerful; it is in the unleashing of this power in our lives that Christian faith finds the basis for its optimism. This is not, however, a matter of education or of re-education, but of remaking (i.e., conversion).[43]

Our destiny lies not in our own hands but with God. Our salvation (or in educational and philosophical terms, the full realization of our humanity, our selfhood, or our personhood) does not lie in subduing nature, transcending or outstripping the animals, effecting social goals through social means such as education or cultural advance; rather it lies in responsiveness to God and the experience of divine power through that response. It is not that human efforts are meaningless, says Calhoun, but that they are not ultimate. They require both something beyond them and something permeating them in order that one may realize one's true excellence and one's ultimate destiny in life.

It is only as persons orient their being in and from God that they find the fulfillment and integrity for which they long. There is, it is true, a sense in which one must grow and develop in terms of one's capacities and potentialities. But there is also a very real sense in which one must die to self in order to find one's true self. The New Testament insists that life comes through death, that the path to life in Christ lies through death with him. This is the scandal of Christianity; it is a proposition offensive to reason. Human intellect neither discerns nor effects this process of transformation. Rather the truth of the matter is that it participates in the transformation. The intellect too is transformed for it is no abstract quality; it is integrally a part of the person who is given his genuine being through identification with the death and resurrection of Jesus Christ. The person whole and entire is renewed; this renewal determines how he shall use his intellectual powers in his further growth and fulfillment. The possibility is now open for these faculties to become an instrument of the higher life aiding one in one's fuller understanding and grasp of it. The intellect cannot give one new life; it can, however, serve to enhance or to frustrate its operation within a person. Conversion is a reorientation of one's life; as such it speaks to the motivation and direction of the educational experience. Moreover, it involves a receptivity to a new power of life and growth coming not from within a person but from God.

1. How does one's relation to God modify and determine his possibilities for realizing true personhood?

2. How does this relationship establish or limit one's freedom, responsibility, morality, values, goals and aspirations?

3. What place does conversion have in the process of realizing true personhood and how is it related to the educational process?

Conclusion

We have briefly examined the question of the meaning of human existence in relation to various aspects of the environment. This is, admittedly, a presumptuous undertaking, for the ultimate meaning of being human escapes us. However, this does not excuse us from ever new attempts at scrutinizing the mystery of life. As Christian educators, we are committed to keep trying for our understanding of the educational task depends profoundly upon how we view the matter. I have tried to sum up the significant questions at the end of each section which have served to focus my treatment and which may give direction to the reader's further reflection. The clues, in my judgment, to the educational implications of each of the five areas we have considered are as follows:

1. Personhood and nature: the capacity for transcending and modifying the environment.
2. Personhood and the animals: the capacity for rational reflection.
3. Personhood and society: the capacity for personal identity and for community.
4. Personhood and culture: the capacity to create, transmit and judge culture.
5. Personhood and God: the capacity for relationship with God through the response of faith.

---

[1] Robert L. Calhoun, *What is Man*? (New York: Association Press, 1952), 45. See also B. F. Skinner, *About Behaviorism* (New York: Vintage Books, 1976) and B. F. Skinner, *Beyond Freedom and Dignity* (New York: Bantam/Vintage Books, 1972).
[2] *Ibid.*, 46.
[3] *Ibid.*, 47.
[4] Ibid., 47.
[5] Michael Polanyi, *The Study of Man* (Chicago: University of Chicago Press, 1963).

[6] *Ibid.,* 41ff.
[7] The above are my summary of the basic arguments which Calhoun presents in his total treatment of the subject in *What Is Man?*
[8] Bertrand Russell, *The Scientific Outlook* (London: George Allen and Unwin Ltd., 1931), 279.
[9] Bertrand Russell, *Education and the Good Life* (New York: Boni and Liveright, 1926), 145.
[10] Bertrand Russell, *Principles of Social Reconstruction* (London: George Allen and Unwin Ltd., 1916), 25-43. This same book was published in New York in 1917 by the Century Company under the title, *Why Men Fight.*
[11] T. E. Jessop, "The Scientific Account of Man," *The Christian Understanding of Man* (London: George Allen and Unwin, Ltd., 1938), 29.
[12] Michael Polanyi, *The Study of Man*, 11.
[13] *Ibid.*, 13.
[14] *Ibid.*, 13.
[15] *Ibid.*, 14.
[16] *Ibid.,* 18.
[17] *Ibid.*, 31.
[18] Emil Brunner, "The Christian Doctrine of Man," *The Christian Understanding of Man*, T.E. Jessop, ed., 153-161.
[19] Robert L. Calhoun, "The Dilemma of Humanitarian Modernism," *The Christian Understanding of Man*, T. E. Jessop, ed., 73.
[20] Polanyi, *The Study of Man*, 60.
[21] *Ibid.*, 60.
[22] W. M. Horton, "The Christian Understanding of Man", *The Christian Understanding of Man*, T. E. Jessop, ed., 231.
[23] Calhoun, "The Dilemma of Humanitarian Modernism," 74ff.
[24] Emil Brunner, *The Word and the World* (New York: Charles Scribner's Sons, 1931), 114.
[25] Calhoun, "The Dilemma of Humanitarian Modernism," 76.
[26] Brunner, *The Word and the World*, 31-32.
[27] H. H. Farmer, *The Servant of the Word* (New York: Charles Scribner's Sons, 1942), 39.
[28] *Ibid.*, 79.
[29] *Ibid.*, 79.
[30] *Ibid.*, 39.
[31] *Ibid.*, 38.
[32] John Macmurray, *Persons in Relation* (London: Faber and Faber Ltd., 1961), 42-43.
[33] Emil Brunner, *The Divine-Human Encounter* (Philadelphia: The Westminster Press, 1943).

[34] Paul Mininger "Culture for Service," *Mennonite Quarterly Review*, (January, 1955).
[35] Roger Mehl, "Faith and Culture," *The Student World* (No. 1, 1955), 120-131.
[36] Mininger, "Culture for Service," 11.
[37] *Ibid.*, 13.
[38] *Ibid.*, 10-11.
[39] Brunner, "The Christian Doctrine of Man," 156.
[40] Calhoun, *What Is Man?*, 60
[41] Brunner, "The Christian Doctrine of Man," 161-166
[42] Calhoun, "The Dilemma of Humanitarian Modernism," 71.
[43] Joseph Haroutounian, "A Protestant Theory of Education," in John Paul von Grueningen, ed., *Toward a Christian Philosophy of Higher Education* (Philadelphia: The Westminster Press, 1957), 24-44.

11

Conversion in Religious Development

One of the most fascinating of human experiences—and one which has been studied and described from many points of view, and seems at first so subjective, complex and diverse as to defy all objective scientific description—is the phenomenon of conversion. And one of the most popular misconceptions which a serious study of this subject dispels is that conversion is merely an extreme emotional orgy indulged in by certain religious groups. It is clear that what can be a normal and wholesome experience in the healthy development of a personality has been exploited in unwholesome ways not only by religious but also by political opportunists. These aberrations, however, ought not blind us to the genuine nature and possibilities of conversion.

It has already been intimated that conversion is not uniquely a religious phenomenon. The efforts of the Chinese Communists in converting a huge nation in the space of a few short years to a new political ideology have been watched by the Western world with abhorrence both as regards their goal and their methods but with grudging admiration withal for their obvious success. The conversion of intellectuals by methods not primarily intellectual has been particularly instructive and frightening. The relative ease with which the Communists broke down numbers of prisoners of war in the Korean conflict has caused great concern among Western military strategists and concerted efforts are being made to prepare trainees to resist the psychological pressures to which they are sure to be exposed if captured.

Nor as a religious phenomenon is conversion uniquely Christian. A.C. Underwood has ably shown that conversion is a common experience in such religions as Hinduism, Early Buddhism, Islam, and in the religions of Greece and Rome. And in Christianity itself, while the necessity for and importance of conversion may be stressed more by the revivalistic sects, genuine cases of conversion are by no means restricted to these groups. In fact, there is no evidence to show that there is a greater incidence of true conversion with lasting effects in these circles where a sense of urgency for a vivid experience is fostered than elsewhere in the Christian church. Church history is replete with examples of conversions of outstanding men such as Paul, Augustine, Luther and Wesley, none of whom were converted under circumstances approximating modern American revivalism. Their conversions are both similar and dissimilar, thus making it impossible to stereotype the experience and to reduplicate it in the lives of all other people by the use of appropriate techniques. Conversion is much too complex and its dynamics within the personality too deep for this to be possible. We should also be warned against assuming that all persons will have such a spectacular or distinct experience that will leave an indelible impression in the consciousness as was the case with these men. There are many ordinary Christians whose experience is just as real, though not so obvious and striking.

There are a number of perspectives from which a study of conversion might be attempted. Dr. William Sargant has attempted a physiological study of conversion in his book *Battle for the Mind*. His interest lies with the brain and nervous system; that is, he is exploring the physiological mechanisms which influence human conduct—that part of a person which he shares with the other animals. Thus he limits his study to "physical or psychological stimuli, rather than intellectual arguments, which seem to help to produce conversion by causing alterations in the subject's brain function."[1] The research of Pavlov with dogs has, he believes, proven very instructive in this regard and he is deeply indebted to Pavlov for his insights on conditioning and the effect this has on the brain and consequently on behavior. Sargant is, of course, quite conscious of the usual reaction to Pavlov's theories that "men are not dogs", but insists that there is sufficient relevance in these studies that they dare not be ignored. He holds that the ideological struggle which the world is now facing may eventually be won by those who are willing to profit by them.

While no extended theological critique will be attempted here, one cannot help but register the conviction that conversion, understood theologically, is not a matter of conditioning the mechanisms of the brain and the nervous system. On the other hand, there is no theological reason for denying that physiological changes do take place in conversion.

A second point of view from which to study conversion is psychological. There is a real wealth of literature available written from this point of view. At the turn of the last century Edwin D. Starbuck attempted an empirical study of conversion based on an inductive analysis of solicited testimonies of religious conversion. Both the narrow limits of this study (there were 192 cases and practically all are American Protestant) and the method of studying and reporting the evidence (there are no fewer than 32 statistical tables and 14 graphs charting various aspects of the conversion experience) raise the question, for this reader at least, of the validity of his findings. One is impressed, however, to discover that more recent studies have not essentially contradicted his main conclusions. William James made extensive use of Starbuck's manuscripts and conclusions in his Gifford Lectures on Natural Religion at the University of Edinburgh, later published as his well-known *Varieties of Religious Experience*. Contemporary writers on the psychology of conversion still refer to Starbuck's research and acknowledge its significance.

A third approach to this subject is theological. Here one attempts to describe what happens in conversion primarily from the point of view of God's action upon the individual rather than in terms of physiological and psychological causes and effects. To attempt a psychological description is not necessarily to deny the activity of God but is merely to view conversion from the human point of view, that is, to study its causes and effects (mental, emotional, moral, etc.) within and upon the human subject. It is interesting to note the great care which most writers (including James and Sargant) take to explain what they are trying to do so as not to give offense to religious persons who might feel that they are trying to explain away the reality of God's activity in conversion. James insists he is making in his study no spiritual judgments, only existential ones, and does not wish to be regarded as irreverent in dealing so objectively and scientifically with facts which many feel to be too sacred for such handling.

This paper limits its study to conversion as an experience of religious growth. The basic approach is to view conversion from the human point of view while keeping always in mind the theological perspective. This writer heartily concurs with the position of Canon Bryan Green that

> The Christian is never a self-made man, and his experience is never purely psychological. His conversion is the work of God and happens when God meets him in grace: he appropriates and accepts what God by grace has done for him, and knows himself to be a new man in Christ Jesus. That is why a note of assurance rings through the New Testament. What the converted man knows is not that he has made himself a Christian through his own effort, but that God has done something for him through Christ, and done something within him by the Holy Spirit. His certainty is in God and in what God has done.[2]

One very important observation made by Starbuck and verified by subsequent studies is that conversion is primarily an adolescent experience. On the basis of his returns already referred to, as well as a study of almost eight hundred cases of conversion contained in the files of the Drew Theological Seminary, Starbuck concludes:

> We may safely lay it down as a law, then, that among the females there are two tidal waves of religious awakening at about 13 and 16, followed by a less significant period at 18; while among the males the great wave is at about 16, preceded by a wavelet at 12, and followed by a surging up at 18 or 19.[3]

Owen Brandon reports a recent survey of 700 cases of conversion (half men, half women) in which it was discovered that 36 per cent were converted before age 15; 48 per cent between ages 15 and 21; and only 16 per cent after age 21.[4] He quotes Frank Colquhoun whose report on the Billy Graham effort at Harringay showed that of those who were converted "just over half were young people under the age of 19, the largest age-group being, as one would expect, the 12-18."[5] The precise age within adolescence varies as it is dependent on factors both within the individual and in the environment. The expectation of a given community and the influences it brings to bear on individuals will cause the average age of conversion to be at variance with another community whose expectations may be quite different. The changing climate of theological opinion and expectations within a given community through a period of time can also affect both the average age and the type of experience. A case in point would be the New England of Jonathan Edwards and the New England of today.

G. Stanley Hall[6] has set up a comparative chart showing the average age of conversion established by a number of researchers, including Starbuck. In all but one, 16 is the age of most frequency. The report of a Rev. E.P. Hammond reflects his own "results" in revival work with children. His deliberate expectations and efforts have resulted in lowering the average age of conversion to 10. Hall's judgment is that Hammond "cultivates precocity" and in the light of all the other evidence one is justified in being skeptical of the genuine quality of such conversions.

The possibility of genuine conversion prior to the usual period of adolescence cannot, of course, be categorically denied; however, it is safe to assert that it will be the exception rather than the rule and that the child capable of conversion will be precocious in other areas of his development as well.

With regard to post-adolescent conversion, while none would deny that it is possible, the statistical evidence shows that it becomes increasingly unlikely that an individual will experience conversion as he grows older. The habits are more firmly fixed and the dynamics of the personality less susceptible to new patterns, especially sharply contradictory ones, as the years go by.

The weight of the statistical evidence causes us to raise the question of why adolescence is the age of greatest religious impressionability. Why are adolescents more susceptible to conversion than pre- or post-adolescents? From a physiological point of view, there are a number of significant developments which affect the psychological makeup of the adolescent. Physical growth is rapid, certain glands and other organs of the body mature, and most obvious of all is the arrival at puberty. The boy is becoming a man and the girl a woman and the time for beginning to accept the responsibilities of adulthood is here. The course of his adult life will now largely be determined as a number of important decisions are faced and made. At the same time, the adolescent must consolidate all the gains of childhood, the integrating tendencies which have appeared at each stage of his developmental history, outlined by Sullivan in order of their appearance as: the need for contact with the living, the need for tenderness, the need for the interest and active participation in his play of significant adults, the need for compeers, the need for acceptance, the need for friendship, and finally in adolescence the need for a loving relationship with a member of the other sex.[7]

This is the period described by Hall as the shift from an autocentric to a heterocentric way of life,[8] by Coe as the creation of the real self,[9] by Starbuck as the birth of a larger self,[10] and by still others as the period of unselfing. All are ways of describing the transition from self-centeredness to other-centeredness, essential to true religion as understood by the Christian faith, expressed in the cardinal doctrine of Christian love. There is a close correlation between the awakening of the new sexual powers of the adolescent and his growing social awareness. Yeaxlee[11] observes that one of the central points of significance of sex for religious growth in adolescence is that puberty brings with it the "other regarding propensity" in the child. The emergence of this new quality of social consciousness moves the child out of his small self-centered life into a larger social context with its new challenges, demands and rewarding relationships. Of course, some adolescents exploit their sexual powers in self-centered ways, but in doing so they thwart and frustrate the birth of the larger self.

The other significant factor for religion involved here is the emergence of the creative capacity which Yeaxlee insists is a **personal** quality and not merely physical or biological. He quotes Kretschmer's (*Physique and Character*) physiological explanation to show that the sexual impulse is dependent not alone on the generative glands, but in a very intricate way on the whole neuro-glandular system of the body; thus the sexual impulse and the creative capacity are an important constitutive element of the total temperament of an individual.[12] All the powers of emotion, imagination and reason are enhanced and the resultant energies and impulses which are awakened insist upon expression. This is what sets up the tensions and conflicts within the adolescent as he seeks to cope with his awakened powers and express himself in his widening social environment. The conflicts he experiences, both within himself and in his social contacts have led psychologists and other observers of adolescence to call this the period of storm and stress. The adolescent is very conscious of a sense of incompleteness and unrest, and the major developmental task is that of integrating his powers into a well-ordered and manageable unity.

The physiological developments in the brain and nervous system coincide with new powers for abstract thought, essential to spiritual perception. The mind is enabled to see in general terms, to secure a deeper intellectual grasp, and to gain profounder spiritual insight. The adolescent is spiritually responsive, sensitive to his need for an ideal to give his life meaning, purpose, and unity. He scans his environment carefully evaluating all the gods it offers him. The ideals he confronts—many of them conflicting—stand over against his actual condition and increase the anxiety, tension, and guilt he may be experiencing. In embracing an ideal which has the power to give unity to his personality, he experiences conversion. Yeaxlee calls this the formation of a master sentiment, a sentiment being that which is capable of directing the whole person and gathering it around a person or idea.

Johnson describes the psychological characteristics of adolescents which uniquely fit them for meaningful religious experience as follows: (a) personal experiences deepen; (b) social interests broaden; (c) intellectual powers heighten; (d) life purposes lengthen.[13] Youth has a heightened capacity for appreciating the ultimate issues and espousing the ultimate values of life. Worship and communion with God become more meaningful as experiences which in childhood were relatively external and formal become internal and vital. An attitude toward life basically enthusiastic and venturesome makes for fertile receptivity to the call of God into his cause and service.

We are accustomed to think of conversion as a crisis experience, as happening instantaneously. The multiplicity of the descriptions of the conversion experience offered in Starbuck's collection immediately corrects this mistaken assumption. For that matter one has but to inquire among his daily associates to discover that not all have had sudden conversions—that some, in fact, have no conscious recollection of any specific occasion of conversion. This has led to a two-fold classification by some investigators of the "once-born" and the "twice-born." Starbuck was unable to detect any significant difference in the religious life of the two groups which he studied.

> We have found that conversion…was a sudden outburst of religious life and awakening to spiritual insight. It has its correspondence in gradual growth. The character of the experiences in the one group and in the other shade off into each other by imperceptible

> gradations, and correspond in the time at which they occur.... The result which seemed to be attained in conversion, and that which was working itself out during adolescence among those persons who have not experienced conversion are at bottom essentially the same, namely, the birth of human consciousness on a higher spiritual level. This is attended by the awakening of a fuller and keener self-consciousness, and at the same time, by the birth of a social instinct, which leads the person to reach out and feel his life one with that of the larger social, institutional and spiritual worlds.[14]

Strictly speaking, it is not correct to speak of those who underwent a conscious experience as being converted or "twice-born" and of others who are also genuinely Christian as not converted or "once-born." The latter are as surely converted as the former. The reasons for the difference in the relative consciousness of the actual experience can be discovered in the environment and within the psychological makeup of the individual. Revivalistic churches tend, for example, to produce more of the "twice-born" than do the churches which emphasize the significance of confirmation. As to the psychological receptivity of a given individual, both James and Starbuck report on the investigations of George A. Coe with 74 persons to discern the relationship between temperamental types and abruptness of religious change. By a series of tests Coe divided them into two groups—the spontaneous (that is, those who were fertile in self-suggestion) and the passive (those who were more suggestible). The former tended to convince themselves of the impossibility of their experiencing conversion and for the most part had been disappointed in their anticipations. The latter more readily experienced what they were told to expect. In the latter case if there were combined with this characteristic a high degree of emotional impressionability and a tendency to automatisms one could confidently expect to experience sudden conversion of a marked character.[15] James sees no reason why these findings should distress anyone, for his own pragmatic working principle is to pass judgment on a thing not in terms of how it works but in terms of the result. There can be no doubt that different people respond differently to the activity of God in their lives according to their particular emotional and other psychological characteristics, though Coe's study is too limited to establish any claim of finality.

Among those who belong to the "converted" Christians there are variant experiences. By no means do all of them experience sudden conversion. Brandon classifies separately those who experience gradual conversion, those who experience conversion by stages, and those who experience conversion and reconversion.[16] Gradual conversion is defined as that in which there is a period of preparation climaxed by the acceptance of Christ as Lord and Savior, but the process of preparation seems to the person more significant than the actual climax. The process, partly conscious and partly unconscious, is described as one of "gradual enlightenment", or as the "emergence of a new quality of life", or as the "change from formal to vital religion." Conversion, by stages, as distinct from gradual conversion, is a process whereby "the subject is aware of spiritual progress at each stage of the experience, but at none of the stages, except the last, does he reach the sense of attainment or full conscious assurance."[17] In the case of reconversion, there is occasionally the need for a second experience of conversion commensurate with the later stage of development of an individual where his first experience occurred prematurely. The individual may have been completely sincere and may have had a genuine experience commensurate with his capacity at that particular stage of his growth. He finds, however, that his earlier experience does not satisfy his spiritual needs as an adult.

We return once more to a consideration of so-called "sudden" conversions. There are those who insist that a sudden conversion is a psychological impossibility. And all who allow the possibility are prepared to admit that there is usually a period of preparation—sometimes a long period—which is usually subconscious. Admittedly, it is only with great difficulty that a study of the subconscious processes leading to sudden conversion can be made, and the conclusions drawn can only be tentative. The method employed is to examine carefully those aspects of the experience both at the time of the crisis and prior to it which lie above the surface, which are part of the conscious experience and can be put into words. From these one can move by conjecture into the processes at work below the stream of consciousness. Starbuck holds that the conscious and subconscious elements are always present and acting upon each other though the proportionate preponderance of one over the other varies with individuals. He studied his cases specifically to discover what he terms the "conscious concomitant" and divided them into five categories ranging from those in which the conscious element is nearly absent to those in whom the conscious element seemed to be most important. He concludes:

> Without exception, the cases studied, no matter how suddenly the new life bursts forth, have antecedents in thought or action that appear to lead up directly to the phenomenon of conversion. The picture seems to be that of a flow of unconscious life rising now and then into conscious will, which, in turn, sets going new forces that readjust the sum of the old thoughts and feelings and actions. Whether the flow of physiological processes first gives rise to the thought product, or whether the incipient conversion holds a causal relation to the flash of new life and activity, cannot be determined. So much is clear, that before and during conversion the two things go together and interact upon each other. The whole conviction period seems to be a disturbance in the automatic, habitual processes caused by the presence of an incipient, but still dim and confused idea. Life is continually prodded by forces from without. Reverses in life, death, the example of a beautiful personality, ideas from other people, the demands of established institutions, and the like, are frequently mentioned as among the things which shake life from its self-content, and lead it into a recognition of a larger world than its own.[18]

There is a physiological explanation for this which is beyond the competence of this writer and the scope of this paper, except for a brief word. James uses a term "unconscious cerbration"[19] to describe what is going on. In an earlier work, to which Starbuck[20] refers, James says that every mental, emotional, or volitional process has its corresponding effect on the nervous system with new cerebral connections being made and deposits of nervous energy accumulating. These deposits and connections build up a tension which explodes with sudden force at the point of conversion. The nervous tension corresponds to the psychological state of anxiety, unwholeness, and disunity which theologically expressed is the period of conviction for sin. Viewed from any of these points of view, psychologically, physiologically, or theologically, the greater the experience of tension, the greater the release when it comes.

Implicit in the discussion up to this point has been the role of the emotions. One may safely say that a conversion experience is an emotional experience. Invariably, testimonies of conversion contain references to how the subject felt at the point of conversion, prior to it and following it. The emotions experienced are not equally intense for every person, and here again factors both within the individual and in the community help to determine the character and degree of the emotional experience. As one might expect, the more intense emotions such as joy or weeping are more characteristic of the revival cases whereas the calmer emotions such as peace and the feeling of acceptance are more characteristic of the nonrevival cases. This is, of course, a generalization; where the burden of guilt or anxiety has been heavy and the experience of release intense in non-revival cases, the emotional consequence is likewise intense.

The role of the intellect in conversion is surprisingly small. Sargant's candid opinion is that

> ...all evidence goes to show that there can be no new Protestant revival while the policy continues of appealing mainly to adult intelligence and reason, and until Church leaders consent to take more advantage of the normal person's emotional mechanism for disrupting old behavior patterns and implanting new.[21]

He finds that Wesley was quite ineffective in his preaching when his appeal was primarily addressed to the intellect, and that his unusual success is due to his strategy of creating high emotional tensions in his hearers. The effect of the emotional tension was, in Sargant's opinion, to suspend their judgment and to make them highly suggestible. When offered the way of escape, they would quickly grasp it and become converted. Theologically stated, it is necessary for the prospective convert to be impressed with a sense of his sin and need before he can be responsive to the offer of God's salvation. It is true that one can be intellectually impressed with his need, but not be moved to respond because of his pride in his self-determination. An intellectual grasp, in order effectively to move a person to act in response to God's offer, must make its impression on the emotions. Psychology's insistence on the unity of human personality and the close interrelationship between the intellect, the emotions, and the will makes this assertion quite comprehensible.

It will have to be admitted that there are a good many conversions with little or no intellectual content. The apparent lack of theological content in some conversions has prompted one writer to dub these as "pagan conversions." This is probably overly censorious since the testimonies frequently limit themselves to subjective descriptions of what was felt or experienced, making no mention of the theological content of the sermon or personal witness which may have precipitated the crisis. Moreover, it is possible to respond to the love of God out of a deep sense of need without abstracting the process. This is not necessarily to be unaware of what is going on on some level, perhaps quite naively but still very genuinely. Few, if any, theologians would insist that a person must be theologically literate in order to experience genuine conversion. On the other hand, for conversion to be genuinely Christian there must be an intellectual capacity for abstract thought which is necessary for spiritual perception. There is general agreement among psychologists that this capacity for abstraction is a late development reaching its latent fulfillment in adolescence. That is to say, the capacity for abstract thinking does not usually appear before adolescence, though as with all other aptitudes it grows and develops only through its exercise.

As Hall[22] points out, adolescence is the time when youth, exercising this new capacity for spiritual abstraction, begin critically to reexamine their childhood religious beliefs and concepts and to refine them into more mature convictions or to replace them altogether by new ones or by irreligious beliefs. This is the period in life when Bertrand Russell became agnostic. Much depends on the kind of teaching and nurture the youth has received as a child and on the quality of his religious experiences and instruction in this period of his life. The more intelligent and curious the adolescent, the greater will be the role of the intellect in his religious development and his conversion when and if it comes to a sharp focus. We do not conclude, however, that the more intelligent the person, the less emotional the experience. This, as we have already seen, is dependent on other psychological factors, though highly intellectual people tend to have a greater mastery over their emotional reactions, regulating them more rigidly particularly in most public situations.

What is the role of the will in conversion? Starbuck and James distinguish between "volitional" and "self-surrender" types of conversion. In the former, the will is consciously exercised in the direction of the new life, where the individual desires and chooses a higher moral and spiritual way of life and gradually through a process of some length achieves the integration he desires. The selfsurrender type of conversion may also follow the exercise of the will either toward or away from the new life. It is not uncommon for persons who have been vigorously resisting conversion suddenly to experience it, nor is it uncommon for those who have been consciously willing it to be frustrated in their effort to achieve it. In the case of the latter, James holds that too great an effort of the will may be jamming the nervous mechanisms which need to be discharged and released in conversion. He sees a parallel in the common experience of trying to recall a name. The harder we try to recall it, the more it eludes us. Frequently it happens that when we put it out of our minds temporarily, the mechanisms are released and the name comes rushing into consciousness. Starbuck's counsel to the frustrated would-be convert is that

> he must cease trying; he must relax, and let the nervous energy, which has been pent up and aching for some outlet of expression, seek its natural and normal channels—that is, he must fall back on the larger 'Power that makes for righteousness,' which has been welling up in his being, and let it finish in its own way the work it has begun. When the person is at last ripe for the experience, when the lines of growth have been focused to one point, when the imperfect life can no longer assert itself in the presence of the larger life that is seeking expression, the change comes, which means on the psychic side a new spiritual birth. Self-surrender, then, is often necessary in order that the normal tendencies of growth may converge and flow into harmony, and that the point of new insight may be, for the person yielding, the truest organizing center of life.[23]

James and Starbuck conclude that to say "Man's extremity is God's opportunity" is the same thing as to say "Let one do all in one's power, and one's nervous system will do the rest."[24] This is putting the matter very baldly indeed. A theological account is to say that man cannot convert himself by his own will. In the final analysis, he must acknowledge his helplessness and allow God to do for him what he cannot do for himself. For that matter, all his efforts in the direction of the new life—not only the final step—are taken by the grace and help of God.

James[25] notes that even in the volitional type of conversion the process of integration is interspersed with occasions of partial self-surrender, and the final unification is rarely, if ever, achieved without self-surrender at the moment of conversion, although it may be less of a struggle than in the other type. The effort of the will, even though it is striving toward righteousness, is still a human expression of the old life.

> Conscious volition before the change of heart is the willful assertion that life shall still be viewed through the old port-holes rather than from a new vantage ground. It is God and sinful man striving against each other. It is at the point of self-surrender that the deadlock is broken, and the man comes forth into a new world. The act of yielding…is giving oneself over to the new life, making it the center of a new personality, and living, from within, the truth of it which had before been viewed objectively.[26]

Starbuck offers no psychological explanation why the person who consciously exercises his will against conversion falls into the category of the self-surrender type. The obvious implication is, of course, that if such a person is to experience conversion at all it must come about through giving up his will not to be converted. Several investigators have noted that persons who resist conversion vigorously are just as susceptible to it as those who desire it. The reason must lie in the fact that since they are vigorously resisting it, they are obviously already deeply involved in the process and the mental, emotional and cerebral effects on the individual are already creating powerful tensions within him which are crying for release. The more vigorous the resistance, the more powerful the tension. It is well-known that persons under conviction for sin and resisting conversion are "of all men most miserable," to misuse a Pauline phrase. Sargant[27] counsels those who, like Horace Walpole wish to be "preserved from sanctification" to adopt Walpole's attitude toward John Wesley's preaching, that of emotional detachment. Even anger and contempt are no adequate safeguard, for they usually arise only when one is so deeply involved as to make escape unlikely.

We have not been concerned in this paper with interesting sidelights of conversion such as the usual overt influences and motives which precipitate the crisis, nor with a detailed description of the emotions experienced during, prior and following conversion but have limited ourselves primarily to a view of conversion as a normal part of growth in religion. It cannot be emphasized too strongly that conversion, important as it is in giving stability, quality and direction to the personality, is not an experience which displaces the necessity for continuing religious growth. The character of the spiritual growth and the Christian education appropriate for it will be somewhat different than heretofore, but continued growth there must be if the individual is to attain spiritual maturity, "the measure of the stature of the fullness of Christ." (Eph. 4:13).

C.S. Lewis puts it superbly in his own inimitable fashion when he concludes the autobiographical account of his conversion, *Surprised by Joy*.

> But what, in conclusion, of Joy? for that, after all, is what the story has mainly been about. To tell you the truth, the subject has lost nearly all interest for me since I became a Christian. I cannot, indeed, complain, like Wordsworth, that the visionary gleam has passed away. I believe (if the thing were at all worth recording) that the old stab, the old bittersweet, has come to me as often and as sharply since my conversion as at any time of my life whatever. But now I know that the experience, considered as a state of my own mind, had never had the kind of importance I once gave it. It was valuable only as a pointer to something other and outer. While that other was in doubt, the pointer naturally loomed large in my thoughts. When we are lost in the woods the sight of a signpost is a great matter. He who first sees it cries, "Look!" The whole party gathers round and stares. But when we have found the road and are passing signposts every few miles, we shall not stop and stare, or not much; not on this road, though their pillars are of silver and their lettering of gold. "We would be at Jerusalem."
>
> Not, of course, that I don't often catch myself stopping to stare at roadside objects of even less importance.[28]

---

[1] William Sargant, *Battle for the Mind* (Garden City, N.Y.: Doubleday and Company, Inc., 1957), 13.
[2]Bryan Green, *The Practice of Evangelism* (London: Hodder and Stoughton, 1951), 34.

[3] Edwin D. Starbuck, *Psychology of Religion* (New York: Charles Scribner's Sons, 1901), 34.
[4]Owen Brandon, *The Battle for the Soul* (Philadelphia: The Westminster Press, 1959), 24.
[5]Ibid., 24. See Frank Colquhoun, *Harringay Story: The Official Record of the Billy Graham Greater London Crusade 1954* (London: Hodder and Stoughton Ltd., 1955) 233.
[6] G. Stanley Hall, *The Psychology of Adolescence*, V.2 (New York: D. Appleton and Company, 1905), 290, 291.
[7]Harry S. Sullivan, *The Interpersonal Theory of Psychiatry* (New York: W.W. Norton and Co., Inc., 1953), 290, 291.
[8] Hall, 301,305.
[9]George Albert Coe, *The Psychology of Religion* (Chicago: The University of Chicago Press, 1916), 171.
[10]Starbuck, 251-267.
[11]Basil A. Yeaxlee, *Religion and the Growing Mind* (London: Nisbet and Company, 1945), 121-143. For Kretschmer's technical physiological explanation and the implications for religion Yeaxlee draws from it, see especially pages 123-125.
[12]*Ibid.*, 123-125.
[13]Paul E. Johnson, *Psychology of Religion* (Nashville: Abingdon Press, 1959), 90-93.
[14]Starbuck, 354.
[15]James, 240-241.
[16]Brandon, 28-33.
[17]Ibid., 29.
[18]Starbuck, 105-106.
[19]James, 207.
[20]Starbuck, See Wm. James, *Principles of Psychology* 1890, Vol. I, 553.
[21]Sargant, 95.
[22]Hall, 315f.
[23]Starbuck, 115, 116.
[24]*Ibid.*, 113.
[25]James, 208.
[26]Starbuck, 116, 117.
[27]Sargant, 109.
[28]C.S. Lewis, *Surprised by Joy* (New York: Harcourt, Brace, and Company, 1955), 238.

12

Anabaptist Education

The first Anabaptists were a group of disciples of the Reformer Ulrich Zwingli in Zurich who broke with him in the 1520s over the issue of adult (believers') baptism. The Mennonites, the Amish and the Hutterites are their modern-day heirs.

The movement was founded by Felix Manz and Conrad Grebel, son of Jacob Grebel, a member of the Zurich city council. Prior to his conversion, Conrad Grebel had studied at the universities of Basel, Vienna, and Paris, and before the break with their mentor Zwingli, Conrad Grebel and Felix Manz had been intended to teach Greek and Hebrew at the theological school Zwingli was planning.

Grebel, Manz, and their colleagues developed their distinctive theological views through group Bible study, drawing on their knowledge of the Latin and the Greek and Hebrew texts of Scripture. They repudiated their own infant baptism and were rebaptized as adult believers, an unlawful act at that time. They also came to believe that the church should be a separated community, leading most of their followers to oppose the conduct of war and to refuse to take civic oaths.

Their movement attracted many adherents throughout central Europe. Eventually the Zurich city council ordered them to cease holding their Bible study groups, which were seen as subversive of Zwingli's efforts to establish a new theological consensus. The persecution that followed their refusal led to the imprisonment and execution of Conrad and Jacob Grebel and Felix Manz. Over the next few years, thousands of their followers were persecuted, tortured, and executed in a number of cities in central Europe.

Though the movement continued to spread, it was some time before its well-educated leadership could be replaced. In 1536 a Dutch priest, Menno Simons, left the priesthood; he provided organizational and theological direction to the movement for several decades. In these early years, this persecuted minority, always on the move, was unable to set up a formal education program as Luther had done in Germany and Calvin in Geneva.

The exception was the Hutterian brethren, named for Jacob Hutter, communitarian Anabaptists who found a relatively hospitable climate in Moravia. Not only were they able to set up a program to educate their children; they were fortunate to have educational theorists among them in the persons of Peter Riedemann and Peter Walpot. An important educational concept was that of instilling in the children a spirit of *Gelassenheit,* that is, "yieldedness," both a willingness to submit to the will of God and a willingness to accept the authority of the community of faith and its designated leaders. Other values to be inculcated were that of community ownership of goods rather than private holding of property and avoidance of an individualistic, self-seeking attitude.

While other Anabaptist groups did not share the idea of a common purse, the ideal of life in community is one shared by all. This ideal was expressed by them in the practice of mutual aid in the event of illness, accident, death, or other circumstances creating special need. An early illustration is the financial assistance provided by the Dutch Mennonites to their Swiss and German brothers and sisters who migrated to America beginning in the seventeenth century.

The word *community* will be found in most discussions of educational theory among Anabaptist groups even at the present time. The goal of education is not so much individual self-realization (though certainly the development of each person's full potential, i.e., one's God-given gifts, is emphasized) as is the development of skills to function responsibly in community. This includes attention to the history of the community, its values, its sense of purpose (worship and service), its sociology, and its belief system. In recent years, there has been a growing emphasis in the curriculum upon developing relational and communication skills.

The family continues to be the primary community in which Christian faith is nurtured. The basic responsibility for nurturing faith in children rests not with the school or the church but with the families of the church. The role of the school and the church is a complementary one, supporting the efforts of parents. It is, of course, recognized that the parents do not stand alone in carrying out their responsibility. Living in community is strongly emphasized as is the idea that the congregation is a family of families. Anabaptist church groups have been fortunate in maintaining a strong sense of family solidarity. However, as America has become increasingly urbanized, secularization and individualism have begun to erode the sense of community, making family life vulnerable. For this reason, the past decade has seen the development of a variety of family life education programs designed to strengthen family life and to counteract the incidence of family breakup.

To avoid the dangers of being primarily an inward-looking, ethnic group, some Anabaptists have placed a strong emphasis on mission and service in the most recent past. The Mennonites are today present in at least sixty countries around the world, speaking a hundred languages. This growing internationalism has called for an international perspective in the curriculum, particularly on the collegiate and seminary levels. Many Mennonite college students spend a year or at least a semester outside North America studying a culture from within and finding ways to be of service, if possible. Mennonite collegians, for example, were among the first to enter mainland China in the 1980s to serve as teachers of English and learn about Chinese society and culture.

School Education

The Dutch Mennonites were the first Anabaptists to set up a program of graduate theological education. Ministerial students now attend graduate level seminaries operated by several historically Anabaptist-related denominations.

Theological education is also available (especially in Canada) on the undergraduate level in Bible colleges and Bible institutes. Most church-related liberal arts colleges began with the stated purpose of training ministers and other church workers. All continue to offer biblical and religious studies within a liberal arts framework. They also attempt to teach the liberal arts from an avowedly Christian perspective.

There are over twenty Mennonite secondary schools in the United States and Canada. Like the colleges, they attempt to teach the various subjects from a Christian point of view and to encourage their students to enter church and service vocations. Students are strongly encouraged to adopt Christian values such as service and simplicity of life, and an awareness of the poverty, hunger, and suffering in the world, along with the responsibility to alleviate it, is fostered.

On the elementary level, there are at least a hundred schools, approximately half in the state of Pennsylvania. Forty of these schools have been established since 1980, indicating that this is still a growing movement.

No sketch of Anabaptist school education, however brief, would be complete without reference to Christopher Dock. Dock was a schoolteacher in eastern Pennsylvania north of Germantown, the site of the first Mennonite settlement in the New World, founded in 1683. In 1770, his brief treatise *School Management* was published by Christopher Saur of Germantown; it is one of the first books on pedagogy to be printed in the United States. It is said that Dock prayed for his pupils each morning before they arrived and each evening after they left. He was found dead on his knees in the posture of prayer in the fall of 1771. Dock is still held up as an example for Mennonite teachers today, though his pedagogical methods may be out of date, for teaching is seen as more than a profession: it is a high and holy calling, indeed, a ministry.

Congregational Education

Another level of education is that of the Christian education program in the local congregation. The first permanent Mennonite Sunday school was set up in West Liberty, Ohio, in 1863.

In recent years the Sunday school curriculum of several major Anabaptist denominations was a Mennonite-produced one known as the Foundation Series. The title refers to Menno Simons's favorite Bible verse, 1 Corinthians 3:11, "For no other foundation can any one lay than that which is laid, which is Jesus Christ." A serious effort was made by the editors and writers to focus on Jesus Christ and to interpret the Scriptures christologically. That verse appeared on the title page of each teacher's guide and pupil book. The current curriculum is known as the Jubilee Series.

13

Indoctrination

The concept of education as indoctrination has a long and respected history. It has to do with instruction in a body of doctrine, that is, in a system of religious or philosophical beliefs, political ideology, or economic theory. Indeed, at one time, indoctrination and education were synonymous. But indoctrination also has an ambiguous and controversial history, especially in modern times, and has recently been called into question as a valid educational method. John Dewey (1859-1952), for example, rejected its validity as authentic education since in his view education has to do with freedom of inquiry, examination, criticism, and evaluation. Such values are prized in a democratic society; indoctrination, in his view, can flourish only in an authoritarian society.

Educational Models Based on Indoctrination

Before considering this debate further, let us review some educational models based on indoctrination in the older, classical sense of the term. Early Hebrew education as reflected in Deuteronomy 6:4-5 is a good illustration of indoctrination. It was the responsibility of the family to teach the children the Shema, "Hear, O Israel: The Lord our God is one Lord; and you shall love the Lord your God with all your heart, and with all your soul, and with all your might." This was the heart and core of Torah. No effort was to be spared in the inculcation of this view of life in the hearts and minds and spirits of the children. It was not only a system of thought but a way of life.

The members of the family were totally immersed in this way of life. They were reminded of it at every turn—when sitting down, rising up, going out, walking by the way, and coming in. The rituals of the household, the clothing they wore, their feasts and fasts all combined to create a comprehensive environment in which this view of life was both lived and passed on.

The criticism that this way of understanding the world and people's place within it was inculcated without critical reflection would be valid but irrelevant. What alternative worldviews would bring the Hebrew people the *shalom* God intended? What was there to reflect critically about? This was the command of God. Critical reflection such as the kind that later arose out of the prophetic tradition had to do not with the possible superiority of the Canaanite over the Hebrew religion but with how faithfully the Israelites were living out the commands of Yahweh.

A second paradigm of indoctrination is the *Didache,* a late first-century or early second-century catechetical manual for the instruction of new believers in preparation for Christian baptism. The first six chapters in particular serve this function. The document begins with the words, "There are two ways: one of life and one of death." Here is no open-ended discussion of the relative merits of these two ways; nor is critical reflection invited on the validity of the assertion. This is indoctrination, pure and simple.

Catechetical instruction in both Roman Catholic and Protestant traditions through the years took shape in another form of indoctrination, the catechism. It contained questions to be asked of candidates for baptism and answers to be memorized by them. When called upon by the catechist to answer, the catechumens would respond word for word as they had been taught. The intention, of course, was that the meaning of the question and the answer had been communicated and grasped. Still, the possibility that the answer had been memorized and parroted without comprehension was always present. In any case, critical reflection, examination, and evaluation were not intrinsic to this model.

New Pedagogies

John Dewey's definition of indoctrination is "the systematic use of every possible means to impress upon the minds of pupils a particular set of political and economic views to the exclusion of every other."[1] This he rejects. True education, in his view, calls for "the active participation of students in reaching conclusions and forming attitudes.... The active participation, the interest, reflection and understanding of those taught are necessary."[2]

More recently, the liberation pedagogies of scholars like Paulo Freire have called into question in an even more radical manner the validity of those educational models that have transmission of a heritage as their goal. Some refer to this as the "banking" model of education in which the deposit of knowledge and experience of a society or a generation is made available to others. It is not only the method (whether doctrinaire or democratic) that is at issue. It is the question of the content itself. Liberation pedagogies mistrust such deposits as basically flawed for they are the product of particular ideologies (political, economic, philosophical, religious).

The new pedagogy insists that the learners themselves create their own knowledge through their own methods by means of critical reflection on their own experience. Furthermore, the most authentic knowledge will be created by those who have the least to conserve (the poor, the powerless, the vulnerable). It is the wealthy, the powerful, the oppressors whose interests are at stake and who have created the deposits in the cultural banks of any given society. They have the most to lose when the learners give up their passive, dependent role in learning (enculturation) and become actively involved in the process of critical reflection, analysis, and evaluation.

This brief survey of the concept of indoctrination helps us to see that it is not simply a question of one method over against another. It involves us in such deeper issues as epistemology (how we can know what we do know), the sociology of knowledge, and the politics of education. These questions will not soon be resolved and until they are, educators would be well advised to live with the creative tension between freedom of inquiry and the indoctrination inherent in passing on a systematic body of principles and values. Both of these give the human race a considerable advantage over the rest of God's creatures. *See also* Action-Reflection; Catechism; Dewey, John; Didache; Doctrine/Dogma; Liberation Theology; Methodology; Progressive Education; Theology and Education; Tradition; Transmission.

---

[1] John Dewey, *Education Today* (New York: Greenwood, 1940), 356.
[2] Ibid., 356.

IV

Theological Education

The task of discernment may serve as one image to clarify the relationship between what the seminary is doing and what the congregation is doing. One of the common tasks shared by seminary and congregation is that of discerning the will of God for our day.

14

Seminary and Congregation: Communities of Discernment

This was the writer's inaugural address as dean of the Associated Mennonite Biblical Seminaries on March 22, 1965. It is reprinted by permission from the July 1965 issue of the *Mennonite Quarterly Review.*

A little over a year ago, upon my election to the office with whose responsibilities I am now charged, I was invited to appear before the Mennonite Board of Education to make a statement concerning my view of the role of the seminary in the life of the church in the years ahead. There is a phrase in current theological discussion[1] which at that time had impressed itself forcefully upon me as an apt description of the nature and primary task of the seminary: *community of discernment.* This phrase continues to impress me as a fertile one for the understanding of what the seminary is all about.

There is a great deal of ferment in the seminaries these days as to what theological education should be attempting and how it should go about it. This was evident at the biennial meeting of the American Association of Theological Schools in Fort Worth last June and is reflected in the current issue of the Association's journal which carries such articles on the general theme, "Models of Theological Education for the Last Third of the Twentieth Century."[2] The faculties of the Associated Mennonite Biblical Seminaries have been deeply involved in the discussion of these issues which have a direct bearing upon our own curriculum which is presently being reviewed.

While I recognize that no one phrase can provide a comprehensive and fully adequate model for the task of the theological school, I would like to have you consider this phrase, community of discernment. The fundamental task of our seminaries, I am proposing, is the task of discerning the Word and the will of God for our day. I would go further and affirm that the task of spiritual discernment is the fundamental task of the church and that the seminary, being a seminary of the church, shares in this task. I am suggesting that a fuller awareness of the nature of the church's task of spiritual discernment will result in *(a)* a clearer understanding of the role of the seminary and *(b)* a greater appreciation of the relation of the seminary to the congregations which also share in the church's discerning task.

As a background for our consideration of the nature of that task, let us look briefly into three communities of faith through which we trace our spiritual heritage.

The Prophetic Community of Israel

No attempt to describe the church's task of discernment in our day could succeed without an awareness of and a profound sense of indebtedness to the prophetic religion of the Old Testament. The person and message of the Old Testament prophets continue to be matters of great interest to those who are concerned with knowing and doing the will of God. There are those who are intrigued with the psychological phenomena of prophetism; others are fascinated by the predictive element in the prophetic oracles; still others are most impressed with the quality and force of the prophets' social concern for justice and equity. None of these, however, legitimate objects of study as they are, quite capture what B. Davie Napier calls "prophetic essence: address to history."

> The characteristically prophetic phenomenon always poses the decisive impingement of Yahweh upon history. This is true whether the prophetic word be invective or judgment, assurance or promise, cry of anguish or confession. This is true whether the prophetic act be concrete, symbolic, or relational. This is true whether the presupposition that Yahweh determines history be conscious or unconscious, explicit or taken for granted, immediately relevant or only of indirect ultimate pertinence. Where this sense of the effective relationship of Yahweh to history is absent prophetism is also absent. Where this is present...there is prophetism.[3]

The prophetic religion of Israel is historical in character not primarily in the sense that it preserved a chronicle of the major events that were a part of Israel's long past and that had shaped its destiny. It is historical in that the prophets of Israel perceived these events as the sphere of God's activity in relation to them. The Exodus was not only a slave people's emancipation; it was a divine deliverance. The wilderness wandering was not only a nomadic existence; it was a divine tutelage. The conquest of Canaan was more than an invasion and a glorious military victory; it was the fulfillment of a divine promise. The exile was not simply the disastrous consequence of a military defeat; it was a divine judgment.

A mere chronicle of these historical events misses their significance as perceived by the prophets. So also does an historical analysis which reports as objectively as possible the causes and consequences of social, economic, political and military factors which undoubtedly were present. What is distinctive in the prophetic interpretation of Israel's historical experiences is the perception of the impingement of the divine activity upon the human course of events, i.e., the intermingling of the divine initiative with the human response. The prophets perceived that Israel's history was determined essentially by the interplay of God's will and the will of his people. The decisions of men and women within their historical situation, with all of the historical consequences of those decisions, were seen as positive or negative responses to the divine will of a righteous and personal God who was directly and immediately concerned with that historical situation and with those human decisions. The prophets saw history as something more than the unfolding of events in the life of a community or a nation; the historical process, for them, was a moral and spiritual process and its interpretation required moral and spiritual insight.

Wherein lay the uniqueness of the prophetic interpretation of Israel's history? Were the prophets keener observers of what was taking place around them than their contemporaries were? To be sure, the eighth-century prophets in Israel were keen in their observations and penetrating in their analyses. They could observe the movement of political currents, the development of international alliances, the buildup of military forces and on the basis of their observations make enlightened suggestions concerning national policy. They were careful readers of the social situation and were able to bring incisive judgments upon the corruption, oppression, and greed that were undermining the very foundations of their social order. As concerned observers of the religious life of Israel, they declared that certain developments in the cultic, ceremonial, and institutional life of Israel were dangerous distortions of the faith of Abraham and of Moses.

As important as their powers of observation and analysis were—and it must be noted that these were important for the prophetic interpretation of history—these alone were not what made their interpretation distinctive. It was not superior intelligence but heightened spiritual perception that sharpened the power and relevance of the prophetic word. These were men and women who had been laid hold upon—who had been addressed by God. God's word of address was directed not alone to their minds but to their wills—indeed to the totality of their very being. They had eyes to see and ears to hear because they were responsive to God's word of address. God's revelation of his person and his will impressed the prophets with the sense of his dynamic presence with them and in the community, not as an interested observer but as a moving force, a personal power, making things happen, accomplishing his purposes in and through them. Their obedience was expressed in their actions and in their words or, shall we say, in their word-acts; they were less conscious of a distinction between word and act than we. They were conscious that the word they were given to speak was a word from the Lord, an authoritative word, a word which itself in precipitating human responses set the very processes of human history into motion.

The Apostolic Community

The members of the apostolic community, like those of the prophetic community in the Old Testament, had this same keen awareness of an active purposing God with whom they had to do. They shared the prophets' vivid sense of the divine impingement upon human affairs; but more than this, they knew themselves to be living in the age of the fulfillment of what the prophets had perceived to be the divine purpose in history, for God had acted decisively in history in the life, death, resurrection, and ascension of Jesus Christ. They perceived that the Christ-event was no mere point on the time line: it was the focal point of all historical events past, present, and to come—the event which had significance for all other events and by which all lesser events were to be interpreted.

Though modern Westerners are prepared to acknowledge Jesus' coming into the world by marking their calendars B.C. and A.D., the significance of the Christ-event, though historical, is not so readily reduced into chronological categories for its significance is not essentially chronological. The Christ-event marks an even more fundamental boundary—the boundary between the old age and the new age. It is however a boundary that is continually shifting for the truth is that the old age has not completely passed nor has the new age fully come. One's relationship to God through Jesus Christ is what determines the age in which one lives. The earliest Christians perceived and confessed that in Jesus Christ God had initiated the new age and that through faith in him they were ushered into it. The transformation was one from disobedience to obedience, from fear to hope, from living with hearts and minds divided and calculating to sharing in the mind of Christ who was willing to take the form of a servant. Wherever human wills remain unsurrendered to the will of God, wherever human minds continue to make judgments from a self-oriented point of view and their hopes derive from what can be humanly predicted and performed there the old age continues its sway.

Those individuals who found themselves standing with Jesus Christ on the boundary between the new age and the old found themselves bound together into a new solidarity with him and with each other. Through their identification with him they became the first fruits and the proclaimers of the new age in which they stood, whose advance they perceived and of whose ultimate triumph over the forces of the old age they were already assured. They gave themselves to the proclamation of God's saving deed in Jesus Christ and called upon people everywhere to repent and be baptized into the community of faith, that ever-enlarging community which owed its allegiance to the risen exalted Christ and acknowledged him as Lord. They perceived and declared confidently moreover that beyond the earthly sphere in which human history is played out lies the sphere of the invisible powers and authorities which claim the allegiance of people in opposition to the claims of God. They understood what modern people have difficulty in understanding—that these spiritual forces use as instruments for their own purposes any and all human institutions which serve as the object of human desires and loyalties. They recognized that these institutions useful and innocent enough in themselves—e.g. all social, political, economic or intellectual systems—may bring one into bondage at the point where one's heart yields its ultimate allegiance to their specious demands, demands which interpose themselves between oneself and God's demands.

The apostolic community perceived that every important decision or act which called into question one's basic orientation toward God was determinative of whether a person stood in the old age or in the new. Further, because those earliest Christians had such a strong sense of the solidarity of the community of faith, they perceived that the decision and act of the individual member had implications for the whole community. "If one member suffers, all suffer together; if one member is honored, all rejoice together" (I Cor. 12: 26). Beyond this they had an overwhelming sense of the cosmic significance of the foothold that the new age had gained upon the earth through their existence as a visible, historical community who confessed Jesus as Lord. They anticipated the day when his lordship would be acknowledged throughout the earth and the heavens and the final victory over the rebellious spiritual powers would be consummated.

There was a strong sense of an approaching consummation when Christ would return in power and great glory and the new age would have fully come. At the same time, they were constantly surrounded by painful reminders that the old age had not yet passed away. The dialectic between the "even now" and the "not yet" of the new age gave them a lively sense of standing at the frontier where God was at work making all things new. They had an eschatological sense of history, a sense of living in the end time, which gave an urgency and a vitality to the way they ordered their lives and their affairs. Both within and without the community, controlled by the Holy Spirit who illumined their minds and gave utterance to their tongues, they proclaimed that God had acted in Jesus Christ, that he was acting now to accomplish his purposes in and through them who acknowledged Jesus as Lord, and that he would continue to act upon the affairs of humanity until he would bring his purposes for mankind into fulfillment.

The Anabaptist Community

All that was expressed in the imagery of the two ages, so vital to the dynamic self-understanding of the apostolic community, found expression in a parallel image in another community of faith through which we trace our spiritual heritage. The doctrine of the two worlds is to the theology of the Anabaptists what the doctrine of the two ages is to the theology of the apostolic community. This, at any rate, is the judgment of Robert Friedmann in a highly stimulating essay, "The Doctrine of the Two Worlds."

Friedmann discusses the often-raised question whether the Anabaptists did indeed have a theology or whether, as some would have it, they were theologically unsophisticated either through choice or through circumstance. His conclusion is that Anabaptism is theological in the same sense that the Synoptics are theological, i.e., not in a formal and systematic sense but in the sense of an implicit theological awareness and coherence.

> A movement of such strength is unthinkable without a definite theological foundation, without specific ideas concerning man's relationship to the divine and the meaning of earthly life. Even if these foundations were not expressed in a systematic way, one must assume that they were implied in all the doings and witnessing of the Anabaptists.[4]

Friedmann further holds that the doctrine of the two worlds may well represent "the deepest layer of the Anabaptist theological outlook"[5] and that its origins are to be found in the teachings of Jesus Christ as these are reported in the Synoptic Gospels from which the Anabaptists drew much of their inspiration.

Friedmann's is an intriguing analysis and is deserving of more critical consideration than it has yet stimulated. The contention that the Anabaptists were not theologians in the formal sense of the term is not and cannot be a matter of debate. However, there is a power in the imagery of the two realms—the kingdom of God and the kingdom of darkness—which both illumines and unifies the various emphases to be found in Anabaptist thought.

One such emphasis, which may be seen as a derivative of the doctrine of the two realms is the distinction between the church and the world discerned by the Anabaptists. The church, as they understood it, is that community of persons who confess Jesus as Lord, are baptized upon the confession of their faith, and are ready to forsake their sinful ways and pledge themselves to a life of obedient discipleship. The world, on the other hand, is that sphere of life where unregenerate persons wield their devices and build their institutions without regard to the will of God. The oath and the sword are symbolic of the worldly order and the necessity of its compulsions and restraints, but in the church one's word is his bond and nonresistant love bears its own constraint.

The tension between two such incompatible communities is but the visible earthly dimension of a cosmic struggle between the two kingdoms—the struggle between God and all the forces of darkness which are ranged in opposition to him. But it is a struggle whose ultimate resolution is assured through the victory Christ has won in his suffering, death, resurrection and ascension. Christ's victory over the invisible powers that govern the kingdom of darkness is a victory that extends to the earthly realm over which they have sought to extend their sovereignty. The world is that sphere of social, political, economic, and intellectual activity in which may be seen the visible historical evidence of demonic influence and of the cosmic struggle for our loyalties which is not yet ended. The church is the historical embodiment of Christ's victory, for it is composed of those who have acknowledged the lordship of Jesus Christ and have been born into the kingdom of God.

An important corollary to the conviction that the kingdom of God is a present historical reality is the Anabaptist insistence that the church is a visible community within history. The implications as seen by the Anabaptists of this understanding of the church in terms of church discipline, in terms of responsibility for the brother and sister and the repudiation of a spurious individualism, and in terms of commitment to discipleship and holy living are well known and require no further elaboration here.

The doctrine of the two worlds, like the doctrine of the two ages, is by its very nature an eschatological concept. The Anabaptist view of history was, accordingly, an eschatological one. The Anabaptists also lived in the tension of the "even now" and the "not yet," for while the kingdom of God was a present historical reality for them yet they were acutely conscious of the historical reality of that other kingdom. It was a tension which gave rise to conflict of various kinds, conflict which in its extreme form led to suffering and even to martyrdom. Only an eschatological view of history in which the larger significance of the suffering of the church could be discerned in terms of the fundamental antagonism between the two kingdoms and the ultimate triumph of the kingdom of God could sustain them. While there was some evidence of eschatological extremism, in the main the eschatology of the Anabaptists was disciplined and subdued and contributed to their capacity for discerning the practical implications of life in the kingdom of God.

The Community of Discernment Today

On the basis of these all-too-brief excursions into three distinct communities of faith through which we trace our spiritual succession, what may be said about the task of discernment? It is to be carried out within a cognitive frame of reference which involves first, the perception that God is acting in human history; second, a lively sense of being caught up in God's purposive activity; and third, an awareness of the eschatological character of our existence. These several dimensions of the task ought not to be conceived as separate and distinct steps in the process of discernment, for closer examination of these three statements discloses them as vitally interrelated, since the second and the third are already contained within the first. That is to say, the perception that God is acting in human history already implies a sense of being caught up in his action for this perception is not open to the disinterested objective observer, but only to those to whom God discloses his act through drawing them into it and making them a participant in it. It is, finally, this participation in God's act which gives to our existence its eschatological character, for God's action is eschatological—it has already begun and it is moving toward its consummation and fulfillment.

Divine Action in Human History

The task of discernment is altogether a dynamic one; the church is both a responsive and an active participant in it. Discernment involves intellectual reflection to be sure, but more than this—and let us say, primarily—it is gathered up in the total response to God of faith, obedience and love.

The perception that God is acting in history is not the perception that a certain specific historical agent (for example, a particular president or nation) is *the* human instrument through which God is building his kingdom on earth. Indeed, the very messianic claims and pretensions of certain political leaders and nation-states may be clearly refuted from such a perspective. Nor does the perception that God is acting in history yield broad generalizations and principles which can be applied in a direct and immediate way to each and every historical situation. Accordingly, the church does not have on the basis of such principles a particular strategy with respect, for example, to the problems of Berlin or Vietnam.

It does not follow, however, that the church has nothing concrete to say with respect to specific historical situations. But the temptation to speak on the basis of a superior knowledge of the particular situation derived from having an immediate awareness of the will of God for that situation must be resisted. So also must the temptation to advocate particular strategies on the basis of the wisdom of the world, taking care only to advocate them in the name of God. The church which truly perceives that God is acting in history knows all too well that effective strategies are based upon calculating self-interest. The truly discerning church is too painfully aware of those many instances in which the cause of a particular nation has been declared to be the cause of God himself to expect much confidence in ecclesiastical pronouncements upon specific military and political undertakings.

What then does the church in any age—in our age—have to say in a concrete way to a particular historical situation? The discerning church will speak of the will of God on the basis of its own experience of the acting, purposing God with whom it has to do. Because each member and all of them together have had their own pretensions and self-interest exposed and brought under judgment, the discerning church can speak with certainty of the judgment of God upon all expressions and manifestations of calculating self-interest whether individual or corporate in every sphere of life. It will not refrain from uttering a prophetic word from the Lord to the nations, including our own nation, when an authoritative word is given to it.

Because each member and all of them together have been delivered by God's action in Jesus Christ from their slavery to the powers of darkness into the glorious freedom of sons and daughters of the kingdom of God, the discerning church can recognize the bondage of those who have their citizenship in the kingdom of Satan. It will recognize and declare, for example, that every economic system, whether capitalistic or socialistic, has within it selfish and demonic tendencies which ensnare those who accept its promises and yield themselves to its specious claims. The god mammon has a way of extracting a full allegiance from those unwary or willing souls who through the inescapable human necessity of participating in the economic order—an order whose function it is to serve humanity's economic needs—have become instead its slaves.

Because they have experienced God's reconciling love in Jesus Christ and had the walls of estrangement between them and their brothers and sisters broken down, the members of the discerning church can speak with assurance about the reconciling work of God. They know that it is not God's will that a man be turned against his brother, that social class be heaped upon social class, and that racial differences be translated into racial conflict, feelings of superiority-inferiority and acts of exploitation and oppression. They recognize that such distinctions arise out of the perspective of this present evil age whose categories of judgment betray its fundamental brokenness and dividedness. The existence of the church in the midst of a broken world as the community of the reconciled is the historical evidence that God's reconciling work is even now going on. The reconciled church will have a sure word from the Lord to bring to every sick human situation which exists apart from the reconciliation to be found in Jesus Christ.

Human Participation in Divine Action

The discerning church has something concrete to say to the historical situation in which it exists concerning the active historical purpose of God on the basis of its own experience of God's purposes. Its discernment both arises out of its lively sense of being caught up in God's purposive activity and at the same time contributes to that growing awareness. As a participant, the discerning church is both responsive to God's initiative and is active in its obedience to the will of God.

The term "obedience" has been a stumbling block to many. It conjures up images of authoritarianism and of a blind, unquestioning submission. The Anabaptists had this word *(Gehorsam)* along with discipleship *(Nachfolge)* as key words in their vocabulary. They have been accused of a wooden legalism in their interpretation of the requirements of biblical obedience and of a naive literalism in their attempt to follow Jesus and obey his commands. Whatever the evidence might be for such charges, it cannot be denied that there was both vitality and validity in their attempt to carry out a full obedience. They insisted that no one can truly know Christ who does not follow him in life.

Let me quote these words from *The Anabaptist Vision:*

> The Anabaptists could not understand a Christianity which made regeneration, holiness and love primarily a matter of intellect, of doctrinal belief, or of subjective "experience," rather than one of the transformation of life. They demanded an outward expression of the inner experience. Repentance must be "evidenced" by newness of behavior. ... The whole life was to be brought literally under the lordship of Christ in a covenant of discipleship. The focus of the Christian life was to be not so much the inward experience of the grace of God, as it was for Luther, but the outward application of that grace to all human conduct and the consequent Christianization of all human relationships. The true test of the Christian, they held, is discipleship. The great word of the Anabaptists was not "faith" as it was with the Reformers, but "following" *(Nachfolge Christi).*[6]

We may well inquire whether such an emphasis was actually an authentic New Testament one. It was indeed if we accept the judgment of a leading New Testament scholar of our time who declared in an address at Harvard University:

> God's disclosure of himself always conveys an absolute imperative: *obedience.* The Gospel proclaims each act of obedience as an act of knowing him in whom was perfect obedience. It proclaims each taking up of the Cross as a step toward fuller knowledge of the grace that is made perfect in weakness.[7]

In other words, in biblical thought to know is to obey. In this respect the Anabaptists had captured—or better still had been captured by—a very profound theological insight.

We cannot here enter into the frequently debated question whether there was an implicit legalism within the strong ethical concern of the Anabaptists. The role of grace in Anabaptist thought has been the subject of recent research on the part of several Anabaptist scholars and it has been demonstrated that the grace-faith relationship was not absent from their writings. But the charge of the critics is not to be turned aside lightly as if it were of no consequence; as faithful and grateful heirs of the Anabaptist vision we do not disavow our heritage by scrutinizing it carefully to discern what may have been communicated in that heritage or alongside it which has given rise to that degree of legalism that has blighted our tradition since the sixteenth century. This may well be one of the major tasks of our generation as the Mennonite church seeks to be a community of discernment in our time and place. The discerning church will seek to discover and maintain the fundamental connection and interrelationship between the authentically biblical emphases of grace and obedience. It will, in full awareness that its true life comes to it as the gift of God, continue to search for and walk along the path of obedience to Christ as this is charted through the twentieth century.

Eschatological Awareness

The last of the three dimensions of the task of discernment sketched at the outset of this section is the awareness of the eschatological character of our existence. There it was suggested that it is the church's participation in God's act which gives to its existence its eschatological character for God's action is eschatological. The apostolic community, it was noted, had a lively sense of standing at the frontier where God was at work making all things new. They had a sense of standing at the point where the new age was invading and overcoming the old. They had a sense of living in the end time when God's purposes will be fully consummated. All this gave them a perspective which sharpened their powers of discernment and affected the way in which they ordered their daily lives.

The Anabaptists also had an eschatological awareness which colored their understanding of their historical situation. It was made vivid as we have seen in the imagery of the two kingdoms. It was decisive in their interpretation of the relation of the church to the world. The Anabaptists were sons and daughters of their time and situation. Their eschatology was, as we have said, determinative of the way they interpreted the relation of the church to the world. But so also did the particular historical circumstances in which they lived. Their historical situation had its influence upon the way in which they approached the Scriptures—the presuppositions they held, the questions they asked, the conclusions and decisions at which they arrived, and the applications to their situation which they made.

One of the unfinished tasks of scholarship and research is the task of inquiring into the hermeneutic of the Anabaptists, both their express articulation of their methods of interpretation of the Scriptures and the implicit methodology by which they operated. As might be expected, and as historical research up to this point has revealed, there is considerable variation in the hermeneutical approaches of various Anabaptist leaders. While the task of historical reconstruction is of continuing significance, it should not be expected to yield a hermeneutic which is fully capable of opening the Scriptures for us in our day. For we too are sons and daughters of our time and place and must courageously and honestly come to terms with our presuppositions in approaching the Scriptures, our degree of openness, the methodological principles with which we work and the character of the responses, decisions, and applications to our situation which we make. With respect to the authority of the Scriptures for faith and life there can be no uncertainty if we are to be considered the faithful heirs of the Anabaptists. This certainty does not release us from the necessity of the process of working through and articulating a hermeneutic for our day; it remains, however, the fundamental premise with which we begin and upon which we build. In my judgment, there is no task deserving of greater priority than this one if we are to be a community of discernment in the midst of the twentieth century.

The eschatological awareness of the Anabaptists is one which we can and must share. We do not conclude from this that we must see the relation between church and world in precisely the same terms as they did, for their perceptions were historically conditioned even as ours must inevitably be. This does not mean that our perceptions are superior to theirs. It does mean, however, that we cannot simply borrow their categories and their conclusions and apply them unexamined to our own situation. The task of discernment for us involves a reconstruction, insofar as this is possible, of the historical situation within which they decided and acted. It involves critical reflection upon the process through which they moved in arriving at their conclusions and decisions. It involves a re-examination of the Scriptures from which they drew their inspiration and direction in arriving at their decisions and actions. It involves a reconstruction of the method of interpreting the Scriptures by which they arrived at their conclusions and applications so that we may be in a better position to assess their validity as applied to their situation and to ours.

Seminary and Congregation

The task of discernment, insofar as it is a human task, may be described as moving along a continuum which we shall call the "continuum of discernment." Along the continuum, and within the cognitive frame of reference which we have discussed, two types of human activity are appropriately carried on in reciprocal interplay—critical reflection on the one hand and that kind of purposive action on the other hand which issues out of the response of obedience to God. It is important that these two be seen as belonging on the same continuum, for separating them too sharply as distinct activities can only have unfortunate, even disastrous, consequences so far as the task of spiritual discernment is concerned. Neither can be a pure act in the sense that it does not in some measure engage the other. To know God, as we have acknowledged, is to obey him. The true knowledge of God does not come about primarily through the exercise of human reason but through God's self-disclosure to those to whom he makes himself known. The true knowledge of what God is now doing in the world does not finally yield itself to disinterested observation and objective analysis but is given to those whom God catches up in his purposes and in whose lives the fruits of an obedient response to the will of God are abundantly evident.

The Discerning Seminary

We have spoken thus far of the discerning task of the church and have made no distinction between seminary and congregation. Insofar as seminary and congregation faithfully reflect in their life and work their participation in the mission of the church of Jesus Christ, they participate in the church's task of discernment. The task of discernment may, it is hoped, serve as one image to clarify the relationship between what the seminary is doing and what the congregation is doing. One of the common tasks shared by seminary and congregation is that of discerning the will of God for our day; both function along the continuum as communities of discernment.

But do they function in precisely the same way? I think not. There is a difference in the way in which they approach the task of discernment. The difference, however, is not an essential or intrinsic one; it arises out of the particular situation or context of each community. That is to say, the seminary is not constituted in quite the same way as the congregation is. It suffers from certain limitations which the congregation does not share. During a three-year cycle there is almost a complete turnover of its student population. Nor does its population reflect the whole range of the personal richness and variety that is to be found in the congregation; its ranks are largely drawn from a limited stratum of the membership of the congregations. Its functions are largely restricted to those of an intellectual nature, with the very intensity of the academic demands calling for a measure of withdrawal from the ordinary round of involvements in the affairs of life.

But the seminary also enjoys certain advantages which the congregation does not enjoy and these have their implications for the way in which it approaches the task of discernment. In the seminary there are brought together persons who have developed through years of disciplined study and effort certain skills for critical reflection—reflection upon our biblical, historical and theological heritage and reflection upon the present life and task of the church in the world. These persons, working in a setting that is conducive to reflection, have a distinct contribution to make in a discerning church.

To say that the seminary's function is more reflective in character, and that the congregation's function is more operational in character, might seem at first blush to express the distinctiveness well. It is true that the seminary is a school, a community of inquiry. There are its professors with their powers of observation and their tools for exegesis and historical reconstruction, and their ability to read the contemporary human document. There are the libraries, the lectures, the seminars, and the vigorous discussions both inside and outside the classroom as mind meets mind. The congregation, on the other hand, is a community which gathers for worship and fellowship and scatters for acts of service and deeds of mercy in the name of Christ. Each community has its characteristic posture, whether reflection or action. But to see each community only in terms of its "characteristic posture" is to indulge in an oversimplification. What is even more unfortunate is for each community to function only in terms of its characteristic posture, and to destroy thereby the rhythm of the reciprocal interplay between reflection and action through which spiritual discernment is granted.

Theologizing, to be sure, involves intellectual effort but a theology of discernment is not essentially the product of intellectual effort. Here we come upon the greatest danger that lies implicit within our work in the seminary. The seminary is, as we have noted, a community of intellectual inquiry, and the basic content for this activity is the Christian message, the gospel. Now the gospel is given not as something to be analyzed and discussed so much as it is a Word to be obeyed, to be received with humility and in faith.

In this community, then, we must become and remain sensitive to the fundamental contradiction of our task. There are within it subtle yet profound temptations, for there is always the tendency that we make out of the gospel *it-truth*—that is, truth which can be discussed, analyzed, handled, objectified, kept at arm's length—a word over which we stand in judgment rather than that word standing in judgment over us. But the gospel is essentially *Thou-truth,* where the living Lord breaks through at the most unexpected times and places confronting us with his word of judgment or of healing.

However, we are called to our intellectual responsibilities in spite of the contradiction, the temptations, and the subtle snares of our calling, and we commit ourselves to them gladly and with eager expectation. For does not the great commandment affirm that we are to love the Lord our God with all our heart and soul and **mind** and strength and our neighbor as ourselves? Richard Niebuhr saw the distinctive task of the theological school as "the intellectual love of God." If we are to understand the Word of God as it comes to us in our situation today, we cannot be intellectually slothful in our hearing of it. Provided that we remain alert to the implicit dangers of our work, we must seek to enter into the understanding of the Christian message with all the critical powers at our disposal. The corrective to the tendency toward intellectual objectifying is to be found in a greater degree and quality of personal participation in the total response of the church to the Word and will of God.

The Discerning Congregation

A sharp separation between reflection and action also has its perils for the congregation, for sheer activity is something quite different from that kind of purposive activity which springs from an obedient response to the will of God. A congregation whose busy schedule and program does not provide for serious study of the Scripture and reflection upon its present mission in the world becomes vulnerable to a host of spiritual foes which readily prey upon it—foes which include such enemies to spiritual health and vitality as traditionalism, legalism and institutionalism. Such a congregation does not profit from the perspective and the strength which might be gained from a critical awareness of its spiritual heritage and the historical tradition in which it stands. It is instead the prisoner of its tradition, a tradition which instead of renewing and being renewed through the lively interaction of the present with the past becomes a dead weight. Such a congregation readily gets entangled in the snares of legalism, that deadliest of all the foes which oppose and frustrate the grace of God. A congregation not given to reflection will fail to discern that eternal life is not guaranteed by even a multitude of good works but that it must be received purely as a gift. A congregation not given to reflection will fail to discern that, although the church—being a visible human community—may develop institutions to express its life and carry out its program, it cannot ignore the dangers of institutionalism. Institutionalism, in current theological discussion, does not refer to the creation of institutions as such, i.e., practices, laws, customs, sacraments, offices, organizational structures and the like; it refers rather to the sin of absolutizing the relative, of granting to institutions an ultimacy which is not properly attached to them, of displacing God with the structures which were originally intended for the service of God.

Conclusion

The congregation is not only a community which acts; it must also be a community which reflects and which shares in the fruits of the process of reflection which goes on in the seminary. The seminary is not only a community which reflects; it must also be a community which acts in response to the will of God and which thus participates in the renewing activity of a renewing God.

The images of the eye and of the hand can be helpful in understanding the discerning function of the seminary and the congregation; however, these images serve to clarify rather than to obscure the interrelationship of the two only if they are held within the larger image of the body of Christ. For all of us are members of Christ and of the community of faith over which he is Lord before we are scholars or pastors or laymen or administrators. And being held within that new solidarity which the apostle Paul describes by means of the analogy of the body, none can say with any conviction:

> Because I am not a hand, I do not belong to the body; or
> Because I am not an eye, I do not belong to the body.
> If the body were all eye, how could it act?
> If the body were all hand, how could it see?
> The eye cannot say to the hand, I do not need you.

Nor can the seminary and the congregation truly be communities of discernment unless hand and eye, purposive activity and critical reflection, fulfill their complementary functions in whatever mutual proportion may be appropriate to each community.

The task of discernment is the task of the church. It can be accomplished only by a community which, renewed through being caught up in God's renewing work, perceives the present purpose and action of God. The task of discernment can be accomplished only by an eschatologically oriented community which, although historically rooted in this time and place, is situated between the times where the new age is pushing back the old, and on the frontiers where the kingdom of God is overcoming the kingdom of Satan.

---

[1] See, for example, J. Lawrence Burkholder, "The Peace Churches as Communities of Discernment," *The Christian Century* (1963), 1072-75.
[2] Articles by George F. MacLeod, Franklin H. Littell, Walter D. Wagoner, Ernest Cadman Colwell, Charles L. Taylor, and W. S. Taylor, *Theological Education* (1965), 1:81-117.
[3] B. Davie Napier, *Prophets in Perspective* (Abingdon, 1965), 59.
[4] Robert Friedmann, "The Doctrine of the Two Worlds," *The Recovery of the Anabaptist Vision*, ed. Guy F. Hershberger (Herald Press, 1957), 105.
[5] *Ibid.*, 106.
[6] Harold S. Bender, "The Anabaptist Vision," *The Recovery of the Anabaptist Vision*, 43.
[7] Paul S. Minear, "Revelation and the Knowledge of the Church," being the Dudleian Lecture for the academic year 1953-54, Harvard University, and published in the Harvard Divinity School Bulletin, 31.

15

Theological Education in the Free Church Tradition

The faculty of the Associated Mennonite Biblical Seminaries has recently engaged in a two year study of the foundations of its program of theological education.[1] Through this study there has emerged the conviction that not only the *content* but also the *context* of the curriculum must be shaped by our theological convictions. At the heart of the Free Church commitment is the understanding of the church as a covenant community based on the free and voluntary response of faith to God's offer of grace. The central reality around which the program of theological education is shaped is the purpose of God in history to create a covenant people for himself. The organizing principle of the curriculum is the attempt to discover and to realize what it is to be the faithful people of God now—what forms that peoplehood should take in the congregations and in the seminary—with a view to setting up programs and structures that are an appropriate expression of that guiding vision.

The context for theological education is therefore not first of all the university but the community of faith. The theological school stands, to be sure, in the academic tradition as well as in the ecclesiastical tradition; however it is the Judeo-Christian tradition (as expressed through the Free Churches in this instance) which is the true home of theological education and provides the basic clues for shaping the form, substance, and style of our enterprise.

Obviously, the theological school is indebted to the university as well as to the church for its shape and character. From the university it learns intellectual rigor, integrity, and objectivity. It learns how to handle the tools of modern critical scholarship and it enjoys the fruits of that scholarship as it tries to understand the social and cultural environment in which the church carries out its mission. But the religious tradition in which the church stands reminds it of the subtle temptation in every human enterprise, especially the intellectual one, to human pride. In attempting to objectify the content of Christian faith and establish the categories by which it can be handled, manipulated, made to hold still and lie at our disposal, we encounter grave peril. The truth of the gospel is that which confronts us and makes us responsible. In fact, the truth of the gospel is not at bottom "it-truth" at all but "Thou-truth; it is God himself in Jesus Christ who confronts us in and through the text of Scripture as it is read in the community of faith and calls for decision: yes or no. The response of faith draws men and women out of their isolation into covenant community.

The Model

One of the major results of the faculty study was a model for theological education which is based upon a commitment to the understanding of the church as the people of God.

Theological Characteristics

The people of God are a ministering community. Ministry, as it has been defined in this study, is the exercise of the spiritual gifts given to the total people of God. To realize this, it is necessary to discern the gifts, develop skills in exercising them, understand how they contribute to the whole task of God's ministering people, learn how to live in community and minister in community, and determine the most strategic way and place in which the gifts of a particular individual should be deployed. This also involves the decision as to whether or not a given individual should fulfill his ministry as a professional minister which is a strategic question rather than first of all a theological one, since the presupposition is that every baptized believer is already a minister.

The "Christian ministry" is present in all its theological fullness wherever the people of God are gathered and members are obedient in the exercise of their gifts. The occasion for calling a professional minister[2] or ministers arises when the task in a given community to which a congregation addresses itself calls for skills not resident in the congregation or for skills potentially resident but in need of being mobilized. The professional minister is not to displace the ministry of the people of God but to mobilize and supplement it. The particular shape that that ministry will take will not be standard in every situation but will be special in each case as determined by the constellation of gifts in the congregation and the task of the congregation in the larger community.

The people of God are a worshipping community. The basic pattern of Israel's worship was the covenant form. Each occasion of corporate liturgical activity was the occasion for decision, for a renewal of the commitment to follow God in obedience and faith. It began with the recital of God's great deed (deliverance from Egypt) and it ended with the solemn acknowledgment of God's leadership of the community which was implemented through the prophetic proclamation of his word. Prophetic preaching involved the recital of God's gracious act, the setting forth of God's demand and claim, and the call for response including the reminder to the people of God's law as Moses had reported it to them. Behind this emphasis on the proclaimed word there always lay the certain conviction that God was at work through it, effecting his historical purpose in creating a people for himself, a community whose life together was both a model for the nations and a foretaste of what was in store for all mankind.

The radicality of the biblical faith, says Millard Lind,[3] is precisely at the point of worship: the affirmation that community can be founded upon and maintained by God's act of grace to which the community responds by the corporate acts of worship. The Free Church operates by structures which are founded upon grace and which receive direction from the volitional act of the worshipping community. This means that worship must be central in the Free Churches and is in fact the foundational political structure from which the congregation orders not only its internal life but involves itself in the world. The Free Church should not see itself as disestablished, but as God's establishment, a this-worldly community brought into existence by God's act of grace to which it responds in free commitment, discerning and doing the will of God in its corporate existence, invading from the vantage point of grace (experienced in worship) the alien structures of this world.

Christian worship involves the renewal of the covenant in which the members of the worshipping community acknowledge with gratitude the sovereign love of God in releasing them from slavery and bondage and in creating those who were "no people" into a people for himself. It calls for a thankful response to God in which the community renews its promise to discover and obey his will. The content of God's will may be summarized in his command to live in responsible love for the brother and for the neighbor. The specific applications of this command must be discerned each day so that the common life and the common task both within and beyond the community may be ordered according to the will of God.

The seminary community provides opportunities for corporate worship so that the covenant relationship with God and with those to whom the members are thus bound is deepened and strengthened. So long as the covenant relationship is the basic informing and shaping reality, the worshipping group is free to experiment with any liturgical forms which assist it in celebrating that relationship. It is of the genius of the Free Church tradition to encourage creative experimentation in the setting up of the liturgical offering for each service of worship. There is no one binding pattern on the one hand nor, on the other, a commitment to sheer spontaneity, though the latter should not be ruled out if the Spirit of God leads in the moment for "where the Spirit of God is, there is liberty."

The people of God are a witnessing community. The message of the gospel is that the power of God was let loose in the world when Christ was raised from the dead and was installed at the right hand of God victorious over "all rule and authority and power and dominion...not only in this age but also in that which is to come" (Eph. 1:19-23). The church, which is the body of Christ, "the fullness of him who fills all in all" is called to share in the cosmic triumph and to shout the emancipation proclamation all over the world. The "principalities and powers" have been brought to their knees by the conquering suffering servant and their capacity to enslave and destroy has been overcome in Christ and in the community that confesses him as Lord. The social, economic, and political structures which are the expressions within history of the "principalities and powers" tend toward the retention of their autonomy apart from Christ and in so doing refuse to acknowledge the cosmic victory which Christ has won and the church embodies and proclaims. To the extent that these visible, historical structures are the expression of human pride and self-centeredness they rob us of our highest destiny and fulfillment under God and must be challenged in a prophetic way.

The ability to interpret the will of God in our time calls for active participation in the event which is our faith, the event of God's creation of a people This means that the seminary community may not be excused from participation in the living response of the living church. While we do not deny that the characteristic activities of the seminary are study and reflection, it must be asserted that study and reflection should be carried on in the context of living engagement in the mission of the church. The Bible itself reflects the living engagement of its authors and subjects in mission; it cannot be properly interpreted apart from living engagement. The Bible accommodated itself to the human thought forms of its day, expressed itself in the vernacular idiom, and addressed itself to the issues raised by the encounter of biblical faith with the social order.

The people of God are a universal, worldwide fellowship. The message of the gospel conveys the good news not only that the "principalities and powers" have been subordinated to God in the victory of Christ's resurrection-ascension but that man's alienation and hostility which have separated him from his creator and from his neighbor have been brought to an end (Eph. 2:14-16; Col. 1:13-23; 3:9-11). Christ's victory has created "in himself one new man (symbolizing reconciliation and unity) in place of the two (symbolizing separation) so making peace." The former social distinctions which were both cause and effect of the alienation and hostility which characterize human existence apart from Christ's victory are now done away with. In their place there is a new social reality, the body of Christ which is made visible in the church. In the body of Christ, all social distinctions based on geography (east or west), nationality or ethnic origin (tribe and tongue and people and nation), sex (male and female), culture (Jew or Greek), economic status (slave or free man), or religious background (circumcised or uncircumcised) are seen as having no ultimate significance for "all are made one in Christ Jesus."

Curriculum Characteristics

The curriculum calls for learning in the context of Christian community. The knowledge which is to be communicated and learned through the curriculum is basically relational in character, and its mastery and comprehension involve relationships. The learner who comprehends this kind of truth and responds to its claim upon his life is drawn into community and learns through participation in community.

This calls for a different orientation of the members of the learning community toward each other than would be required if their intellectual search were directed toward purely objective material whose secret can be determined by disinterested observation and analysis which leave the discoverer unchanged in his being. The relationships of faculty to students are not properly characterized as wisdom-ignorance, initiate-novice, teacher-learner but as partners in the gospel and fellow partakers of the grace of God. Teachers and students together make up a hermeneutic community, each sharing what insight has been given him for the testing and the edification of the whole company.

The curriculum calls for learning in the context of personal commitment. Knowledge in the biblical sense is relational and demands response. To live in the knowledge of God is to live responsibly in community. Knowledge of this kind is moral and calls for moral commitment, the termination of suspended judgment. The knower is called to leave his objective neutrality and is drawn by his decision into his subject matter which changes his being. This is the epistemology of obedience expressed by the Anabaptist, Hans Denk, who said, "No one may truly know Christ who does not follow him in life." In other words, to know is to obey and to obey is to experience more and more fully the grace of God in one's life.

The seminary curriculum may appropriately be thought of not primarily in terms of information to be assimilated but in terms of decisions to be made. A student's progress may be charted in terms of moral as well as of intellectual growth which is the primary criterion of measurement in most schools, including theological schools. The context of a particular decision cannot be maneuvered and structured into a curriculum or schedule. Nor can the response of the person be structured if it is to be fully free and fully authentic. However, the expectation that encounter will take place and decision will be demanded can be made a part of the life of the seminary in every aspect of the program both in and out of the classroom. The koinonia groups, forums, and chapel services in particular are set aside for searching out the will of God in matters large and small and for determining appropriate responses, personal and corporate.

The curriculum calls for learning to take place through participation in a pilgrimage. The community of faith is not only an historical event; it is also a present reality. It is in this fact that we find the true relationship between history and experience; their unity is discovered through present participation in that community which has a long memory and whose Lord binds past and present together. For this reason, it is a false dichotomy to place **content** and **experience** in juxtaposition. The whole emphasis is placed upon experience but experience which is not idolatrous with respect to the present. The God who acts is the one who acted in the past, who continues to act in the present, and who will continue to act until he brings his historical purpose to gather a people for himself to its consummation.

Although God's historical purpose does not waver, the historical scene is characterized by change. Since all of life in its personal, social, and political dimensions is in constant process of change, the task of understanding, appropriating and transmitting the Christian faith is an ever-changing one. The learner is seen not so much as one who has assimilated the wisdom of the ages but as a participant with all the faithful in a pilgrimage of obedience through the modern wilderness where landmarks change but where the "pillar of cloud" (and of fire) is seen and followed.

Learning in such a context will emphasize experience, analysis, and evaluation. The faith of the learner takes shape and is tested in living encounter with all that meets him in the world where men live: poverty and affluence, propaganda and prejudice, war and peace, illiteracy, illegitimacy, brokenness, and restlessness. The learner has not truly learned until he can recognize these issues and speak a meaningful word to them. The test of authentic theological reflection is to be found in the way the heritage and the human predicament are brought to the point of convergence.

The curriculum calls for learning to take place through geographical scattering. Just as the activity of God in calling out a people for himself is not limited to any one time in history (it spans the centuries), so it is not limited to any one place. The ethnic or cultural enclaves which all too often pass for authentic congregational life do not adequately comprehend the universality of God's people. How may the seminaries express in their community life this catholic vision?

Although this program is not predisposed against the concept of clustering which is currently being widely advocated among leaders of theological education in North America, it is not dependent on that strategy alone. It advocates a policy of scattering students to a number of centers so that it can be truly said that the world is our campus. While representatives of the larger Christian fellowship beyond North America will be brought as churchmen-in-residence to the Theological Center, students will be encouraged to participate in the Transcultural Experience which provides opportunity to experience at firsthand the life and witness of the younger churches. The Off-Campus Theological Term makes possible participation in the life of other ecclesiastical traditions than the ones with which the student is most familiar. In the Clinical Pastoral Education Term, the student will become a member of a closely-knit group of persons from several denominational backgrounds who will be exploring their total body of experiences, past and present, with a view to self-understanding and greater sensitivity to other persons. This involves the convergence of experience and reflection, theological and behavioral disciplines, theoretical and practical knowledge. The Urban Ministries Program is similar in some respects and also calls for learning "on location" away from the seminary campus, as does the Congregationally Supervised Pastoral Education Program.

The curriculum calls for learning to take place through the pursuit of a diversity of professional goals. The program is based on an understanding of Christian ministry which is not dependent on the presence of a professional minister in the congregation to give theological integrity to its existence. It is a strategic question for the congregation whether to call a professional minister(s) to its staff. This will involve the assessment of its total resources and the determination of its mission. When a call is issued, it will be done with a clear awareness of the way in which the professional minister(s) will supplement and enhance the ministry which is already being carried out by the ministering congregation. Similarly mission boards and other denominational agencies will call for persons whose job definition has been carefully worked out and focused upon the specific task to be done.

The model presupposes that the congregations will develop through a careful self-study particular program emphases appropriate to their situation. They may call for the ministry of a professionally trained person to supplement the resources of the congregation in such ministries as evangelism, Christian education, hospital visitation, counseling, etc. The professional minister (if one is called) should be set free to function primarily in the area(s) of his competence giving priority to it (them) in terms of his time and resources. This would mean that other areas of the congregation's life and ministry would be carried largely by the nonprofessional ministers in it. His particular ministry is carried out in the context of the total ministry of God's ministering people.

The determination of financial support patterns is primarily a pragmatic kind of issue based on the local situation. The appropriateness of congregational financial support for a particular ministry must be measured in each situation completely on the basis of the needs discerned and the resources available. Congregational priorities will determine whether the minister(s) who will be supported are formally trained or not and whether the supported function is that of preaching, teaching, counseling, visiting, evangelizing or other.

Large congregations may be in a position to support a staff of several professionally trained ministers whereas smaller congregations may wish to cluster and engage a professional minister to give leadership in a particular area of ministry to which they have agreed to give priority. A single professional minister may also function appropriately in a given congregation provided care is taken to avoid the kind of generalized, all-inclusive role symbolized in recent years by the term "pastor." The counseling role may be both specialized and shared by a group of members in the congregation; the same is true of the teaching role, the administrative role, and of other ministering roles. This model presupposes that in the training of the professional minister the ministering roles will be shared to the fullest extent possible. It assumes further that the number of specialized roles carried by a given minister will be kept minimal according to the appropriate limits of his ability and the resources of the congregation in which he serves.

This approach to ministry avoids the standardization which the current generation of ministers is finding unacceptable. It makes possible a greater diversity of roles than has been thought desirable or feasible to this point. In the congregations, this calls for a new set of skills and a new basis for decision-making in the calling of staff ministers. These are the very skills which are needed in any case for the congregation to discern its mission and mobilize its resources effectively.

In the seminary, this calls for the provision in the curriculum for students not preparing for professional ministries as well as for others to learn a great variety of professional skills and combination of skills. It should be clear that a given candidate will not be expected to master the whole range of ministering skills. He may become proficient in only one or two, or he may develop ability in the exercise of several depending on his native capacity. What is important is that he develop a superior mastery of these skills and the ability to train and supervise others in the congregation. Above all, he must have a vision of the total ministering church exercising all the spiritual gifts and a practical knowledge of how ministry in community is carried out.

The curriculum calls for additional skills on the part of faculty members beyond competence in a particular theological discipline. The theological teacher who participates in the enterprise of equipping persons to minister in community must cultivate his own capacity to be a teacher in community. He must have an appreciation for the unity not only of the mission of the church but also of the task of theological education which prepares men and women for that mission. The theologian-teacher is expected to develop a high degree of proficiency in the exercise of his discipline and to practice it in the service of the total mission of the church.

The greatest contribution which can be made to the development of the student's ability to minister is accomplished by putting the resources and insights of a discipline (Bible, history, theology, ethics, homiletics, education, etc.) at his disposal at the point of his greatest readiness to learn. To sense the teachable moment, the teacher must know the student well just as he knows his own discipline well. It requires consummate skill to effect the convergence of subject matter and learning readiness and the student himself will carry much of the responsibility to have this happen. The material to be learned will be both organized systematically and presented existentially when it is appropriate to the situation. The purpose of the coming together of the teacher, learner, and content at the moment of teachableness is to advance insight, develop skill, foster self-awareness, and nurture faith and commitment. While such convergence with its promotion of true learning is all too rare in formal education and must be received with wonder and gratitude as a gift when it happens, its occurrence can be anticipated with greater frequency if disciplined attention is given to it.

The teacher who comes to his work with the expectation that genuine learning can be promoted as well as received with gratitude will tend to be flexible and relaxed; he will encourage experimentation, analysis, and evaluation and will be able to adjust his material and his approach to the emerging situation. He will be concerned for the personal development of his students in all their areas of growth not limiting his concern to the intellectual alone. Such a teacher will have the capacity to appreciate diversity of experience, piety, personality, academic disciplines, and professional goals.

Supplementary Program

The following program elements have been designed to supplement and complement the curriculum of instruction given by the faculty:

Theological Center. A program which brings visiting churchmen to the campus for short periods in residence to serve as role models and to participate in the teaching-learning process in a variety of ways.

Experience in Christian Community. During each semester in residence the student will be expected to participate actively in the Experience in Christian Community. This experience (to be taken with curricular seriousness) consists of four major elements: (i) K (koinonia) groups which include students, faculty, staff, and spouses; (ii) Forum, a weekly meeting of the entire community for discussing issues of Christian concern. This follows the eating of a common meal; (iii) Worship services in the chapel provide for the renewal and celebration of covenant community. Worship is not only doxological but also dialogical. It should include in addition to prayer and praise the opportunity for mutual admonition; (iv) Commissioning is the formal occasion for the recognition of the students' spiritual gifts and the commitment by the students to the work and ministry of the church.

Supervised Experience in Ministry. All students, whether or not they are preparing for professional ministries supported by the church, participate in field work assignments in congregations or community agencies. In addition, students preparing for specialized ministries participate in one or several assignments. (i) Supervised Experience in Ministry Seminars which include also individual supervisory sessions with the instructor. This approach maximizes the potential of the teachable moment as it arises in an actual ministering situation. (ii) Congregationally Supervised Pastoral Education requires a year of supervised ministry in residence in a congregation selected for its ability to provide learning resources so the student can explore the range of his potential ministering skills and develop his gifts to a high level of proficiency. (iii) Clinical Pastoral Education may be taken in a center accredited by the Association for Clinical Pastoral Education.

Off-Campus Theological Term. The student is encouraged to study for one term in another seminary in order to become acquainted with a theological culture different from his own by being plunged into a context shaped by that other theological tradition.

Transcultural Experience. This term abroad enables the student to be an observer and a colleague in a mission and/or service program. It is intended as an internship in the life and mission of the church overseas and is designed to break down the student's narrow ethnocentrism and sensitize him to the church-world encounter as well as to help him gain a broader world perspective.

0verseas Mission Training Center. The Center is a cooperative enterprise of the training and sending agencies of the church designed to prepare overseas workers whose field and assignment have already been determined by the calling church and the sending board. The director tailors the curriculum for each student to suit his unique needs, utilizing the program resources of the seminary and of other schools and universities in this country and in the country to which the candidate is assigned.

One's statement of purpose should, no doubt, appear in the introduction rather than the conclusion of an essay. In this instance, however, we present it as a summary of our intention which underlies the variety of activities and experiences which constitute the curriculum of the seminary.

> It is the purpose of the seminary to be a Christian community of scholarship and discipleship in the Free Church tradition. It is the responsibility of this community to interpret the continuing

> significance of the vital elements in its heritage in the light of the Scriptures and to witness to them in conversation with the larger Christian fellowship and with the world. To this end the seminary has developed a program for the equipping of Christian men and women to participate in this task and to serve the churches in this country and abroad in a variety of professional and nonprofessional ministries informed by this vision.

The foregoing statement, while not all-inclusive, is illustrative of the concern to keep the focus of attention on the larger goal which is to participate with God in what he is doing in the world, that is, creating a covenant community, a people for himself. All curricular decisions, faculty appointments, admissions policies, graduation requirements—in short, all policy decisions must be determined in the light of this fundamental affirmation and contribute however indirectly to this end. These programs and structures must be kept under scrutiny constantly so that a judgment can be made whether they continue to be an adequate instrument of the purpose for which they are intended.

---

[1] This study made possible by a generous grant from Lilly Endowment, Inc., was published in Ross T. Bender, *The People of God: A Mennonite Interpretation of the Free Church Tradition* (Scottdale, Pa.: Herald Press, 1971). A fuller elaboration of the elements of the model and the theological foundations undergirding it is contained in that publication.

[2] The professional ministry is marked by (a) special training, (b) special functions, (c) full-time employment, (d) full salary, (e) regulation by peer group standards.

[3] Associated Mennonite Biblical Seminaries Professor of Old Testament.

16

Christian Education in Theological Education

My assignment, as I understand it, is not to be an apologist for the place of Christian education in theological education, presenting vigorous arguments to convince you that it has a valid and honored place as a discipline among the other theological disciplines, for of this you are already convinced. Assuming as we do its past and continuing validity in the program of the theological schools, our question is how Christian education may make its distinctive contribution to the whole process of theological education and how it may in turn be shaped by that process.

Theological education is in considerable ferment today. Many seminaries are in process of re-examining and revising their programs with all the stress and strain that this review and revision brings. I visited a number of seminaries to learn at first hand of some of these curriculum developments; printed releases from the member institutions of the American Association of Theological Schools are further evidence that many modifications and innovations are under way. Most of us know about all this from first hand experience in our own faculties. But the ferment itself is not alone what impresses me; it is the amazing congruity among the theological schools along certain lines of curriculum planning. Indeed, such is the congruity that future historians will undoubtedly posit a common source for these currents of thought. Such a source (let us call it "N") will necessarily be recognized as the Niebuhr-Williams-Gustafson study of theological education in Canada and the United States[1] sponsored by the American Association of Theological Schools and financed by the Carnegie Corporation of New York. This study gathered together the various "oral traditions" and put them into documentary form thereby giving direction and impetus to the several stirrings that were already evident among the schools prior to the publication in 1956 of the first part of the report.

Not all of these developments have a direct and immediate significance for Christian education as a discipline within the curriculum of the theological school; however, I have in this paper attempted to identify some of those which do and to elaborate their implications for Christian education.

1. An emphasis on the wholeness of the learning experience is being stressed. Truncation and fragmentation are increasingly deplored.

The problem of unity in theological education is threefold:

(a) there is the problem of the logical cohesiveness of the material to be studied;
(b) there is the problem of establishing the connection between the Christian heritage and the personal experience of the seminarian; and
(c) there is the problem of establishing the connection between the Christian heritage and the task of the church in the modern world.

Each of the several areas of study represented in the curriculum of the theological school has its own inner norms of consistency which relate the various parts to one another in an ordered whole. The student who encounters all these disciplines and attempts to gain some mastery in his study of them is faced with a large task to comprehend not only the inner consistency of each one but also the interrelationships among them. As the curriculum has been expanded to include in addition to courses in Bible, church history, theology and preaching such fields of study as worship, music, Christian education, social ethics, missions and evangelism, speech, counseling, group dynamics, philosophy of religion, psychology of religion and sociology of religion the problem has been intensified. How shall the student find the unifying principle to a comprehensive, unified view of the Christian heritage as he struggles with these varied approaches to studying it? For that matter, where is the faculty that has resolved this problem and reflects this resolution in its course of study? Niebuhr, Williams and Gustafson report that "there is no doubt of the widespread concern among students and faculty for some universal rationale and logic of internal relationships to order the diversity of the theological studies."[2]

How does the concern for logical unity in the curriculum affect the department of Christian education? First of all, as an integral part of the program of theological education Christian education must regard itself as a theological discipline. In an earlier period, there was a tendency for the theoretical basis for religious education to be non-theological, even in some instances anti-theological. But the work of men like H. Shelton Smith, James Smart, Lewis J. Sherrill and Randolph Crump Miller has established a trend toward a theological orientation in Christian education theory which is to be applauded and encouraged. That it has been possible to bring educational theory into greater congruity with theological modes of thought is due in large part to the "humanizing" of theology that has taken place. By this I refer especially to the serious attention that some theologians have given to the findings of the life sciences and to their attempts to build bridges between these disciplines and theology. The work of Paul Tillich upon which Lewis Sherrill has built in *The Gift of Power* is a good illustration of what I have in mind. Sherrill's educational theory is theological, not in the sense that it is systematic or dogmatic theology but that it considers the educational issues in the light of the Christian revelation and its several themes. It is theological, moreover, without ignoring or rejecting sociological and psychological theory which educational theory must also take into account. Christian education is itself a bridge and it finds those theological systems which are themselves attempting to build bridges the most congenial to its own purposes.

Building educational theory on the bridge between theology and the life sciences is not without its perils. The Christian educator cannot realistically be expected to be equally at home in these other areas as well as proficient in depth in his own field. Nor can he simply adapt and incorporate the methodological principles and the findings of these other disciplines into his own discipline. He must find his starting point and his organizing principle within his own discipline, a discipline which is operational in its primary orientation. Whereas theology and the life sciences tend to be primarily descriptive in their view of human nature, for example, Christian education is interested in the question of human nature in order to discover what and how one may become what one is intended to be.

One of the perils to which Christian education is vulnerable is an uncritical borrowing and selection of categories and perspectives from other disciplines for its own purposes. On what basis shall it make judgments concerning the validity of these categories and systems of thought? A possible approach to overcome this problem would be for the

Christian educator to come at his discipline through another discipline in which he has gained scholarly proficiency. In the case of the Christian educator on a theological faculty, that discipline should be theology (biblical, systematic or philosophical) but it must be the kind of theology that is already sensitive to the actual human situation today. By approaching educational issues theologically, Christian education will maintain its close connection to the other departments of the seminary. Its distinctive subject matter will emerge from the practice of the teaching ministry in the local congregation as it draws its content, direction and methodology from the Christian heritage. The very attempt to draw its content, direction and methodology from the Christian heritage of necessity drives the discipline of Christian education to seek answers from outside the Christian heritage for that heritage was not designed to answer all its questions. However, as Christian education looks to the life sciences to find additional help in answering its questions, it goes with a basic perspective with which to judge and evaluate what it finds there. The Christian understanding of what it means to be human, for example, as grounded in the Christian revelation and elaborated in Christian theology is normative for Christian education theory though it requires further elaboration and supplementation by contemporary readings of the human document.

One of the contributions of Christian education to the theological enterprise is to be found in its very necessity to bring theology and the life sciences into conversation. Through this meeting, both parties in the conversation may be enriched and strengthened. Theology becomes more viable and credible as it is humanized through the encounter between the heritage of the past and the modern analysis of human existence. At the same time, it brings a word of hope from the past and the beyond to bear upon the understanding of the human predicament which empirical observation and analysis alone cannot uncover.

In some theological schools, there is a growing emphasis upon interdepartmental cooperation in certain courses with teams of teachers from several departments working together. Professors of Old Testament and New Testament studies are called upon to assist the professor of homiletics; professors in the field of sociology of religion are called upon to work in the field of social ethics. Where the theological school is located in a college or university setting, the professors of sociology and psychology may be called on to do some team teaching or give special lectures; specialists in the fields of education and communication theory are also valuable resources for theological education.[3] The department of Christian education should be ready both to initiate and to support all efforts within a given faculty to implement interdepartmental and interdisciplinary approaches for it finds this very necessity implicit within itself.

One other issue of practical importance for curriculum planning which arises from considerations about the logical cohesiveness of the material to be mastered has to do with flexibility or rigidity in fixing course requirements. It centers on the question as to how a student may best be helped to find the key to unlock what Niebuhr calls the "logic of internal relationships to order the diversity of the theological studies" and "the internal consistency of the Christian understanding of life."[4] Some theological schools either through despair of finding such a key or out of the conviction that the student is in the best position to find it himself turn the student loose in the forest of the curriculum without the guidance afforded by a highly structured program. Other schools prescribe the course of studies rather carefully with a minimum of electives. Such programs would seem to suppose that the key has been found or is at least implicit within the structure and it remains only for the student to find it and make it explicit in his own theological understanding. It is apparent that no one solution satisfactory to all the theological schools has been found. It may well be that Christian educators with their technical knowledge and experience in curriculum planning on other levels may find from within their corpus of theory some wisdom which may throw light on the matter.

2. The seminary is increasingly becoming a place for students to find faith as well as to prepare for Christian ministries.

H. Richard Niebuhr, in his discussion of the search for the essential unity in the Christian heritage which can give unity to the theological curriculum suggests an important clue which takes us beyond the concern for logical unity:

> The search for this internal consistency of the Christian understanding of life involves many subtle questions. Superficially it is possible to outline a scheme of studies in which each has its place and in which the relationships are formally stated. Such a

> theological encyclopedia can display a rational order and designate the relationships of all human inquiries to the theological themes. But the real key lies in the nature of the Christian faith itself and hence beneath the surface of any formal scheme. Because the Christian faith has at its center a personal response to the reality of the creative, redeeming, and inspiring God, the unity in our faith must be found through personal discovery of the ultimate reality which shapes the whole of life.[5]

The necessity for personal response implicit within the Christian faith introduces a unique dimension into theological education which is not found in other forms of professional education. The theological student is faced with a fundamental ambiguity and a subtle snare as he approaches his studies for the gospel which lies at the core of the Christian heritage is given not so much as subject matter to be critically scrutinized and carefully systematized as it is a word to be believed and obeyed. The student is, however, summoned to his task of critical inquiry and analysis in spite of the snare and the ambiguity for what Niebuhr calls the "intellectual love of God'' is also a Christian calling which he cannot escape; he should be encouraged to enter into it gratefully and reverently and with all the intellectual diligence of which he is capable. There is a large body of intelligible content in the Christian heritage the study of which enhances his appreciation of that heritage and helps him to make it his own.

How may we help our students to avoid the pitfalls of their calling? We can caution them to beware of becoming spectators only as the drama of redemption unfolds before them and invite them to take their place along with us on the stage as participants in the drama—coming to know at first hand the meaning of judgment and grace, guilt and forgiveness, alienation and reconciliation. We can help them to develop a theological vocabulary and the modes of thinking and being which make their use of this vocabulary authentic. Our students, if they are to have a faith to proclaim and a faith to share, must have more than a theological vocabulary and mindset; they must also have a faith to confess. Theology, for all its profundity and complexity, is a relatively easy matter to articulate and to communicate, but a living faith is not so readily quickened and nurtured, at least not in a school. Both are essential ingredients in the equipment of the student—theological clarity which gives articulate expression and direction to Christian experience and personal faith which gives vitality and immediacy to theological reflection.

The importance of the role of personal faith in developing theological understanding cannot be too strongly emphasized. The seminaries are increasingly recognizing that the personal response of faith must be a continuing one and that the Christian commitment of the seminarian must be nurtured so that it will remain commensurate with his intellectual growth. More than this, the seminaries are discovering that seminarians are coming to their studies with greater questions of personal faith and doubt than in an earlier period. Perhaps this is the fruit of the growing secularism of society in general and of the university in particular. It may be that the anxieties of life in a nuclear age are creating deeper uncertainties among youth in general, including potential seminarians, than ever before. It may be that the current generation of seminarians is more sophisticated intellectually than an earlier one and is demanding a greater measure of intellectual rigor in answering the questions of faith. It may be the result of the failure of the church to be prophetic and courageous as it addresses itself to the social order or it may be the disillusionment that has become widespread with respect to the viability and relevance of the institutional church which have caused misgivings to arise concerning the very faith the church professes and proclaims and by which it orders its life and its institutions. It may be that the programs of the Sunday school and the youth groups and the campus religious foundations have been seriously inadequate.

Whatever the cause or complex of causes may be, the seminaries are beginning to recognize and assume their responsibility for the quickening of faith and the nurturing of the commitment of their students. This places a large burden upon the resources of the seminary and has certain implications for the character of its program. The seminary must be a school but it must be more than a school; it must be a community of faith where the gospel is proclaimed and lived. Some at least, if not all, of the functions of the local congregation must be exercised in the seminary community.

While it cannot be maintained that Christian educators stand alone among their colleagues in their concern and responsibility for the nurturing of the Christian commitment and growth of the theological student, they can be held to greater account when this dimension of theological education is ignored. The historian or the systematic theologian can be faithful to his task without expressing this concern but the Christian educator finds the imperative for his responsibility deeply embedded within his very discipline; he brings both a practical concern and some body of experience as to how Christian commitment and growth are nurtured. These are significant resources within a faculty as it seeks to meet this new dimension of its responsibility to equip its students intellectually and spiritually for their tasks.

3. There is a growing concern to relate the whole enterprise of theological education to contemporary issues that the church faces in society.

There are three circles of issues with which the church is properly concerned and for which her ministers require that kind of theological education which will enable the church to be prophetic as it addresses them.

(a) The first circle of issues might be called national and international issues—war and peace, poverty and affluence, exploding populations, malnutrition and starvation, international relations, race relations, propaganda and prejudice, automation, unemployment and leisure, relationships between church and state, and capital punishment, to identify some of the major ones.

(b) The second circle of issues arises out of the increasing acceptance by the church of her responsibility to carry out her ministry in the inner city. By doing so, she faces the problem of ministering to "the disinherited" and of how to communicate the gospel to them in terms which they can recognize as authentic. Here too the problems of poverty, of slums, of inadequate housing, of illiteracy, of illegitimacy, of broken families, of racial prejudice and discrimination, of restless underprivileged people, of school dropouts, of drug addiction, of prostitution, and other forms of sexual perversion take on a more immediate and less abstract aspect.

(c) A third circle of issues, while identifiable, is not totally distinct from the first and the second. It might be identified as encounter with the philosophies and ideologies of our day. Some of these are of the more sophisticated, coolly intellectual type; others are more of the hotbed variety, both virile and aggressive, clamoring for our loyalties. They are encountered in the university and in the political forum; they have their orientation in the left and in the right. They leave no area of life untouched whether politics, or economics, or sociology or theology.

As the church attempts to address itself to such complex issues as these it discovers not only that its action programs are of the "too little and too late" variety but also that all too often they fail to identify and work at the real issues. A profounder approach to the problems involves reflection and this in turn involves theological insights as well as sociological and other kinds of analysis. Theological understandings of social responsibility and the meaning of human community must be worked out in conjunction with sociological analyses of power structures; psychological findings about basic human drives for power, for status, for acceptance, for sex, for meaning, for pleasure, for fulfillment, for success, etc., must be understood in terms of theological understandings of sin, guilt and anxiety and the fundamental brokenness of humanity, individual and corporate, as well as in terms of the acceptance, redemption and reconciliation that is to be found in Christ. These are two illustrations of the necessity for finding the points where various approaches to understanding the human situation interpenetrate one another.

Reflection alone, however, is not a fruitful approach to resolving the problems of the nation and of the inner city. There is a necessary rhythm between reflection and action; it is in the reciprocal motion between the two that the lights begin to flash and the truth of the matter is discerned. Incarnation and compassion become meaningful theological categories only when they are born out of Christian identification with and involvement in the miseries of humankind; there lies within these experiences the raw material for theologizing. A theology born out of this kind of encounter is likely to be vital and relevant for it must bridge the gap between the world of the first century and the world of the twentieth century and it must submit itself to the critical testing of both worlds.

What are the implications of the above considerations for Christian education? First of all, Christian educators must make their contribution along with their colleagues to finding ways of bridging the gaps between the first century and the twentieth, between theology and the other disciplines, between reflection and involvement. Christian education must learn from the attempt of theological education to close these gaps and must attempt to incorporate these learnings in its approach to

Christian adult education for the local congregations. The way in which the process of comprehending Christian truth proceeds on the Christian adult education level may be less theoretical and more action-oriented, but it cannot afford to be less profound. Indeed, we should not conclude that all the wisdom will flow one way—from the seminary to the congregation; there may well be and there certainly should be a reservoir of experience upon which theological formulations may draw arising from the obedient response of Christians who have gained certain insights into issues of Christian concern through their participation in vital programs of Christian adult education.

Another implication for Christian education is to be found in the consideration that some of these issues suggest educational concerns. The issues of prayer and the teaching of religion in the public schools, federal aid to private education, shared time classes are all issues of national importance; they are issues which Christian educators should be discussing and debating and helping to resolve. The issues of religious and racial prejudice are of primary concern to Christian educators. It is their responsibility to inquire where and how prejudice is communicated and how positive attitudes toward those with whom we differ may be taught. It is their responsibility to scrutinize rigorously all church school curricula for evidences of prejudice and intolerance and to draw attention to these issues to curriculum planners and to those who may be teaching in the church school.

Many of these issues suggest areas of content for church school curricula which are seeking greater vitality. One denominational educational commission, facing serious criticism and discontent with respect to the adult uniform lesson series, is seeking to rescue that series from irrelevance by relating it more directly to these living issues. Representatives of other agencies and boards of the denomination, particularly the social action groups, have been invited to participate in a careful scrutiny of the uniform outlines to discover those lessons which best lend themselves to a study of living issues informed by the biblical text. The same commission is launching some pilot projects known as "Project Consensus". Several adult church school classes are being selected for the experiment; procedures are being worked out carefully for their use in selecting a problem, finding resource persons to assist them with their analysis of the problem, arriving at consensus, and in acting upon that consensus.

Issues such as automation, unemployment and leisure, capital punishment, recognizing and coping with propaganda of various types—these are but a few samples of the many issues which Christian adults must come to terms with if they are to understand the world in which they live and to live effectively within it. Issues such as poverty, illiteracy, illegitimacy, morality—private and public, suggest education and action programs for the local congregation. Ideological issues from the fields of politics, economics and philosophy may suggest curriculum items for some adult classes as well.

The Christian education department can be one channel for feeding these issues into the curriculum of theological education. As theological educators find the way of illuminating these issues in the light of the Christian heritage, Christian educators can be the channel for communicating those procedures and insights which emerge into the curriculum of the church school. Their concern for adults might also cause them to support continuing education programs for the laity sponsored by the seminary.

4. There is a growing awareness of the need for the improvement of the teaching-learning experience.

In recent years, some theological schools have been giving attention to improving their methods of teaching. The lecture method is giving way to make room for an increasing number of seminars and encouragement is being given to independent study by those who can profit from it. Case study methods and verbatims are being used; clinical training is offered by many seminaries. A limited use of audio-visual aids is being made. Team teaching is being introduced.

Many Christian educators make use of a wide range of effective teaching techniques in their courses and undoubtedly some of them share their knowledge and experience with their colleagues. The introduction of new techniques and methods of teaching, as valuable as this is, is not the most important contribution that Christian educators can make toward the improvement of the teaching-learning experience. More basic than methodology is the theory of Christian learning within which specific teaching-learning experiences can be planned. An adequate theory of Christian learning should be comprehensive enough to illuminate teaching-learning both in the church school and in the theological school. The discontinuities between Christian adult education and theological education are not so great as might generally be supposed.

Probably there is no such thing as a unique, distinctively Christian theory of learning. I would like, however, to propose for your consideration a theory of learning which is appropriate to the study of the Christian heritage either in the congregation or in the seminary. This theory arises from the distinctiveness of the material which forms the content of the Christian heritage. In a previous section we have acknowledged that while the gospel lies at the core of the Christian heritage, it comes to us in a cultural matrix (i.e. history, literature, language, etc.) which forms the intellectual content for critical scholarly study. The approach to the study of Greek and Hebrew is not essentially different from the approach to the study of other ancient languages. Methods of teaching and learning the biblical literature and the biblical history, for example, are not essentially different from methods applied to secular materials of the same kind. It is for this reason that the theological teacher is free to profit to some extent from the theories of learning and the methods of teaching that his colleagues in other subject matter fields use. Having allowed that biblical literature and history are just that (literature and history) we have not said all that must be said. They are certainly not less than that; they are something more, for in a way that is not equally true of secular literature and secular history, biblical history is **our** history and biblical literature is a portrayal of **our** lives. When we read it, we are reading about ourselves and about the community of faith in which our lives are set.

The study of the biblical literature and history is a process of self-discovery, a process which is illumined by the personal encounter with the God of whom the Bible speaks, to whom it points. He is not merely one historical figure among many historical figures of the past. He is one who enters into relation with people **now** as **then**. This encounter transforms the study of the biblical text from a scholarly, academic, objective exercise into a personal experience with the living God who breaks through the written page and personally confronts us. This confrontation becomes an experience of judgment and of grace, of demand and promise, of address and response.

Against this backdrop, permit me to sketch in a few brief strokes a theory of learning which consists of three major parts, parts which are not sharply separate and distinct but which lie along a continuum. The first stage is that of exploration which gives way to decision-making which gives way to action.

LEARNING = EXPLORATION → DECISION-MAKING → ACTION

The Learning Continuum

The first stage (exploration) involves a study of anything that lies within the Christian heritage (the Bible, church history, the creeds, theology, etc.). It involves also a careful reading of the contemporary human situation with special reference to one's own particular place and circumstances in relation to the whole. The third step in stage one is to bring together the past and present, the content and the present experience. What are the continuities which bind these worlds together? It is at this point that one may discover that the history of Adam is his own history, and the history of Israel is the history of his own people. A bridge which spans the centuries begins to be built across which he can travel at will for both ends of the bridge are anchored in one world, his own world. As he travels back and forth he discovers that much which has happened or been written in the intervening centuries is of help to him in discerning the continuities that stretch from the first Adam through the second Adam to the contemporary Adam which he discovers in himself.

As one studies the biblical text, he discovers that he brings a host of new questions arising out of his present situation to the text. He has living questions to which he is seeking living answers. Then, to his surprise, he finds that he is not the only questioner. As he reads the text openly and honestly, he discovers that the text begins to address some searching questions to him. The questioner becomes the questioned and is called upon to give his answer. God, the living God, confronts him, addresses him with his word of judgment and of grace, and demands his answer.

Stage two involves decision-making. This dimension is essential to Christian learning. As we noted earlier, there may be some kinds of learning, some fields of study, which can be mastered without demanding commitment, in which judgment may be suspended indefinitely, but in Christian learning the call to commitment cannot be silenced. Continually the learner is being raised to her feet and asked to decide. One cannot know the will of God or discern the mind of Christ in dispassionate objectivity. She may gather some facts about God or about his people in history, but she cannot know God or comprehend the inner secret of God's people without coming off the bleachers of suspended judgment or out of the laboratory of objective detachment.

Stage three is the logical conclusion of stage two. Decision-making in the Christian sense is not only agreeing but acting; it is not only believing, but doing. When we speak of faith, we really mean faith-in-action, faith translated into life. To know God is more than to grasp certain facts about him; it is to be in a living, responding relationship with him in which one is caught up as a participant in what God is doing in the world through his people even now.

This theory of Christian learning, while it does not provide a specific pattern for every particular teaching-learning situation, does suggest, it is hoped, a framework and a progression whose marks might be reflected in each particular context. Within the program of theological education, there is a greater emphasis upon scholarly tools and procedures (knowledge of Hebrew and Greek, syntax and grammar, the exegesis of literary texts, historical reconstruction, philosophical analysis etc.) In the case of Christian adult education, the emphasis is less upon critical scholarship (though its fruits are becoming increasingly available to lay persons) and more upon decision and action. In addition, while most lay men and women may bring less scholarly insight to the process of exploration (stage one) they bring a wide range of insight and experience from their everyday involvement in the structures of society which also serve as raw material for a Christian understanding of contemporary life and the role of the church in the community. Christian adult education **is** theological education in a congregational context and is enriched by the fruits of technical theological scholarship. Theological education in the seminaries, for its part, must be carried out in the awareness that Christian truth can only be discerned in the larger context of a living, responding church to which the seminaries are related in a vital way.

The concept of a learning continuum may be of some help in resolving the classic conflict between **content** and **experience** as organizing principles in the curriculum, a conflict well-known to Christian educators and increasingly being felt in theological faculties as greater emphasis is put on field education and clinical training. The conflict is less intense in church school curriculum planning today than in an earlier period, nor need it be a disruptive factor in planning the program of theological education.

There is a growing awareness in the seminaries of the necessity for stressing the convergence of theory and act. Such modifications in the curriculum as have been made to facilitate this convergence, however, have not been very radical and have left the traditional disciplines largely intact. A much more radical proposal is now being made by Jesse H. Zeigler, Associate Director of the American Association of Theological Schools who brings, among other perspectives, a Christian educator's point of view to the enterprise of theological education. He proposes that the curriculum of the theological school of the future will be organized around those life situations which have the greatest capacity for provoking theological reflection. The analysis of the racial upheaval in Watts, California, for example, might serve to precipitate the search for a theology which is viable and credible and which will guide the church in its contemporary mission. Professors and libraries will serve as resources to the students as they seek to identify the issues involved in the fundamental human predicament behind the present problem and to find answers which can guide programs of action. Professors will be relieved of the task of organizing and presenting to their students material which is already found in the literature. They will be freed for research and writing on the one hand and for stimulating and directing their students in their search on the other. In addition, they will have more time to participate actively in the church's program as the church becomes more actively involved in addressing itself to the problems for which Watts stands as a representative example.

The merits of Zeigler's proposal and all the practical problems of curriculum planning it anticipates remain to be debated and tested. Certainly it is a creative and provocative suggestion and we may expect to hear a great deal more about it.

Conclusion

Christian education does have a significant place in theological education. Christian educators bring a point of view and many of the professional skills which are essential to planning and carrying out the educational enterprise. They have a special contribution to make in curriculum planning and building for they bring a technical knowledge of principles of scope, comprehensiveness, sequence and balance and of the importance of clarity and unity in the establishing of an objective. They have a concern for maintaining a close relationship between the seminary and the congregation and between the Christian heritage and the present human situation. They are a resource in the seminary which attempts to nurture the Christian commitment as well as to stimulate the intellectual growth of its students.

Of course, when Christian educators are mere pedagogues, they do not represent a significant resource on their faculties any more than any other pedant among their colleagues. But when they are theologians and educators after the manner just described, they bring to their work the quality of living scholarship which may contribute to the renewing and revitalizing of theological education in our day.

---

[1]Three books and a series of five pamphlets which were distributed to the member institutions of the American Association of Theological Schools between April, 1954 and April, 1956 emerged from this study. The first one—a volume of essays, *The Ministry in Historical Perspective*, edited by the research staff—was not a part of the official report. The second one was published in April, 1956 by Harper and Brothers of New York under the title *The Purpose of the Church and its Ministry: Reflections on the Aims of Theological Education.* The third one was also published by Harper and Brothers in 1957 under the title, *The Advancement of Theological Education.* H. Richard Niebuhr was assisted in this study by Daniel Day Williams of Union Theological Seminary, New York and by James M. Gustafson of Yale University Divinity School.

[2]H. Richard Niebuhr, Daniel Day Williams and James M. Gustafson, *The Advancement of Theological Education* (New York: Harper and Brothers, 1957), 82.

[3] 0f course the contribution can be reciprocal; at Goshen College, for example, seminary professors have presented lectures and participated in seminar discussions in the school of nursing and in undergraduate courses in psychology and social work.

[4]Niebuhr et al., *The Advancement of Theological Education*, 82.

[5]*Ibid.*, 82.

17

The Meaning to the Seminaries of the Changing International Situation

To propose to comment with any significant degree of accurate perception on the changing international situation is a presumptuous undertaking for the view from Elkhart County is somewhat hazy. To comment further on the significance of all these changes when perception of the actual facts of the matter is limited is even more presumptuous. To comment still further on the meaning to the seminaries of all this strikes me as being well-nigh perilous.

How is any lay observer of world events to speak of what he sees with any assurance that he perceives correctly? Indeed for the most part he does not **see** very much at all except what the international news agencies capture on film and the national television news agencies first edit and interpret, then broadcast. Most of what we observe is through the eyes of others, that is, through the press which does have observers on the spot around the world. There are, in addition, statements made by national political leaders and opinion makers from our own and other countries and with the advent of communications satellites it has become possible on occasion to hear their unexpurgated and uninterpreted points of view directly. When I lived for several years in the New York area, I was able to listen to Channel 13 which gave complete television coverage to the speeches and debates in the General Assembly of the United Nations. More and more Americans, including Mennonites, are traveling and living abroad, but only those who are trained and skillful observers are able to gain more than a superficial impression of what is actually going on in the particular areas where they find themselves.

If it is difficult for nations to develop strategies based on accurate information and a correct assessment and interpretation of that information, how shall the church establish its international strategies, for the fact gathering apparatus of the church is not a very sophisticated one. To be sure, it need not be as sophisticated as that of governmental and news agencies but all too often the church has become unwittingly identified with the purposes and policies of its government both at home and abroad through lack of authentic information and careful analysis. The church with an international mission must be knowledgeable about world affairs if it is to avoid naive or even self-defeating strategies; its educational institutions which prepare workers for overseas assignments must also be adequately informed if they wish to avoid sending "innocents abroad."

The Changing World Situation: Major Issues

Having acknowledged both the difficulty and the necessity of attempting to understand the changing international situation, let me now make a brief excursion into that perilous territory. Here I fall back not primarily on my own observations and impressions gained from a limited amount of travel and reading but upon an address delivered in November 1996 in New York by William C. Olson of the School of International Affairs, Columbia University. The occasion was the celebration by a group of Christian educators of the completion of the Cooperative Curriculum Project in which representatives from our denomination participated. Olson was invited to present a çommentary on the world situation today which constitutes the historical setting within which the contemporary church must carry out its world mission.

In his address, "Mid-Century Plus: What Are the Great World Issues Now?" Olson outlined a novel set of categories with which one might focus the bewildering array of events which press in upon us, both confusing and threatening us in greater or lesser degree. He spoke of (a) headline issues; (b) crisis issues; (c) gut issues; (d) framework issues, (e) agenda issues; and (f) fate of mankind issues. I attempted to test his categories by lifting out a number of current events in the news and classifying them.

(a) Headline issues are the ones posed by the dramatic events of the day and may arise anywhere on the globe, flitting from Djakarta to Peking to Salisbury to Detroit to Watts to Shade Gap, Pennsylvania. Some of these issues are central; others are peripheral as measured by the number of persons affected and how long national or international interest is sustained. The failure that occurred in 1966 during the Gemini space effort is an example of a headline issue; reflection upon its failure focused attention upon the timetable in the race for the moon. At that point many people lost interest and reflected no further upon the issue while others went further and pointed up the fact that the space agency had projected no plan or strategy beyond reaching the moon. Others reflected upon the military and political significance of the space race while only a few were reflective about the metaphysical and spiritual implications of all this. While we laugh off the Russian cosmonaut's claim that there is no God because he went out into outer space and found no signs of his presence, few of us are willing or able to reflect any more profoundly on the matter. Our cosmology requires considerable rethinking and expanding in the light of new scientific discoveries about the nature and dynamic character of our universe.

(b) Crisis issues are those which point up the fact that we have come to a turning of the ways, that the status quo is jeopardized, that old answers and policies are no longer adequate and that decisions must be made and courses of action initiated.

(c) Gut issues are what 0lson calls the "bread and butter" issues, not in the sense of trivia but in the sense of famine and starvation. It is one of the ironies of our time that America is embarrassed with a food surplus while some other nations are starving. This issue, too, affords the possibility of reflection on a variety of levels ranging from political and economic considerations to the profounder level of reflection about social responsibility in the light of the gospel.

(d) Framework issues have to do with regional and international alliances and with the establishing of foreign policy. Old frameworks like the North Atlantic Treaty Organization and the Warsaw Pact are in process of radical revision at this very time.

(e) Agenda issues are those which have actually brought together responsible persons to discuss and negotiate matters of difference which all parties concerned have an interest in reconciling. The debates in the United Nations center around an agenda which may be read as a barometer of most of the world's storm centers. The Carnegie Endowment for International Peace publishes each year a listing of current issues being debated by the General Assembly; this compendium serves as a convenient guide to persons who wish to inform themselves about what is going on in the world.

(f) The fate of mankind issues are those posed by the explosion of another nuclear bomb by China or by a show-down confrontation of great powers such as took place between Russia and the United States in the Cuban missile crisis. The Geneva disarmament conference is an illustration of an agenda item which is at the same time a fate of mankind issue.

It is obvious that these categories are somewhat arbitrary and that a given issue may be categorized in more than one way. I mention them only as an illustration of one way of attempting to focus the bewildering array of events and issues with which we are confronted. They provide a crude but helpful way for the lay person to get a hold on his world, at least to understand it if not also to make some impact upon it although this may seem to him to be a remote possibility.

Olson spoke of war and peace, racism, and nationalism as being the major issues which threaten world order. He identified certain constellations of interests which were driving some countries together and others apart. He pointed out that whereas revolutionary fervor and opposition to imperialism provide emerging nations with a common cause, the constructive task of nation building introduces a narrowly nationalistic spirit which threatens effective regional integration. The failure of the Arab states and of the emerging African countries to federate are vivid examples.

National myths and illusions constitute yet another set of issues which must be recognized as realities. That is to say, China may in fact not be able to survive a nuclear holocaust but that she believes that it is possible to do so and bases her foreign policy upon it must be accepted as hard fact. India has had, until recently, her illusions that she is an effective international force through her moral influence alone which more than compensates for her lack of military strength. Indonesia has been extremely vocal in making anti-imperialistic statements while at the same time and without any apparent sense of contradiction seeking to extend her empire to include Malaysia. Americans, Olson pointed out, also live by their illusions among them being the belief that all international crises can be settled by military means and that most countries can be bought through the foreign aid program. Perhaps the greatest illusion of all is the one based on frontier legends and projected on international affairs which assumes that in every situation there are good guys and bad guys and the good guys always win. There is very little comfort and support to be found in history to support this point of view but the illusion is very powerful and still persists.

The impact of science and technology was also traced in terms of their effect in forcing us out of our "parochial national cocoons." Olson pointed out that whereas politics has used science in many ways to advance political, diplomatic and military goals, scientists and technologists have not in any significant way modified politics.

Olson assumed no responsibility to tell us what is the responsibility of the church in the face of all these issues apart from encouraging the church to be adequately informed and to avoid policy recommendations (usually based on inadequate information) which are the responsibility of statesmen and government officials.

The Church in a Changing World: Establishing the Point of Contact

We come now to this question ourselves, for any understanding of the meaning to the seminaries of the changing international situation must arise out of the framework which the church establishes in addressing itself to great world issues. In light of the fact that these issues are so complex and far reaching, it would be futile to suggest that an effective strategy for the church as it attempts to address itself to these issues is dependent upon a complete and thorough comprehension of them. Rather, the church must seek to establish the point of contact between its concern and world events. It must assume a particular posture toward them arising not so much out of the vagaries of the changing scene as out of its perception of its mission in and to the world. If such a posture and point of contact can be established, the church may begin to view the changing international situation, comprehend it and address itself to it from that vantage point.

One tempting possibility which presents itself to the church is retreat and withdrawal in the face of all that storms and threatens on the world scene. By this I refer not to a physical or geographical withdrawal which has indeed been attempted in our own history, but a pietistic withdrawal into a focusing of attention upon the "spiritual." There was a preview in the May 17, 1966 issue of *Look* magazine of a book entitled, *Pius XII and the Third Reich.* The book is written by historian Saul Friedländer and is a study of Nazi-Holy See diplomacy based upon material found in the German Foreign Office archives as well as material secured from British, French and Israeli sources.

Friedländer reports on an interview between Joachim von Ribbentrop, Reich Minister for Foreign Affairs and Pope Pius XII who received him in the Vatican on March 11, 1940. von Ribbentrop began by asserting that Germany and the Vatican must seek to reach an understanding concerning relations between them and that "agreement on fundamentals" was possible. However, he went on, Germany was for the moment preoccupied with the war so that a "comprehensive clarification" would have to be temporarily postponed. In the meantime,

> ...it must be borne in mind that an understanding between National Socialism and the Catholic Church depended on one cardinal prerequisite, namely that the Catholic clergy in Germany renounce political activity in any shape or form and confine themselves exclusively to the cure of souls. Today, the Catholic clergy in Germany do not as yet seem to have fully realized the necessity of so radical a distinction. In Germany, he said, the Catholic Church had appropriated positions and powers of the most varied kind, which could not be reconciled with the absolute necessity that the Church restrict itself to the cure of souls.

With respect to the key issue at stake, namely the extermination of the Jews, the article asserts on the basis of documented evidence that the Pope did in fact have limited information about what Hitler was doing though he was not in possession of all the facts of the case. The Pope exhausted his private fortune and in addition solicited the aid of Catholics in North America to help European Jews to migrate to South America. However, he made no public protest nor did he attempt to change Hitler's policy. Most of you are aware of the controversy excited by the Broadway play, *The Deputy*, in which the charge was presented in dramatic form that the Pope was negligent in his responsibility to speak out against Hitler's policy to exterminate the Jews. Friedländer's work is a documented historical treatment of the same charge which can now scarcely be denied.

Now one must acknowledge that the Pope's act in assisting the Jews to migrate to South America was a genuine and sacrificial act of Christian charity. Indeed is this not similar to our own approach to suffering and injustice in the world? Is this not the way to describe what we are doing through our relief efforts—binding up wounds, clothing the naked, feeding the hungry, housing the homeless, comforting the bereaved, resettling the refugees? And is this not an authentic response to our particular historical situation in the light of the gospel? I am unaware of any opposition in the Mennonite churches to this program. But if we were to advocate a public statement protesting the American military presence in various hot spots around the world in terms of its economic, social and political consequences, we would arouse instant controversy. In fact such controversy already is evident in our church papers even though no official agency of the church or spokesman for the church has uttered such a protest in the name of the church. I point this out simply to indicate that there is a considerable body of opinion among Mennonites that the church's business has to do with the "cure of souls" and in addition with acts of mercy but that these constitute the boundary of its legitimate sphere of activity.

Our theology of discipleship and our traditional formulation of the relationship between the church and the world (including our position on church and state) have tended to emphasize the personal or private aspects of the Christian life. This has, in fact, been one of the strengths in the Mennonite perception of how to be a Christian in the world. But it must be admitted that we have not been able to demonstrate in a clear and convincing way how our method of handling a line fence dispute between two neighbors applies to a boundary dispute between two nations like India and China. Nor have we been able to translate clearly how reconciliation between brothers who have a difference may be extended to reconcile groups of persons who come from different racial backgrounds. In privatizing the faith, the church has reduced and truncated the gospel although the real intention in many cases has been to be faithful to the gospel and not to compromise it. There is a growing body of nascent theological opinion among Mennonite scholars that the question of the church's responsibility toward the political, economic and social order requires a new and searching appraisal. The assumption of "realistic theology" that Jesus addressed himself to the private sphere of life and to the field of interpersonal relationships and that he did not speak to issues affecting the corporate structures of society has not been as critically challenged by Mennonites as it should be.

The Role of Theology in the Mission of the Church

To attempt to do much more than to identify the problem goes beyond both the scope of this paper and the competence of its writer. What I have to offer here will be in the nature of supplementary comments which may make a small contribution toward determining the direction in which we must move to establish the point of contact. The point of contact is not to be found in terms of an abstraction or an idea. The point of contact does not have to be artificially established for it is already at hand; the important question becomes how the church is to shape that contact into the kind of encounter in which God may confront the world. This is a theological question and calls for theological reflection and this is where the seminaries may participate. Reflection and involvement establish the necessary rhythm that marks all authentic Christian theologizing.

Herbert C. Jackson, director of the Missionary Research Library in New York has expressed this insight well in an article entitled, "The Missionary Obligation of Theology" which appeared in the May-June, 1965 issue of *Practical Anthropology*. He asserts quite correctly that "Christianity is an event: the event of God's dramatic and visible intervention into human history by becoming a human being—the Incarnation; the event of the self-disclosure of God…; the event of the new creation wrought in man and in society by the lordship of the ascended Christ." (123) He goes on to speak of a second consideration which must be seen in relation to the event character of Christianity and that is the "theologizing trait of religious man." Jackson observes that while **event** and **theologizing** should be integrally related to each other, they have been for the most part "parallel but largely isolated aspects of our faith." As a consequence, theology has all too often been barren and impoverished and rather than giving impetus and direction to the church in its mission to the world it has side-tracked the church from concentrating on its mission. Jackson does not deny theology a valid place in the church but asks that it assume its rightful role of "providing prophetic insight into the implications of the event character of Christianity." (126) Theology has a "missionary obligation", but that missionary obligation as Jackson perceives it is not to provide what used to be called "the biblical basis for missions", nor to establish a theological rationale for the stewardship of men and money in the missions program of the church. It is not even that of establishing a section on missiology in systematic theology alongside the other themes.

"The missionary obligation of theology is that of constituting theology not as a set of formulations but as a dynamic inquiry functioning always in tension at the frontiers where Christian faith meets unfaith or the denial of the will of God in social righteousness or non-Christian religious systems and cultures." (129)

> Missionary theology would be a continuing inquiry into how God is encountering people who are not his, or not fully his, and into how he is acting in the midst of the world with its multifarious societies, none of which is by any means even approximately his.
>
> Missionary theology would cause the church to hover constantly on the brink of the encounter with the non-Christian: the non-Christian person, the non-Christian social or economic or political situation, the non-Christian culture. Such theology would be contemporary and relevant and vibrant—and missionary.
>
> Theology would in truth undergird the event-quality of Christianity, and would bring the church, in the living sense of her members, into true "partnership in obedience," not with some other group or institution but with the Holy Spirit. Contemporary biblical studies have drawn attention clearly to the twofold fact that the God of the Bible is the "God who acts," but that he also provides the interpreter of these deeds, so that man can discern between the ordinary events of ongoing history and the "mighty acts" of God in history. Thus in Christian theology we have both deed and word, both of which are oriented toward the redemption of men. (130)

By his insistence on keeping the event character of the Christian faith central in the church's theologizing, Jackson has set up an important hermeneutical principle. Those who would interpret the will of God and the mind of Christ for our day must be deeply involved in the event which is our faith, that is, in what God is now at work accomplishing in the world. The interpreter must be caught up as a participant in God's act; he must be a living member of the living responding church for it is the existence of the church in the midst of the historical stream of events that is the historical manifestation that God is indeed acting in history. The biblical evidence that God was acting in history is to be found in that he called out a people. The covenant community which God created and brought into existence was, to be sure, one community among the various communities existing in the time and space continuum we call history. But it was more than this for it represented a genuinely new reality within history and was indeed a living, visible testimony of history's possibilities. It was to show forth the shape of the divine intention for all historically conditioned communities and this intention was to be expressed not apart from but in and through all the aspects of historical existence, that is, in the economic, social and political areas of life.

The missionary obligation or character of theology as it has been defined is not compartmentalized into "overseas" and "home" areas of concern. James A. Scherer deplored what he called a "three continent mentality" in an address entitled, "The Church as Mission: Reassessment for Theological Education" presented at the Consultation on Theological Education held under the auspices of the Division of Overseas Ministries of the National Council of Churches at Stony Point, N.Y. on January 8-11, 1965. He held that the missionary enterprise must be stripped of its "salt-water mythology" and that the missionary issues which theology must contemplate arise out of the attempt of the church to be faithful in its mission irregardless of its geographical location. Among the issues which Scherer identified were the following:

(a) the missionary structure of the local congregation which provides the locus for the essential task of the church. Theological schools should not be found training congregational leaders with two sets of assumptions—that overseas congregations are missionary and that home congregations need not be geared to implement the missionary task. What is called for is a radical rethinking of the very nature of the congregation's reason for being as well as the forms that being takes.

(b) the pattern of the church's ministry including the role and calling of the laity. The seminary curriculum must take into account emerging forms of Christian ministry in which the whole congregation participates and which reflect the richness of the gifts Christ has given to the church. This calls for a measure of flexibility which is not easy to achieve. Added to this must be an awareness of the wide variety of forms of congregational life and kinds of local situations in which churches around the world find themselves.

(c) the Christian witness to men and women in the secular world. Charles C. West, Professor of Theology at Princeton Theological

Seminary also presented an address at the Cooperative Curriculum Project meeting in New York to which I referred earlier. Dr. West spoke about how the Christian and the church must face the realities of the gospel in a secular society. The process of secularization, he stated, has resulted in the loss of our capacity to make ordered sense and to see coherence in the world. Various social institutions, including the family, seem to be losing their capacity to give coherence and meaning to life. Life is seen as a complex and impersonal network of functions and interactions and the meaning of freedom and responsibility is hard to discern. The older metaphysical systems with which persons rationalized their existence and within which they made their decisions and ordered their affairs have been stripped away. Life in a secular society is exposed and vulnerable and many lack the courage and fortitude which they are now called upon to summon forth that they may assume total responsibility for their own destiny. They look in vain within the social order which is our own creature for any signs of promise or hope.

The theological school is faced with the responsibility of helping to discern the meaning of the biblical doctrines of creation, redemption and vocation in the face of a secular world and to learn how to communicate that meaning to those whose primary frame of reference is this-worldly.

(d) the Christian witness to those of other faiths. One of the most serious lacks in seminary training has been in the area of equipping people to witness to persons representing the various major religions of the world. It is not that there are not courses and literature available; it is the lack of personal encounter with such people to which I refer. Whereas there has been abundant opportunity to encounter the secular world (and it has been largely a missed opportunity), there has been little occasion to enter into living conversation with the Buddhist, the Moslem and the Hindu. The one sent out to minister to persons of these faiths has largely had to learn to do so on his own.

(e) the seminary as a Christian community. There is a growing recognition among seminaries that the seminary itself must be a genuine Christian community if it is to train men and women for mission with any measure of integrity and of effectiveness. It is not enough to have a correct doctrine of the church; the ecclesiology which the seminarian learns is communicated not only by what is said in the systematic theology class but even more by what is expressed in the life of the seminary in its totality.

Seminary Education and the World Mission of the Church

The consideration that the seminary must be an authentic Christian community has profound significance at a number of points but especially so in terms of our earlier insistence that **theologizing** and **event** must be kept in close relationship. This means that neither the seminary program nor the seminary student may be excused from participation in obedience, that is, in the living response of the living church. This does not deny that the primary function of the seminary is study and reflection but it does mean that study and reflection must be carried on in the context of living engagement in the mission of the church. The Bible itself, which is at the heart of our study, reflects the living engagement of its authors and subjects in mission; how can it be properly interpreted apart from living engagement? It accommodated itself to the human thought forms of its day, expressed itself in the vernacular idiom and addressed itself to the issues raised by the encounter of biblical faith with the social order. We must be quick to confess that we in the seminaries have not yet learned all that this implies in terms of the restructuring of our program, but we are eager and ready to learn. We are ready to learn along with our entire denomination and its various agencies as they are increasingly moving out to confront our own society and as they are developing a worldwide awareness and operational frame of reference. We want to assume insofar as we are able that same frame of reference and that same awareness in order that we may adequately prepare workers for the home church and the church in other lands. Among the dimensions of our program which are contributing to a larger social awareness are the following:

The faculties of the Associated Mennonite Biblical Seminaries have concluded in the process of reviewing the program of instruction that "Mennonite theological education ought to reflect a sensitivity to and an awareness of the current human and world situation." Each professor tries to be alert to current situations and experiences which bear upon his discipline and inform it. We will be looking for ways in which to provide clinical training for our students not only in the context of hospitals but also in the context of industry, etc.

One of the members of our faculty is a member of the board of the Urban Training Center in Chicago. Several students have participated in the summer program at UTC. Several students have spent a summer in New York City working in the East Harlem Protestant Parish. The seminary has approved this assignment for field work credit. Each year the class in Evangelism spends a number of days in a workshop in Chicago. For many students this is the high point of their seminary career. This year the class in Evangelism studied the possibilities of setting up a coffee house ministry in Elkhart. Through their efforts, this ministry will soon become a reality. An organization has been effected which includes members of the Elkhart community.

Each year Mennonite Biblical Seminary engages in an exchange program with a Negro seminary in Atlanta. An MBS student attends classes in Atlanta and a southern student studies in Elkhart. Recently our visiting student shared with us very candidly his own impressions and observations of the experience of living and studying in the north.

Among the dimensions of our program which are contributing to a larger world awareness are the following:

Each year there are several international students in the student body of our seminaries. They come with a different set of presuppositions than those usually reflected by most of our students. Each year there are several missionaries on furlough in the student body. They come with a set of questions different from those they asked when they were first students in our schools. There is an increasing number of students who have had overseas experience in PAX, TAP and Voluntary Service programs. The presence of all these persons in our schools effectively challenges any tendency which may be present to think in narrowly North American terms. In addition, we have a small but growing number of students who interrupt their theological studies for a hitch of service or travel overseas. One student elected to take a year of studies at Union Biblical Seminary in Yeotmal. Several students participated in an East-West Encounter in East Germany and in Prague. The discussions dealt with issues of Christian concern in a world that is politically and ideologically divided. Most of the teaching faculty have had overseas study, teaching or other service experience in their background or have traveled extensively abroad. Perhaps slowly but certainly very steadily there is emerging in our schools an awareness and concern that is global in its scope.

A more recent development in our program has been a "visiting scholar in residence" plan which attempts to bring to the campus as opportunity affords visiting scholars from abroad. Dean K.C. Mathew of Union Biblical Seminary, India spent two weeks in residence. He gave several special lectures, visited classes and participated in informal discussions with students and faculty. The purpose of these encounters was:

1. to provide for ecumenical and international dialogue;
2. to develop an awareness of the Christian church in India; and
3. to stimulate international Christian interest and concern.

Dean Mathew is a member of the Mar Thoma church of South India; his presence among us was much appreciated.

A second visiting scholar was Dr. Zdenek Trtik, Professor of Systematic Theology at the Hus Theological Faculty in Prague. He shared with us most candidly the problems of the Christian church in a Communist land and also exhorted us about the perils of being the church in our land. He also presented a most provocative and stimulating address, "The Responsibility of the Church in the Epoch of World Revolution."

One of the new dimensions that I observe moving into the thinking of our church with respect to its worldwide mission is a recognition that the church in North America is not only the **sending** church while the church in other lands is only the **receiving** church. To be sure, the mission of the church is an international mission and by that very token there will appropriately continue to be a sending of fraternal workers, but this sending will be moving both ways. In those situations where leadership has not yet been adequately developed it would obviously be unwise to send the best national leaders to North America. Nor at this point in history is the church in North America in need of financial and material assistance. However, let us be grateful to the younger churches for the spiritual renewal which has come to the older churches as a direct consequence of the privilege of bringing them the gospel and sharing with them in the experience of observing the gospel take root and grow in a new culture. They have taught us many things about what it is to be the church in mission and there is much more to be learned from them if we have the humility to hear them.

There will continue to be areas of the world to which the church will be sending workers, some of whom the seminaries will be expected to prepare. It is gratifying to see the wide range of talents and skills which can be used in the church's mission around the world and to see the responsiveness on the part of so many persons to dedicate their skills to this ministry. The diversity of ministries and skills which are called for puts a tremendous strain on the capacity of any school to provide an adequate training program and we are under no illusion as to our limitations in this regard. There are, however, some things which we can do and there are some things which we can do better than other things. We have been reviewing our program of studies which is designed to prepare persons going into overseas missionary service. While we recognize that the worldwide mission of the church calls for many specializations, we believe that the field of specialization offered by our seminaries should be limited to the area for which we are best equipped—the spiritual and theological preparation of the missionary which makes him an effective witness to the gospel by word and life. If he is to specialize in mass communication or translation or the preparation of Christian literature, he should seek this kind of training elsewhere, preferably during a furlough after he has become aware of his context, its needs and his gifts in relation to his particular assignment.

In light of this, it would follow that the missions curriculum should not be a separate and distinct one at all points for the qualifications of the overseas missionary are for the most part essential for pastors at home, or for that matter for all persons engaged in world mission at home or abroad. All need to be "detribalized," to learn "cultural flexibility," to learn how to get along in difficult interpersonal situations, to gain skill in communication, to develop deep convictions and spiritual warmth, to become "mature in Christ."

Persons who come to seminary with a broad liberal arts education (whether in the humanities or the life sciences) are already well on the way to developing the qualities that have been described. The additional disciplines to be found in biblical, historical, and theological (both systematic and practical) studies will help to round out these qualities. Significant help in gaining cultural flexibility can be given by offering courses in cultural and missionary anthropology. Their function would be to serve as means to this end rather than to prepare persons to be experts in anthropology. Similarly, elementary courses in linguistics could provide help in learning the skill of communication and in mastering a foreign language. Courses in the history and theology of the missionary enterprise of the church continue to have a significant place in the curriculum. Area studies of countries and continents where the Mennonite church is at work are appropriate as are courses in ecumenical theology, Roman Catholic theology and living religions of the world.

In addition to the program of instruction, there are a number of extracurricular areas which require consideration and strengthening:

1. The seminary must become a genuine Christian community in which the person can realize his "authenticity" in Christ.

2. The seminary should find ways of helping students with their interpersonal relationships. Don Jacobs believes that the student should be deliberately immersed in inter-personal situations which are difficult and demanding.

3. The seminary should strive to cultivate an international atmosphere. This means more students from abroad, more students with overseas experience in PAX, Voluntary Service, etc., more missionaries on furlough in the student body, more faculty members who have traveled, studied or served abroad, more awareness and discussion on international issues.

4. The seminary should provide transcultural experiences for its students and faculty. To quote from Robert Lee's letter[1] to Atlee Beechy, "Perhaps, education beyond the academic must call for some kind of an existential encounter with a live situation...in order to discover whether our framework of reference can stand on its own or remain on untenable cultural props." Transcultural laboratories could readily be set up in the summer months in Quebec, New York, Chicago, St. Louis, Texas, Mexico, Puerto Rico.

5. The whole program and life of the seminary should consciously be carried out in the framework of world mission. This could have some implications for the existing curriculum in terms of courses to be added or deleted or in terms of course content and approach. These implications will be discovered as the total framework becomes more consciously world mission oriented.

Conclusion

In conclusion, let me share with you two brief statements which I found in my reading in preparation for this assignment. Since both are such excellent statements, I could not decide between them and decided to share them both.

The first is a statement drawn up by the Second Consultation on Theological Education in Southeast Asia and quoted by Peter G. Gowing in an address at a Consultation on Theological Education held at Warwick, New York, March 4-5, 1966. The theme of the Consultation was, New Challenges to Seminary Teachers in a Rapidly Changing World.

> The new concern for society and culture does not mean a radical rejection of the traditional disciplines taught in a theological curriculum. It does, however, mean a radical re-thinking of these disciplines, relating them to one another, to the ministry committed to the People of God, and to the world in which this ministry is to be exercised. Courses need to be related to the thought forms, the culture patterns and the burning contemporary problems of the society in which the theological school has been called to serve.

The second quotation is taken from Charles C. West's address in New York to which I have already referred. Professor West affirmed that

> ...theology is born out of our reflection on the missionary obedience of the church. This means that the process of education and the discovery of the Church's mission are at heart identical. We are concerned in both with a response which bears witness to the reality which we believe controls our existence. That is right which bears this witness. Our task then, is to discover the form of our faith, of our living relation to the reality of Christ which can and does control the destiny of man from outside the circle of our culture, our customs, and our desires. This is the heart of Christian mission and education, and the source of all meaningful theology.

---

[1] Several years ago Atlee Beechy wrote to a number of graduates of Mennonite schools in overseas assignments and asked them, "What is the role of the Mennonite college in preparing persons for effective participation in world mission?"

Notes on the Essays

1. Could Any Work Be More Important?

This address was presented at a Christian Education Workshop at Camp Friedenswald in November 1990. The title is borrowed from a special edition of *Newsweek* magazine which asks that question rhetorically with reference to the passing on of the cultural heritage to each new generation of children.

2. Nurture: Passing on the Faith

This article was published in *Gospel Herald* (March 6, 1990). Reprinted by permission.

3. The Family: A Setting for Education

This paper was presented in various settings including a variation of this theme which was given at a meeting of the Mennonite Secondary Teachers Convention at Laurelville Mennonite Church Center, September 29 - October 2, 1983 under the title, "Dinner Tables and Classrooms."

4. The Teacher: Example, Revealer, Change Agent

Based on notes from a classroom lecture, "Jesus, the Master Teacher," this paper was presented at a Christian Education Workshop at Laurelville Mennonite Church Center.

5. The Teaching Ministry of the Church

Prepared for a class in Foundations of Christian Education at AMBS, this article was an adaptation of a longer paper entitled "*Kerygma* and *Didache*" presented in a seminar at Yale University Divinity School in April 1961.

6. Teaching the Bible in the Congregation

Presented at a meeting of the faculties of the Council of Mennonite Seminaries in August, 1969 at Aspen, Colorado, this essay was included in the Text Reader series of the Institute of Mennonite Studies edited by Willard M. Swartley, *Essays on Biblical Interpretation: Anabaptist-Mennonite Perspectives* (IMS 1984). Reprinted by permission.

7. The Sunday School: History and Purpose

This paper was originally given as a classroom lecture at AMBS in the course, Foundations of Christian Education.

8. The Relevance of Some Aspects of Piaget's Theory for the Teaching Ministry of the Church

Originally presented to a Research Seminar of the AMBS teaching faculty on March 16, 1994, this paper grew out of the writer's research in the Piaget Archives at the University of Geneva during the 1979-80 academic year and the summers of 1982 and 1992.

9. The Aims of Education

This paper was originally presented in a seminar on educational philosophy in the philosophy department of Yale University Graduate School in January 1961.

10. On Being and Becoming a Person

Originally presented at a Philosophy of Christian Education Conference at Bethel College, North Newton, Kansas in August 1963 under the title, "Life and its Setting," this essay was revised and retitled in October 1982.

11. Conversion in Religious Education

This paper was presented during a seminar on Growth in Religion at Yale University Divinity School during the second semester of the 1960-61 academic year.

12. Anabaptist Education

This article is reprinted from *Harper's Encyclopedia of Religious Education*, Iris V. Cully and Kendig Brubaker Cully, ed. (Harper & Row, 1990) 27-29. Permission granted by Harpercollins Publishers.

13. Indoctrination

This article is reprinted from *Harper's Encyclopedia of Religious Education*, Iris V. Cully and Kendig Brubaker Cully, ed. (Harper & Row, 1990) 321-322. Permission granted by Harpercollins Publishers.

14. Seminary and Congregation: Communities of Discernment

This was the writer's inaugural address as dean of the Associated Mennonite Biblical Seminaries on March 22, 1965. It is reprinted by permission from the July 1965 issue of the *Mennonite Quarterly Review.*

15. Theological Education in the Free Church Tradition

This article appeared in the journal of the Association of Theological Schools, *Theological Education* (Winter 1973). Reprinted by permission.

16. Christian Education in Theological Education

This article appeared in the journal of the Religious Education Association and the Association of Professors and Researchers in Religious Education, *Religious Education* (January-February 1967). It was presented at the annual meeting of the latter organization in February 1966. Reprinted by permission.

17. The Meaning to the Seminaries of the Changing International Situation

This paper was presented to the May 1966 meeting of the Council of International Ministries (Mennonite).

Ross T. Bender

In his lifetime, Ross T. Bender has contributed much to the church—as pastor, writer, theologian, educator and administrator. "He has character that is built on faith," one of his former students now colleague says.

Ross was born June 25, 1929, in Tavistock, Ontario. He married Ruth Steinmann in 1950; they have five children and seven grandchildren. He studied at Toronto Teacher's College and the University of Western Ontario before completing his bachelor's degree at Goshen College, Goshen, Ind. He also earned Bachelor of Divinity and Master of Religious Education degrees at Goshen College Biblical Seminary in 1956. He then earned Master of Arts and Doctor of Philosophy degrees at Yale University. Post-graduate work was completed at the University of Pennsylvania and the University of Geneva, Switzerland.

The church has been the focus and context of Ross's work. He has served in pastorates in Waterloo, Ont.; Lansdale, Pa.; and Lakewood, Colo. He also has served the Mennonite Church and his home congregation, College Mennonite Church in Goshen, in many ways.

In addition Ross served more than 26 years at Associated Mennonite Biblical Seminary in various roles, including 15 years as dean. He was the first person to serve as dean for both Goshen (College) Biblical Seminary and Mennonite Biblical Seminary. This put him in a key position to bring together the curricula of the two seminaries and thus helped to further a closer association and the move of GBS to the Elkhart campus in 1969. At AMBS, he also served as professor of Christian Education and director of the Institute of Mennonite Studies. Ross retired as Dean Emeritus of AMBS in 1996.

Among his special assignments for the Mennonite church are the following: Member, Mennonite Commission for Christian Education, 1963-71; Chair, 1967-71; Executive Secretary, Mennonite Board of Congregational Ministries, 1972-74; Moderator, Mennonite Church General Assembly, 1981-83; President, Mennonite World Conference, 1984-90.

Special ecumenical assignments included the following: Member, Association of Theological Schools Executive Director Search Committee, 1978-80; Research Associate, Office of Family Education, World Council of Churches, 1979-80; Ecumenical Participant, General

Assembly of the Presbyterian Church (USA), June 1983; Co-chair of Seminar on Baptism, Peace and the State in the Reformed and Mennonite Traditions, October 1989; Co-chair of Theological Conversations between the Mennonite World Conference and the Baptist World Alliance, 1989-92.

Academic honors, fellowships and listings include the following: Rockefeller Doctoral Fellow at Yale University, 1960-61; Lilly Scholar at Yale, 1960-62; NIMH Post-doctoral Fellow at the University of Pennsylvania Division of Family Studies, Department of Psychiatry, School of Medicine, 1970-71; and two faculty research grants from the Association of Theological Schools in 1961-62 and 1979-80. He was listed in Outstanding Educators in America, 1970; Leaders in Education, 1970; and Who's Who in America, 1984-present.

In addition to his published articles, he has authored and co-edited three books: *The People of God: A Mennonite Interpretation of the Free Church Tradition* (Herald Press, 1971), the report of the Study Project to Develop a Model for Theological Education in the Free Church Tradition which he directed; *Christians in Families: Genesis and Exodus* (Herald Press, 1982), in the Conrad Grebel Lecture Series; and *Baptism, Peace and the State in the Reformed and Mennonite Traditions* (Wilfrid Laurier University Press, 1991). Co-editor with Alan P.F. Sell.

Ross is a member of the Religious Education Association and the Association of Professors and Researchers in Religious Education.